INTERNATIONAL MONEY

Postwar Trends and Theories

INTERNATIONAL MONEY

Postwar Trends and Theories

Second Edition

PAUL DE GRAUWE

Oxford University Press • Oxford
1996

Oxford University Press, Walton Street, Oxford OX2 6DP

Oxford New York
Athens Auckland Bangkok Bombay
Calcutta Cape Town Dar es Salaam Delhi
Florence Hong Kong Istanbul Karachi
Kuala Lumpur Madras Madrid Melbourne
Mexico City Nairobi Paris Singapore
Taipei Tokyo Toronto
and associated companies in
Berlin Ibadan

Oxford is a trade mark of Oxford University Press

Published in the United States
by Oxford University Press Inc., New York

British Library Cataloguing in Publication Data
Data available

Library of Congress Cataloging in Publication Data
Grauwe, Paul de.
International money : postwar trends and theories / Paul de
Grauwe. — 2nd ed.
Includes bibliographical references and index.
1. Foreign exchange. 2. Economic history—1945 I. Title.
HG3815.G72 1996
332.4'b—dc20 96–6178
ISBN 0–19–877513–X (Pbk.)
ISBN 0–19–877514–8

Typeset by Graphicraft Typesetters Ltd., Hong Kong
Printed in Great Britain
on acid-free paper by
Bookcraft (Bath) Ltd., Midsomer Norton, Somerset

PREFACE TO THE SECOND EDITION

Since the publication of the first edition of *International Money*, a number of important changes have occurred in international monetary relations. One is the increasing degree of international financial integration. During the 1980s many countries in Europe and in Asia opened up their capital markets to the rest of the world, so that they now confront the new opportunities and rigours offered by highly integrated and sophisticated world capital markets. Second, the last major multilateral attempt at fixing exchange rates, the European Monetary System, collapsed. These developments are not without significance for the behaviour of exchange rates and for the conduct of national monetary and fiscal policies.

In this second edition, therefore, emphasis is given to these developments. More particularly, we study in greater detail than in the first edition why fixing exchange rates will always run into problems. In addition, we analyse more thoroughly the importance of perfect capital mobility in international monetary relations.

Not only have changes occurred in the real world, also theorizing about the world has undergone important changes. The most important one is most probably the decline of the efficient market hypothesis and the rational expectations theory. Evidence has been accumulating that foreign exchange markets are not efficient and that expectations are not formed according to the rational expectations paradigm. In the first edition we already stressed this. Subsequent empirical and theoretical research has confirmed that a better way to understand the working of the foreign exchange market is to build on the assumption that economic agents are rational in a limited sense. We develop these ideas more thoroughly in this edition.

In working on this second edition I have profited from many discussions with colleagues and students. In particular, I am grateful to Stanley Black, Ralph Bryant, Claudia Costa, and Harris Dellas for their comments and suggestions. I also thank Danny Decupere for research and Francine Duysens for secretarial assistance.

P. D. G.
March 1996

CONTENTS

LIST OF FIGURES

LIST OF TABLES

ABBREVIATIONS

ARIMA	*autoregressive-moving average process*
BIS	*Bank for International Settlements*
CEPS	*Centre for European Policy Studies*
CPI	*consumer price index*
EMS	*European Monetary System*
G-5	*Group of five major industrial countries*
IMF	*International Monetary Fund*
NAIRU	*non-accelerating-inflation rate of unemployment*
OECD	*Organization of Economic Co-operation and Development*
OPEC	*Organization of Petroleum Exporting Countries*
PPP	*Purchasing Power Parity*
RMSE	*root mean squared errors*
SDR	*Special Drawing Rights*

THE FUNDAMENTALS OF MONEY:
NATIONAL AND INTERNATIONAL

1. Introduction

The development of a modern economy would not have been possible with-out the use of money. This is also true at the international level. The use of a monetary instrument which is acceptable as a means of payments and as a unit of account to participants in international transactions is a prerequisite for the development of international trade. Without a means of payments and a unit of account, international trade has to revert to barter.

The basic problem of a barter economy is that an individual wishing to buy something does not know whether the product he supplies in the exchange will be acceptable to his counterpart. A great deal of searching will be involved in finding the person who has exactly the reverse desire in exchanging these products (the 'double coincidence of wants'). Thus, barter hampers international trade by imposing large search costs.

These benefits of money are well known. They are realized both in national and international transactions. The puzzling thing is that despite the obvious gain from the use of one money, it appears to be quite difficult to introduce one money in the international economy which will be acceptable to everyone. If the benefits of using one money in international trade are so obviously large, why don't we observe it? What are the problems that have made the introduction of a generally acceptable means of payment and unit of account more difficult at the international level than at the national one? Answering these questions is one of the tasks of this book. In order to do so, we have to start by concentrating on the basics of money.

2. Characteristics of money

A *first* fundamental characteristic of money is that it is very much like a *collective good*. That is, the benefit of money to an individual derives exclusively from the fact that others also use it. Contrary to a private good which has a utility to an individual whether or not others also consume it, money has no utility whatsoever when used by only one person. In order to have value to an individual, it is necessary that others also use it. And the larger the group of people using the same money the greater the utility to that individual.

In this connection, Tobin has compared the utility of money with that of a language. A common language, like a common money, is useful because it is used by many people. It becomes more useful as a means of communication when shared by an increasing number of individuals.

As is well known from economic theory, problems arise when a collective good is supplied in private markets. One of the main reasons is that it is quite often difficult to induce individuals to contribute voluntarily to a collective good system, when it is hard to exclude them from its use. When collective goods are supplied by voluntary contributions, too many individuals will refuse to pay for the system if they know they cannot be excluded from it. In other words there will be too many free riders.

There is a *second* characteristic of money, however, which changes the nature of the problem, and makes money a *very special collective good*. This is that the users of money can be made to pay quite easily. Everybody who uses money will have to hold money balances. These money balances (cash, demand deposits) carry no (or a relatively low) interest rate, so that the user of money pays by the fact that he forgoes a higher interest rate on other assets. As a result, there exists a mechanism in the supply of the collective good which avoids the free riding problem which we encounter with many other collective goods.

The preceding implies that it will be profitable for private agents to supply money services. The source of their profits lies in the fact that money holders are willing to pay a price for the service in the form of a low return on these money balances.

We now come to a *third* characteristic of money. The willingness to hold money balances is based on the *confidence* of the holder that these assets will not lose their value. In order for a particular money to be accepted, economic agents must be confident that the supplier of this asset will not do things that reduce its value. If they fear that this may happen, they will not voluntarily hold these money balances. This raises a very fundamental problem for the supplier of money: how to convince the holder that he, the supplier, can be trusted?

The supplier can solve this problem in two ways. One is by investing in all kinds of confidence building schemes. For example, the supplier can invest in sunk capital (large and luxurious buildings), i.e. physical assets that lose much of their value if the business is discontinued. In doing so the supplier ties his hands. As a result, he also convinces the holder of the money that he will not run away, or do other foolish things. If he did, he would lose these valuable symbols of trust.

Another, and probably more important confidence building scheme is to guarantee that the money can be converted at a fixed price into another asset over whose value the supplier has no control. Such a guarantee existed during the period of the gold standard, when holders of currency could convert their holdings into gold at the central bank. Such guarantees exist today in most countries in that bank deposits can be converted into currency at a fixed price.

As is well known, there is a problem of credibility in such a commitment. Holders of money realize that there might be situations in which it will not be in the interest of the issuer of money to fulfil his commitment. Thus the rule requiring the supplier to maintain convertibility may lack credibility. We will encounter this problem many times during our discussion of the post-war history of international money. The convertibility of the domestic currency into foreign currencies at a fixed price was the main confidence building device used by countries to have their currency accepted in international transactions. As in the old days, problems of the credibility of these commitments quickly arose.

All these confidence building devices are costly, but also necessary to convince the money holder that the supplier of money will not willingly engage in activities which lead to a reduction of the value of money.

Thus, supplying money can be a very profitable business for private entrepreneurs despite the fact that money has the characteristics of a collective good. Suppliers, however, will have to incur costs not only to run the business, but also to build up a capital of trust. Without the confidence in the stability of its value, economic agents will not freely hold money.

A *fourth* characteristic of money has to do with *economies of scale* involved in its supply. This can best be explained as follows. Suppose a country has two issuers of different currencies. (The existence of several suppliers of currency occurred frequently in the early days of the development of paper money). Call these currencies A and B. As the issuers of these currencies are likely to follow different policies, the changes in the value of these two currencies will not be the same. As a result, the price of one currency in terms of the other is likely to fluctuate. The existence of these two separate currencies in the same country reduces the utility of each of them to the residents of that country. Certain transactions will have to be done with currency A, others with currency B. Currency A and B will not be universal units of account and media of exchange in this country.

If then one currency, say currency A, were to gain acceptance for all transactions, its usefulness would certainly increase. As a result, residents of that country would be willing to pay a higher price for currency A if it achieves this general acceptance. This means that there is scope for the issuer of currency A to increase his profitability by expanding the size of his operations, and by supplanting currency B. The same will hold for the issuer of currency B.

We can make this point clearer by recognizing that the supply of money involves a double operation. The supplier issues a liability, which is used as money, and purchases an asset (extends credit). The source of the profit of the issuer of money (the bank) is the margin between the interest rate earned on the asset and the interest paid on the liability. When the liability of the bank gains increasing acceptance as money, the users are willing to pay more for the service, i.e. they are willing to forgo a higher interest rate when holding this money. As a result, the interest margin between the assets and the liabilities of the bank can increase. In this sense the issuer of money profits from increasing returns to scale.

It is important to realize here that the economies of scale in the supply of money are derived from the collective good nature of money which we discussed earlier. Economies of scale arise because the utility of using a particular money increases with the number of individuals using that money. Thus, the economies of scale do not arise because of some technological feature in the supply of money, but rather because of the nature of the utility of money. The economies of scale derive from the demand side. Banks can then exploit these economies of scale by expanding the supply of their money.

3. The concentration of the money supply process

The upshot of the previous analysis is that there will be a strong pressure towards capturing the benefits of these economies of scale. As in other sectors characterized by economies of scale, this will lead either to concentration of the money supply process in the hands of a few, and possibly only one issuer, or by a cartelization of the market. In the first case, the supplier of money achieves a monopoly, which allows him to maximize the interest margin. In the second case several suppliers will make an agreement to tie to each other the currencies they issue, for example by fixing their exchange rates, and by regulating the supply process. In so doing they create one monetary area and increase the usefulness of their currencies. This then also allows them to increase the margin between the interest rate on their assets and on their liabilities.

This process towards concentration and cartelization is not a smooth one. It is characterized by upheavals and crisis. Its dynamics can be described as follows. In order to capture a larger part of a profitable market, the individual bank takes more risk. Its portfolio of assets will be enlarged by loans to less reputable borrowers. Some banks will be successful in this policy of enlarging their market share. Others are less fortunate when some of their borrowers fail to repay their debt. This sets in motion a bank crisis, when the holders of the currency issued by this bank present their holdings for conversion in hard cash (gold for example). Not all the holders of the currency issued by the bank can be satisfied, since the bank typically covers only a fraction of its liabilities by cash reserves.

The rest of the story is well known from the history books. The failure of the bank to convert its liabilities into hard cash triggers a domino effect. It undermines the confidence in the whole system, and it can set in motion a general run on the banks. Even banks with a sound portfolio of loans will not be spared, and will be faced with a liquidity problem resulting from conversions of their liabilities into hard cash. This was a recurrent feature of American monetary history during the nineteenth century. When the dust settles, fewer banks will be left. Those that remain will have a larger market share and will be more profitable. The cycle can start all over again.[1]

4. Money and state monopolies

This tendency towards concentration of the money issuing business is inevitable and follows from the dynamics engendered by the large economies of scale involved in supplying money. It leads to another phenomenon: the involvement of the state in the money supply process. The pressure of the state to take over the business will mount with each crisis. This follows from the fact that each crisis leads to losses for a large number of people, who are holding worthless paper. The popular outrage will form the political basis for government action. In addition, the banks who are left over after a crisis have an interest in preventing newcomers from entering the market. Although this tendency is prevalent in many markets, it is especially important in the banking sector, where large externalities occur during every bank crisis. As mentioned in the previous paragraph, during a bank crisis the sound banks are affected by the run on their cash. They have, therefore, an interest in preventing banks from engaging in unsound banking practices. They will call for government control on these banking practices. This will usually involve making entry into the business more difficult.

Few countries have resisted this pressure from the public and from the banking community. As a result, in all countries of the world the government has gradually acquired more control over the money supply process.

In most non-industrial countries of the world this has led to complete nationalization of the money supply process. In those countries, the state has acquired a monopoly power to issue currency *and* deposits. In most industrial countries, however, some division of labour has been found between the state and the private sector. The government has the monopoly power over the issue of currency only. Private banks have kept their position in the money supply process by issuing deposits.

An important question here is why the same phenomena that have led to the nationalization of the supply of currency have not led to the nationalization of the supply of deposits in the industrialized world. Two features have made this

---

[1] There is an important literature on the advantages but also on the problems of monetary regimes based on the free supply of currency. For a survey see Laidler (1992). The best known proponent of such a system is Hayek (1978). See B. Klein (1974) for a formal analysis.

possible. First, and foremost, after the great banking crises of the 1930s when deposit holders attempted massively to convert their deposits into currency, the monetary authorities have reacted by providing a lender of last resort service to the banks.[2] This effectively guaranteed that sound banks which faced a liquidity problem during a banking crisis, would be able to obtain all the currency needed to satisfy their deposit holders. The existence of this guarantee was itself sufficient to eliminate these banking crises.[3]

A second feature of the division of labour between the public and the private sector in the money supply process has to do with economies of scale. By effectively imposing one currency on the whole country, and by guaranteeing that deposits could be converted into that one currency, the government made sure that the economies of scale in the supply of money were fully exploited. Whereas in the old days an individual bank could profit from these economies of scale by expanding its scale of operation, this is no longer true in the present system. In the system which now prevails in most countries, small and large banks issuing deposits capture the same benefits from the economies of scale involved in creating money. There is therefore no natural advantage gained by being large. The economies of scale in the money supply process have been made external to the banking firms.[4]

This is an important aspect of the system arrived at in most industrialized countries. It makes it possible to have many banks who compete without the inevitable tendency towards monopolization of the supply of deposits. This division of labour between the public and the private sector in the money supply process is an ingenious construction. It allows the benefits of competition to be reaped, and at the same time it avoids the problems inherent in a completely free banking system.

This can also be summarized as follows: the government supplies the public good aspect of money. This means that national money is the unit of account and the medium of exchange acceptable to all residents of the country. By doing this, the government allows the economies of scale to be exploited fully. The private banking sector can then in a sense 'free ride' on the existence of a nationally accepted numeraire and supply deposits in the same numeraire. There is no need for these individual banks to acquire a monopoly position to fully capture the economies of scale. As a result, the great turbulence inherent in such attempts to acquire a monopoly position are avoided.

---

[2] In the 19th cent. Walter Bagehot had already provided the theoretical basis for such service; see Bagehot (1917). It took a major crisis to convince the US monetary authorities to follow Bagehot's advice.

[3] Many countries also added to the lender of last resort function deposit insurance schemes. These helped to convince the deposit holder that his assets in the bank were safe. Both the lender of last resort facility and the deposit insurance scheme solved a major confidence problem inherent in private banking. See Laidler (1992).

[4] It should be stressed that we consider here only the economies of scale arising from the collective good nature of money (the demand side). There are other sources of economies of scale in the supply of money (e.g. diversification of risk) which can still be captured when individual banks increase their size.

5. Money and inflation

The monetary institutions arrived at in most countries solved the major problem of a competitive money supply system: its unstable character. It created, however, a new one: *inflation*.

In a competitive system there is an automatic control on the over-issue of currency. An individual bank which wishes to expand its loan portfolio faster than the other banks will have to reduce the interest margin between its loans and its liabilities. Since the currency it issues carries a zero interest rate this means that the bank has to reduce the loan rate to expand its activities. In so doing its operations become more risky. The currency issued by this bank will become riskier than the other currencies in circulation. They all carry the same zero interest rate, however. As a result, economic agents will be tempted to convert the currency of the over-issuing bank into hard cash or into the other currencies. This will force the bank to curtail its business, or to close its doors.

As argued earlier, this process may lead to a lot of disturbances and crises. It will, however, not lead to generalized inflation.[5] Things are quite different when the state has taken over the supply of currency. As with the private issuer, the government will occasionally be tempted to quickly expand credit and thus the supply of currency (for example to finance a war). This will lead to the same reactions by the currency holders as in the previous case: they will want to convert the currency into gold or into another (foreign) currency. The main difference between the private issuer of currency and the government is that the latter can declare the currency to be inconvertible without going broke. In contrast to the private issuer, the government can coerce its citizens to use the inconvertible currency as a domestic unit of account and medium of exchange. As a result, there are no checks anymore on the issue of currency by the government. Inflation will be a recurrent phenomenon.

6. International money: how different from national money?

We have sketched the major features of the money supply mechanism in individual countries. We must now come to the implications for the international monetary system.

---

[5] If the hard cash (e.g. gold) into which the currencies are convertible becomes more plentiful, we may have inflation. This source of inflation, however, can be said to be external to the operation of the free banking system. Several recent papers have shown that free banking in general leads to lower inflation than a monopolized banking system. See Baye, *et al.* (1993).

At the international level several currencies compete. No single country has been able to impose its currency on the whole world. The major problems which we encountered in our discussion of the money supply process within a country also appear at the international level.

We can classify these problems as follows. First, there will be problems arising from the collective good aspect of money. Second, there will be problems of confidence and credibility.

6.1. Money as an international collective good

An individual country (and its banking system) which manages to have its currency accepted over a wider range of international transactions provides a collective good service to the world. This country (or rather the banking sector of this country, including the central bank) will be able to capture these benefits by obtaining a larger spread between its assets and liabilities. As argued earlier, this leads to economies of scale in the supply of an international money. There are therefore incentives for the suppliers of national moneys to extend the reach of their moneys beyond the national boundaries.

Thus, as was the case during the development of the national currencies, strong competitive forces will also exist at the international level between the suppliers of different national currencies. Up to now, however, and contrary to what happened within countries, this has not led to an international monopoly for one currency. As a result, the full benefits of using one money have not been realized at the international level. What are the reasons for this different evolution?

The answer has to do with the different political environment at the national and the international level. At the national level governments invariably took over the supply of currency, for the reasons analysed in the previous sections. At the international level, there has been a conspicuous absence of a central authority which is able to monopolize the currency issue. Since it is highly unlikely that such a world government will come about in the near future, one has to conclude that the supply of currencies at the international level will remain a highly competitive business.

Another important difference between the national and the international development of money follows from the fact that national governments have maintained national niches where the local currency is enforced by the power of the state. As a result, the competitive forces and the economies of scale which naturally tend to lead to the disappearance of many currencies, were held in check by these local monopolies.

On the whole, however, the basic forces in the supply of international currencies are competitive. They, therefore, also lead to a lot of volatility. Much of the history of international money has been characterized by attempts by national governments to provide some institutional structure aimed at mitigating the effects of this competition.

6.2. International money and the confidence problem

How does the issuer of a national currency convince potential foreign users that it is a currency which will keep a stable and predictable value? Such confidence on the part of the foreign economic agents is necessary for them to willingly hold the currency. If these foreign agents fear that the issuing country may follow policies which will reduce the value of the currency, they will not hold it. Since there is no international authority with the power to force the use of that currency in international transactions, it will disappear as an international medium of exchange and unit of account. Thus, a national currency can graduate as an international currency if there is confidence that it will maintain a stable purchasing power.

This confidence, however, does not come freely. Economic agents do not trust promises of governments. This is true both at the national and the international level. In order to convince distrustful economic agents of his good faith, the supplier will have to invest in confidence building devices. The most common is to announce that the national currency will be freely convertible *at a fixed price* into another asset, over whose value the issuing country has no control. This other asset has most often been gold, or other national currencies. In committing himself to such a convertibility, the issuer is 'bonding' himself, i.e. he is tying his own hands so as to convince the foreign holder that he can do no harm to the value of the currency.

The recurrent problem with such a commitment is its credibility. The issuer may announce today that his money will be convertible in gold or in foreign currencies at a fixed price, but what guarantee does the holder have that this commitment will be honoured in the future? No international authority exists which can force the issuing country to honour its commitment. We face here a very fundamental problem of the international monetary system. It has been called the 'time consistency' problem. As will be clear from the following chapters, it is at the core of any explanation of the difficulties of setting up a stable system.

This *time consistency* problem can be described as follows. The issuing country will at each point in time compare the benefits of continuing its commitment towards (fixed price) convertibility with the costs of doing so. The costs of maintaining convertibility in general derive from the fact that the issuing country must subordinate its monetary policy to the requirements of convertibility. What this implies in practice will be analysed in the next chapter. It is almost inevitable that there will be moments at which the issuing country will find the costs to be larger than the benefits. In that case it will decide to renege on its commitment. Since the holders of the currency know that this is the calculus made by the issuing country, the commitment towards (fixed price) convertibility will have a low credibility.

The problem is a very general one because the other currencies which could be used in international transactions suffer from the same credibility problem. Economic agents will have to evaluate how credible these different commitments are. This will lead to recurrent confidence crises, when economic agents re-evaluate these commitments. When this happens, large movements in and out of particular currencies will occur.

We can summarize the preceding discussion as follows. Strong competitive pressure exists for individual countries (and their banking systems) to extend money services to the rest of the world. This competitive pressure derives from the economies of scale inherent in the supply of money to the world (which, as we saw earlier, derives from the collective good nature of money). In this competitive battle those countries that extend their money to a larger part of the world gain an advantage.

In order for a country to be a successful supplier of money to the rest of the world, it must convince foreign holders that this money will keep a stable value. This can be achieved, for example, by offering a guarantee to these holders, involving the promise of convertibility into another asset (gold or foreign currencies). However, the credibility of such a commitment is always dubious, as the holders of the currency realize that the issuing country may act opportunistically and refuse to honour its commitment under certain contingencies.

It follows that the international supply of money is likely to be a bumpy road. On the one hand, many countries compete to reap the benefits of supplying money. On the other hand, they face the continuous distrust of money users who will switch in and out of currencies at the whim of slight changes in confidence in these moneys. Thus, a competitive international money supply process is likely to exhibit a lot of volatility and recurrent crises.

Box 1.1. The economics of standards: an application to money

Some of the problems associated with the origins of money can also be found in the way standards are established. Take the example of a word-processor program like WordPerfect or MS-Word. These programs are privately produced. They are certainly private goods in that the exclusion principle can be used to make individuals pay for acquiring the product (like money). At the same time however there is a public good aspect in these programs in that the utility I derive from acquiring and using, say, MS-Word also depends on the number of consumers who use MS-Word. The reason is that MS-Word is, like a language, a means of communication. If many other people (e.g. my publisher) use the same program I can easily transfer texts. If I use a program that few others use I will have little utility from this program even if it is superior.

This public good aspect of word processors creates economies of scale separate from the technical economies of scale that derive from the fact that producers of software incur large development costs. These technical economies of scale typically lead to declining average cost curves. The economies of scale discussed here derive from the demand side: as the number of users of a particular program increases, new users will be willing to pay a premium over and above the price they are willing to pay for programs with a smaller number of users (assuming the same quality). These economies of scale will be exploited by the software companies.

It is clear that this feature must lead to concentration effects. The most useful program will be the one that is used by everybody, much in the same way as the most useful money would be the one that is used by the whole world. Must this necessarily lead to one program taking over the whole market and becoming the sole standard? Not necessarily. We observe an interesting development in the word-processing market. At some point, when the number of competing major programs is not too large, it becomes attractive for the individual producers to attach conversion routines in their programs allowing the customer to easily translate his texts into the competing programs' language, and to import texts created by other software programs. In so doing, the producer dramatically enlarges the domain over which his customers can communicate. Today all the major programs have these conversion utilities embedded in their architecture. As a result, the user of say WordPerfect or MS-Word can effectively communicate with (almost) all users of word processors without incurring significant conversion costs. This development then allows the market to find an equilibrium with several relatively large producers. The dynamics of concentration can stop here.

The remarkable thing is that the free market of word processors has achieved this equilibrium in which only a handful of programs have come to dominate world-wide, in a relatively short period. How come such an equilibrium appears to be so much more difficult to realize in the sphere of money? In order to answer this question it is good to recognize that in the sphere of money similar features as in the word-processing market are now in existence. In particular, as indicated earlier, the moneys of almost all industrial countries have similar conversion facilities as the major word-processing programs. These conversion formulas increase the usefulness of national moneys.

Not all conversion formulas are the same, however. Some are more costly than others. Two features are important here to determine the cost of conversion. First, the degree of freedom with which the conversion can be done. Second the existence or not of a price guarantee at conversion. In general the least costly conversion is one where the exchange of money is completely free (no exchange controls) at a fixed price. All other formulas, for example free convertibility at a flexible price, create more costly conversions, and therefore reduce the usefulness of the national money.[6]

We return to our original question which we now rephrase as follows. Why are not all countries going for the least cost conversion formulas? The answer has to do with problems of credibility of promising conversion at a fixed price. And here the word-processing market and money become quite different. In the word-processing market, producers encounter no credibility problem when they sell a program allowing their customers to freely (and almost costlessly) import and export texts from and into other programs. The conversion program is a technical formula that once installed cannot be changed. Things are very different with money. When the monetary authorities promise to convert the national money into a foreign currency (or into gold in the old days), this promise will always be in doubt. We will come back to this problem to analyse the reasons underlying this inherent lack of credibility of a fixed exchange rate commitment. Here we stress that the monetary authorities will find it more difficult than the word-processor producers to develop conversion facilities which effectively create one standard with all the benefits obtained from such a standard. It is likely that in the monetary sphere the solution arrived at in the word-processing market will not lead to a stable equilibrium. The only stable solution that generates all the benefits of having one standard is likely to be one in which only one money exists.

---

[6] These different conversion formulas will be discussed later.

7. Commitment versus coercion in the international monetary systems

The history of the international monetary system of the last 100 years is a sequence of attempts to build international institutions aiming at capturing the benefits of the process of international money creation while at the same time avoiding the crises inherent in this competitive system. It is useful to characterize these attempts by the mix of control (coercion) and commitment the authorities have used. As we have seen earlier, the national monetary systems contain a mix of coercion and commitment. The authorities coerce their citizens to use the national money for domestic transactions. At the same time, there is usually an element of commitment, in that the commercial banks guarantee the conversion of their outstanding deposits into cash. In order to guarantee the credibility of this commitment, the government regulates the activities of the banks.

At the international level we also observe various mixes of coercion and commitment. At one extreme the national authorities control all financial trans-actions of their residents with the outside world, and there is no commitment towards the convertibility of the domestic money into another asset at a fixed price. At the other extreme, the buying and selling of foreign currencies by resid-ents is left completely free, and the authorities commit themselves to convert their currencies into another asset (gold or foreign currency) at a fixed price. In between these two extremes we can have systems with few commitments towards convertibility (at a fixed price) and very little control over international financial transactions.

Usually the existing systems will involve a mix of these two characteristics, coercion and commitment.[7] During the post-war period the world experienced systems with very different mixes of coercion and commitment. It is fair to say that the world has moved towards less coercion *and* less commitment especially since the 1980s. In the following chapters we analyse these systems. Before we analyse the post-war system, however, it is useful to study its antecedents, in particular the international gold standard.

8. The international gold standard

The international gold standard which was in existence during the last part of the nineteenth century until 1914 was a monetary arrangement among the major countries of the world. Its main feature was that each participating country com-mitted itself to guaranteeing the free convertibility of its currency into gold at

---

[7] It is clear, however, that in order for a national currency to become an international money, the mix will have to contain relatively little coercion. The reason is simple. Foreigners cannot be coerced by the national authorities, and will not be interested in holding a currency that cannot be acquired and disposed of freely. Thus, for a currency to graduate to the level of international money, control over the sale and purchase of that currency must be held to a minimum.

a fixed price.[8] In the terminology we just introduced, it was a system with commitment and with little coercion. This combination of commitment towards convertibility and absence of controls had important implications.

First, residents of the participating countries now had at their disposal a domestic currency which was freely convertible at a fixed price into an asset (gold) acceptable in international payments.

In day to day transactions the detour of gold was superfluous. The fact that each currency was convertible into gold at a fixed price also made it possible that each currency was convertible into all others also at a fixed price. Professional arbitrage would make sure that when one unit of, say, currency A was worth one gram of gold, and one unit of currency B was worth half a gram of gold, currency A would be worth twice as much as currency B. Economic agents could then directly convert one unit of currency A into two units of currency B, without the trouble of first having to buy gold and then sell it. (Actual shipments of gold only took place when the exchange rate of currencies A and B got out of line with the exchange rate implicit in the gold prices of the two currencies.)

As a result of this international arrangement, each participating currency became effectively an international currency. An importer, for example, who wanted to buy foreign goods could use his own money to make the transactions, and could work out the cost in his own currency. Thus, the effect of the arrangement was to provide a collective good, international money, to all participants. This was beneficial not only in terms of greater efficiency. It also helped to stabilize the international monetary system. The economies of scale inherent in the supply of money were made external to individual countries' banks. All these banks (whether small or large) could now capture the benefits from the existence of one *de facto* international money. They did not have to expand their size to capture these benefits. As a result, the upheavals of a competitive banking system where individual banks try to grab the benefits of large size were avoided.

Second, the participating countries had to accept some rules ('the rules of the game') for this system to be workable. These rules can be illustrated by an example. Suppose one country experienced a faster increase of the supply of the domestic currency. (This could be due, for example, to a large increase in government spending which is financed by issuing currency.) As a result, domestic prices tended to increase faster than foreign prices. This, in turn, stimulated imports (which had become relatively cheap) and made exports more difficult (which had become more expensive). The trade account deteriorated. This had important implications for the foreign exchange market. There was now an excess demand for the foreign currency. The domestic banks which had to supply these foreign currencies to their customers bought them from the central bank by reducing their cash reserves. The central bank, however, did not hold foreign currency but held gold only.[9] It used the latter to obtain these foreign

---

[8] For a recent historical analysis of the international gold standard, see Eichengreen (1995).
[9] This does not mean that they held no foreign currencies at all. Most of their international reserves consisted of gold.

currencies from the foreign central banks. When the transaction was completed, the domestic central bank had lost gold to the benefit of the foreign central bank.

The monetary effect of this transaction was that the domestic money stock had declined. Residents now held less domestic currency (which they had sold to obtain foreign currency). The counterpart was a decline in the gold stock of the country. The rules of the game now implied that the country should allow the money stock effectively to decline. Or put differently, it allowed the money stock to move in the same direction as the gold stock. This rule ensured that domestic prices would start declining again and that the trade account could return to equilibrium.

It can easily be seen that this rule was necessary to ensure continuous convertibility of the domestic currency into gold. Suppose the country did not apply the rule. As a result, when the gold stock declined the central bank took action to ensure that the domestic money stock did not decline. This involved increasing the cash reserves of the commercial banks (which had declined in the previous transaction). The important implication of this policy was that the domestic price level was permanently above the foreign price level. As a result, the country was faced with a continuous deficit in its trade account, and, therefore, a permanent excess demand for the foreign currency. Thus, it also follows that the central bank continuously lost gold, until the gold stock was completely depleted. A run on the gold stock of the central bank was likely to occur, however, before the stock was depleted, forcing the authorities to close the gold window.[10]

We conclude that the rules of the game were a necessary condition for ensuring convertibility. In addition, the rules of the game had a positive effect on the credibility of the authorities' commitment towards convertibility. The fact that the authorities applied the rules of the game could be considered as visible evidence that they were serious about maintaining convertibility.[11]

Despite the rules and the apparent seriousness of the authorities to maintain convertibility, the system did not survive the First World War. Why not? The answer is the same as the answer to the question why during the history of national money, the monetary authorities invariably came to a point where they refused to honour their promise to convert currency into gold. The best historical example is the inconvertibility of sterling which was instituted during the Napoleonic Wars.

---

[10] There is an important literature analysing the timing of these runs on the central bank which will be discussed in Ch. 4.

[11] There has been some debate about how seriously major central banks applied the rules of the game during the period of the international gold standard. See Bloomfield (1959), Cooper (1982), and Eichengreen (1995). The evidence indicates that the application of the rule was far from perfect. Nevertheless it can be said that the monetary authorities were usually taking steps towards monetary deflation when large outflows of gold occurred. Also, countries like Great Britain relied on movements of the discount rate to forestall actual gold movements. For example, the Bank of England would increase the discount rate when gold outflows threatened to occur (for example as a result of a deficit in the trade account).

The pressure to finance war activities is generally so high that governments will inevitably finance part of the military expenditures by issuing currency. It is then also inevitable that the amount of currency in circulation will become so large relative to the gold stock that a confidence problem arises and that a run on the gold stock is set in motion. The reaction of the monetary authorities has always been to close the gold window when major disturbances (like wars) occur. As will be seen later, during the post-war period, disturbances of lesser magnitude than a world war led to very similar problems.

At the end of the First World War, conditions were re-established to institute an international gold standard. Although attempts were made by some countries to do so, these failed. This is not the place to analyse the reasons for this failure.[12] The important point to note here is that as a result of this failure, the international monetary system of the inter-war period was characterized by crisis and upheaval. The intensity of the crisis was so great that the conviction arose that a competitive international monetary system would always lead to extreme disorder.

The Second World War, with its physical and economic destruction, provided the basis for the start of a new system. Under the leadership of the US, the blueprint of a new international monetary system was drawn up in Bretton Woods at the end of the Second World War. It came to be known as the Bretton Woods system.

---

[12] Kindleberger (1973) has identified an important problem of the inter-war period, i.e. the absence of a country with a leading position. The UK was losing its role as a world leader, and the US had not yet taken up this role. This power vacuum was an important factor in the unsuccessful attempts at restoring a stable international monetary system in the inter-war period. For a fascinating account of this period, see also the classic work of Nurkse (1944).

FIXED EXCHANGE RATE EXPERIENCES IN THE POST-WAR PERIOD

During the post-war period several major attempts were made at introducing and maintaining systems of currency convertibility combined with fixed exchange rates. The most important one, undoubtedly, was the Bretton Woods system which involved most industrialized nations and which was conceived immediately after the war. Another important experiment was started in 1979 by a number of European countries and led to the European Monetary System. We discuss these two attempts at fixing the exchange rates of convertible currencies. In this chapter we describe the main features of these systems. In the next chapter we ask why these systems of fixed exchange rates did not survive.

1. The Bretton Woods system

1.1. The blueprint

The Bretton Woods system was probably the most ambitious international monetary agreement between sovereign states in history. Its essential feature was borrowed from the international gold standard. As in the latter, the Bretton Woods system relied on a commitment towards convertibility. Domestic currencies were to be made freely convertible at a *fixed price* into an asset over which the issuing countries had no direct control. If credible, this commitment by national authorities would provide the basis for distrustful economic agents to willingly hold national moneys, and to use them in international transactions.

In addition, such a system would allow economic agents to profit, *de facto*, from a world-wide money. Since residents of a country were given a guarantee that their money was freely convertible at a fixed price into other currencies, they could consider the foreign currency as an extension of their own. Thus, if the system worked as in the blueprint, the world would approximate the ideal situation in which there exists one world money. Such a situation would facilitate international trade and development. In addition, the benefits of the collective good, international money, would be distributed to all participating countries alike. As a result, the competitive scramble by the individual suppliers of money to capture the economies of scale inherent in the money supply process would be avoided.

Thus, the Bretton Woods system, as a blueprint, contained a mix of commitment and coercion similar to the international gold standard. The freedom to transact in different moneys was thought to be essential to create a collective good for the world. The commitment towards convertibility at a fixed price was seen as the basis for confidence in the stability of national moneys.

This blueprint, however, was not put into practice immediately. It turned out to be quite difficult to allow transactions to operate freely. As a result, the blueprint was applied much later, in 1958, when the major currencies were made freely convertible into one another. We will come back to the question why the Bretton Woods system was applied only after such a delay. Here we concentrate further on the similarities and the differences of the Bretton Woods system and the international gold standard.

1.2. Gold Standard and Gold-Exchange Standard compared

Where the Bretton Woods system turned out to be different from the international gold standard is in the choice of assets into which national currencies would be convertible. An ingenious two-tier system of convertibility was established, which was known as the 'gold-exchange standard'. At the centre of the system stood the dollar. The US monetary authorities guaranteed the convertibility of the dollar into gold at the fixed price of \$35 per ounce of gold. Contrary to the days of the gold standard, however, this gold convertibility of the dollar was restricted to the foreign central banks only. If private US and foreign residents wanted to convert dollars into gold they had to turn to the private gold market, where no guarantee existed that gold could be bought at \$35 per ounce.

The second tier of the system was the commitment of the monetary authorities of the participating countries to convert their currency into dollars at a fixed price. The latter was called the official exchange rate (or the parity rate). It was supposed to remain fixed, except when the official exchange rate was persistently out of equilibrium. What this means, and how disequilibrium could come about, is one of the subjects of the next chapter.

One may wonder why such an elaborate system of convertibility was necessary. Was it not easier just to return to gold convertibility as it existed during the days of the international gold standard? There are several reasons why such an arrangement had become difficult. First, the distribution of gold across countries was very uneven. After the Second World War, about 70 per cent of all the gold held by the monetary authorities of the world was in the hands of the US. Thus, a credible gold convertibility of the other currencies would have required a massive redistribution of the gold stock. Second, it was generally believed that the existing gold stock would be insufficient to sustain the growing demand for international liquidity. One way to save on gold, then, was a two-tier convertible system, where the key currency would be convertible into gold and the other currencies into the key currency.[1]

One interesting aspect of the gold-exchange standard is that the arrangement provided for a system of 'checks and balances'. The countries outside the US committed themselves to convert their currencies into dollars at a fixed price, thereby linking their monetary fate to the dollar. The right to convert their dollar balances into gold at the fixed price of $35 per ounce of gold, however, gave these countries a considerable power to discipline the US monetary authorities. If the latter issued too many dollars, thereby creating inflation, the other countries could convert their dollar balances into gold. The implicit threat that they would do this was supposed to discipline the US monetary authorities.

1.3. The Bretton Woods system: the second stage in a three-stage story of international money

It is not uninteresting to point out here that the Bretton Woods system followed a general trend in the monetary history of most countries. In the first stage of the shift from a metallic currency to paper money, gold was deposited in the vaults of the banks. In the second stage the gold stock was centralized in the central bank, and the private banks replaced gold convertibility by convertibility of their liabilities into currency (the liability of the central bank). Thus, the gold exchange standard was a transposition of this second stage of national monetary development to the international scene.

The major difference between the national and the international version of this monetary model is that in the former the central bank had a coercive power over the commercial banks. It could, for example, force the banks to hold minimum reserves, to ensure the convertibility of their liabilities into currency. In the international version of this model, the US (the central bank) had no such power over the participating countries. Nor could the participating countries force the US to hold minimum gold reserves to ensure the gold convertibility of the dollar into gold. The whole system of commitments was based on trust.

As will be clear later, the third stage of this monetary arrangement when the central banks abolished the gold convertibility of the national currency, was achieved at the international level during the 1970s. Thus, the history of international money is to a certain extent a rerun of the history of national moneys.

This has important implications. Up to now we have not observed countries

---

[1] During the interwar period similar arrangements were tried out. They were the subject of the Genoa Conference which was held in 1922. One of the recommendations of the Conference participants was to limit the number of countries who would maintain the gold convertibility of their currency. Only the key currencies (in particular sterling) would be required to do so. The other currencies would maintain convertibility into sterling. The explicit rationale for this proposal was the fear of an insufficient stock of gold, and the deflationary pressure that this would exert on the world economy (see Clarke (1973)).

reintroducing gold convertibility into their domestic monetary systems. History seems to be irreversible in this area. Similarly, the third stage in which the international monetary system now finds itself with a complete absence of gold convertibility is unlikely to reverse itself. Why this is so, will become clear in the next chapter when we analyse the reasons for the abolition of gold convertibility during the 1970s.

2. The Bretton Woods system and the 'rules of the game'

The two-tier convertibility arrangement of the Bretton Woods system could only credibly be maintained if certain 'rules of the game' were followed. These rules were in essence the same as the rules that were supposed to be followed during the days of the international gold standard.

In order to describe these rules it is useful to employ the simple textbook model of demand and supply in the exchange market.[2] On the vertical axis we set out the exchange rate, S, which in the discussion here will be called the price of the dollar in units of DM. On the horizontal axis we have the quantities of dollars, Q, bought and sold in exchange for DM. The demand curve, Q_D, is a negatively sloped line, and expresses the idea that when the price of the dollar increases the demand for dollars will decline. One reason is that when the dollar increases in price, German residents will buy less US goods, and therefore reduce their demand for dollars, *ceteris paribus*.

The supply curve, Q_S, is a positively sloped line, i.e. when the dollar becomes more expensive relative to the DM its supply will increase. Here the main underlying mechanism is the activities of German exporters: when the dollar increases in price, German exporters will increase their supply of exports to the US. The dollars earned are sold in the exchange market, so that the supply increases.[3]

The intersection of the demand and supply determines the equilibrium exchange rate. The Bretton Woods agreement now involved the determination of an official exchange rate, together with an upper and lower limit. These limits were put at 1 per cent above and below the official exchange rate (represented by the horizontal lines S_U and S_L in Fig. 2.1). They defined a band of 2 per cent within which the exchange rate could move freely. As soon as the exchange rate was reaching the upper/lower limit the central bank was supposed to sell/buy dollars. This would prevent the price of the dollar from going beyond the limits.

[2] This well-known model has shortcomings. In particular, it relates the *flow* demand and the *flow* supply of foreign exchange to the exchange rate. The modern view (which will be used in later chapters) considers the exchange rate as the price which equilibrates the demand and the supply of *stocks* of assets. Despite these shortcomings we use it here because it is the simplest possible model which is able to illustrate the main point we want to establish.

[3] Note that the supply curve could be backward bending, so that the exchange market becomes unstable. This feature of the model is explained in every textbook on international economics. (See e.g., Caves and Jones (1985).) We do not pursue this complication here. In later chapters we return to issues concerning the stability of the exchange markets, using more appropriate models.

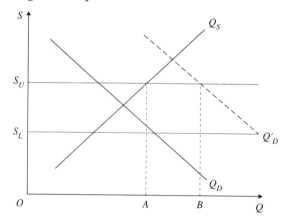

FIG. 2.1. Supply and demand in the foreign exchange market

In order to describe this mechanism in more detail let us assume that due to an exogenous increase in the demand for US products in Germany, the demand for dollars increases. We represent this shock by an upward shift of the demand curve in Fig. 2.1. The equilibrium exchange rate now exceeds the upper limit S_U. The German central bank will have to sell dollars so as to prevent the exchange rate from exceeding S_U. Fig. 2.1 tells us that an amount AB will have to be sold. As a result the total demand for dollars is OB. The supply consists of a component OA (the private supply) and AB (the official supply).

The rules of the game can now be formulated as follows. If this increase in the demand for dollars is a permanent phenomenon, the German authorities must follow restrictive monetary or fiscal policies aimed at reducing the excess demand for dollars. These restrictive policies reduce aggregate spending and therefore also spending for imports. These policies allow the demand curve in Fig. 2.1 to shift back to the left. They also make sure that the equilibrium exchange rate returns to a position within the bounds given by S_U and S_L.

A failure to follow this rule leads to a situation where the equilibrium exchange rate is permanently above the upper limit. Thus if the central bank were to decide not to follow the rule, it would have to intervene continuously, so that its stock of international reserves would inevitably be depleted. The fixed exchange rate of the dollar would not be sustainable.

It is not without interest to point out that the monetary effects of the interventions of the German monetary authorities in the exchange market lead to an automatic application of the rules of the game. This can be seen as follows. The sale of dollars by the Bundesbank is done in exchange for DM, which are presented to the Bundesbank by German residents. As a result, Deutsche Mark are taken out of circulation. The German money stock declines. This decline in the stock of money, in turn, leads to a reduction in spending and a decline in imports. Thus, if the central bank allows this mechanism to operate, it follows the rules of the game.

The major problem of the Bretton Woods system is that the application of these rules is not without cost. For example, the required reduction of aggregate spending may affect domestic output and employment negatively. We will come back to this problem in the next chapter, where we analyse in detail why the Bretton Woods system got into problems.

3. The Pre-Bretton Woods system[4]

The Bretton Woods system as we described it, did not really start operating until 1958. Up to that date most currencies of the industrialized countries remained inconvertible. That is, residents of these countries could not freely buy foreign currencies. Thus, during 1945–58, the monetary authorities applied only one aspect of the Bretton Woods convertibility rule. They guaranteed a fixed price at which they were buying and selling foreign currency. However, they did not allow economic agents to freely buy and sell foreign exchange at the fixed price. The mix between commitment and coercion was biased in favour of coercion.

Why did it take almost fifteen years before the system agreed on in 1944 at Bretton Woods, became effective? What were the characteristics and the problems of this hybrid system? These are the questions to which we now turn.

In order to understand why it took so long to apply the Bretton Woods system in practice, it is useful to study the attempts made by the United Kingdom in 1947 to introduce one of the basic features of this system, the free convertibility of sterling into dollars. As part of an agreement with the US in which the latter extended a loan of $3.7 billion, the UK authorities decided in 1947 to make the pound sterling convertible at a fixed price. Very quickly, however, a speculative crisis emerged, which forced the UK authorities to intervene in the foreign exchange market. In a few weeks the UK international reserves declined by two-thirds. It was clear that speculators did not have the necessary confidence that Britain could maintain the pound sterling at the announced fixed rate against the dollar. After this brief experiment the inconvertibility of the pound sterling was again instituted.

The failure of the pound sterling to weather its first confidence problem was an early signal of the problems the Bretton Woods system would face once the step towards convertibility was taken in 1959. This early failure also convinced the authorities of the European countries that their economies were not ready for the step towards convertibility.

The period from the end of the war until 1959 was characterized by substantial controls on exchange transactions. These controls started right after the war. In an attempt to facilitate imports of capital goods, many European countries maintained overvalued currencies, so as to enable residents of these countries to buy foreign currency (mainly dollars) cheaply. This system made it inevitable that

[4] For an excellent account on this period see Solomon (1977) and Van der Wee (1985).

excess demand for foreign currency (dollars) became a fact of life,[5] and that its purchase had to be regulated.

The result was that currencies were not freely convertible. This had the unfortunate effect that countries had to make sure that their bilateral trade with all the other countries was in equilibrium. The loss of efficiency of such a system was comparable to the loss of efficiency implicit in a barter economy. A country which exported to another country had to accept goods of that latter country in payment, even if these goods were not really desired or were not of the required quality.

It became clear that this bilateral trading system would inhibit the reconstruction of Europe. As a result (and the pressure of the US also helped), the European countries decided to institute the European Payments Union, which can be considered as the first step towards convertibility. Its main feature was that the payments system was multilateralized. Each country's payments and receipts from its trade transactions were centralized with the Bank for International Settlements (BIS). When after one month, a country had a net debtor (creditor) position in the system, it was required to make a payment (receive payment) in gold or dollars. Initially, only a fraction of these outstanding balances were settled with gold and dollars, the remainder being converted into a loan by the creditor country to the debtor country. The fraction to be settled in gold and dollars was progressively increased.[6]

This system certainly removed the worst inefficiencies of the bilateral payments system, and provided the basis for the sustained recovery of the European countries. When at the end of the 1950s, the financial position of the major European countries had improved significantly, the next step towards convertibility into dollars was taken. This convertibility into dollars also ensured that each currency which became convertible into dollars, also became convertible into all the other (dollar) convertible currencies.

It is no exaggeration to state that this step, together with the institution of the European Economic Community in the same year, contributed towards the explosion in the growth of trade in Europe, and to the historically unique growth of the European economies during the 1960s. Despite these advantages the Bretton Woods system collapsed in 1971.

4. The European monetary system

After the disintegration of the Bretton Woods system the industrialized world experienced a great deal of exchange rate volatility during the 1970s.[7] It was felt,

---

[5] This period was one of 'dollar shortage'. Many economists were gloomy about this and predicted a long period of excess demand for dollars. The best-known analysis is by McDougall (1957). It turned out to be completely wrong, as the next decade would be characterized by a dollar glut.

[6] Triffin was instrumental in providing a blueprint for this European Payments system. See Triffin (1957).

[7] In the next chapter we analyse the factors that led to the disintegration of the Bretton Woods system.

especially in Europe, that the high exchange rate variability contributed to the distortion of trade flows and was a source of conflicts between nations. As a result, under the initiative of Helmut Schmidt (the German Chancellor) and Valéry Giscard d'Estaing (the French President), members of the European Community established the European Monetary System (EMS) in 1979.

4.1. The blueprint

The operating principles of the EMS resembled very much those of Bretton Woods. Participating countries committed themselves to keeping their exchange rates fixed, i.e. to limit the fluctuations of these exchange rates between given margins of fluctuation.[8] Thus, one could represent the operation of the system very much as in Fig. 2.1 (which described the operations of the Bretton Woods system). All we have to do is to relabel the vertical axis. We call it now the price of, say, the DM in units of FF. The demand and the supply curves are then to be interpreted as the demand for and the supply of DM against FF. The French and German authorities agreed to define a parity rate (also called the central rate) and an upper and lower limit (S_U and S_L) around the parity rate. The EMS agreement then consisted of a commitment by France and Germany to keep the exchange rate between these upper and lower limits. All the other member countries did the same thing, i.e. they defined parity rates and upper and lower limits for their exchange rate *vis-à-vis* all the exchange rates of the other participating currencies in the system. This led to a matrix of central rates and upper and lower limits around them. Each of these central rates involved two countries and committed them to keep their exchange rates within the prescribed limits.[9]

Let us now return to Fig. 2.1, suitably redefined, to analyse the workings of the EMS further. Suppose that the demand for DM against FF shifts to the right. In order to prevent the exchange rate from increasing above the upper limit S_U, the Banque de France has to intervene in the market and sell DM against FF, in the amount represented by *AB*. If the Banque de France does not hold enough DM to make the intervention, the Bundesbank has to lend the DM to the Banque de France. Thus, France becomes a net debtor *vis-à-vis* Germany. (Note that it is immaterial whether it is the Banque de France or the Bundesbank who makes the intervention. If the Bundesbank intervenes, it will have to sell the same amount of DM in exchange for FF. In that case the Bundesbank acquires FF which is a liability of the French monetary authorities.)

---

[8] We disregard the use of the ECU in the European Monetary System. Initially the ECU stood as the symbol of the new monetary regime in Europe. However, it never acquired a practical importance in the operation of the system. For a more detailed analysis of the workings of the EMS, see De Grauwe (1994) and Gros and Thygesen (1992).

[9] The band of permissible fluctuation was not the same for all countries. The normal band was 4.5% (derived from the fact that the upper and lower limits were 2.25% above and below the central rate). This band was used by Belgium, Netherlands, France, Germany, and Denmark. Italy used a wider band of 12%. Later when Spain and Portugal joined they also used the wider band.

The rules of the game in the EMS were pretty much the same as in the Bretton Woods system. In the case discussed in the previous paragraph, France had to follow restrictive monetary and fiscal policies so as to reduce the excess demand for DM. Alternatively, Germany could follow expansionary monetary policies which would also have the effect of reducing the excess demand for DM. In general the system developed into a regime in which the deficit country (France in our example) was forced to make the adjustment. We return to this issue, because this asymmetry created conflicts in the system which were at the core of its ultimate disintegration.

During the first half of the 1980s, the EMS was a relatively 'flexible fixed exchange rate system'. Countries were not really fully committed to keeping the central rate unchanged. It was felt that if pressures became too high these central rates could be changed, provided the other member countries agreed to the change. Thus, in the example of Fig. 2.1 France could (with the agreement of Germany) decide to devalue the FF (i.e. raise the central rate of the DM), thereby shifting the upper and lower limits upwards. Such 'realignments' occurred frequently until the middle of the 1980s. From 1987 onwards, however, the system evolved into a truly fixed exchange rate regime, in which the member countries were fully committed to keep the central rates unchanged. They managed to do this until 1992–3, when speculative crises erupted, forcing some countries to leave the system. Those remaining in the system decided in August 1993 to dramatically increase the permissible band of fluctuation to 30 per cent (2 × 15 per cent).[10] The system could no longer be called a fixed exchange rate regime.

4.2. The EMS and Bretton Woods compared

As argued in the previous section, the essential operational principles of the EMS were the same as in the Bretton Woods system. Nevertheless there were also some major differences.

First, the two-tier structure that existed in the Bretton Woods system was completely absent in the EMS. Thus, each country was committed to convert its currency at a fixed price into other currencies of the system. None of the countries, however, committed itself to guarantee the conversion of its own currency into some other asset (gold in the Bretton Woods system). Thus, in contrast to the Bretton Woods system, the EMS was a symmetric one in which all countries were treated equally. This did not last, however, and the system gradually acquired asymmetric features (without, however, returning to the two-tier arrangement of the Bretton Woods regime). In the next chapter we analyse why these developments occurred.

Second, the 'commitment technology' was quite different in the two regimes. The EMS can be said to have been a *multilateral* fixed exchange rate regime.

---

[10] The exception was the Netherlands which maintained its commitment to keep its exchange rate *vis-à-vis* the DM within the narrow limits prevailing before the crisis.

This manifested itself in the fact that decisions to realign had to be taken by all member countries together. Thus, when say Belgium wanted to devalue its currency in 1982, the ministers of finance of all the member countries convened to decide about the appropriate new central rate of the Belgian franc against the other currencies. This was not the case in the Bretton Woods system. Each country could decide unilaterally to devalue or to revalue its currency against the dollar. The US essentially did not care. This 'benign neglect' attitude of the US was often criticized. It should be remembered that the US paid a price for this, i.e. it guaranteed the gold convertibility of the dollar at a fixed price.

Another way in which the multilateral nature of the EMS manifested itself was in the interventions in the foreign exchange markets. Each EMS country was committed to intervene in each of the participating currencies, if the exchange rate of that currency hit the limit of the intervention band. In the Bretton Woods system each country would intervene in dollars only, so as to keep the dollar exchange rate of its currency within the permissible band. Thus, the Banque de France only intervened in the dollar market of the FF and the Bundesbank in the dollar market of the DM. Triangular arbitrage[11] made sure that the FF/DM rate would also remain within a given band. The result was the same as in the EMS, i.e. all bilateral exchange rates of the participating currencies remained within a fixed band.[12] The nice thing about the Bretton Woods system is that the multilateral fixing of all exchange rates was possible despite the fact that the central banks only fixed their respective dollar rates. Private arbitrage, itself the result of convertibility, fixed the other exchange rates.

---

[11] Triangular arbitrage is an arbitrage activity in which economic agents take positions in three currencies. This arbitrage ensures that the bilateral exchange rate of say the DM in FF equals the ratio of the dollar rates of the FF and the DM. Thus, if the dollar/DM rate is 1.5 and the dollar/FF rate is 5, then arbitrage will ensure that the DM/FF rate is 3.33 (5/1.5).

[12] It should be mentioned that whereas the permissible band of fluctuation against the dollar was 2% (2 × 1%), it was 4% for all bilateral rates. An example makes clear why. Suppose the DM was at its upper limit against the dollar (+ 1%) and the FF at its lower limit (− 1%). Suppose now that shocks in the market drive the DM to its lower limit against the dollar (it depreciates by 2% against the dollar) and the FF to its upper limit (it appreciates by 2% against the dollar). In that case the DM has depreciated by 4% against the FF. This is also the maximum amount of depreciation possible by the DM against the FF.

WHY FIXED EXCHANGE RATE SYSTEMS COLLAPSE

1. Introduction

The Bretton Woods system and the European Monetary System were attempts at fixing exchange rates of convertible currencies. There can be no doubt that, if successful, these systems were quite attractive. They made it possible to extend the benefits of using one money to many countries. As a result economic agents of, say, Germany or the Netherlands could effectively consider their own currency, the DM or the guilder, to play the role of an international money. If a German or Dutch resident expected to import goods in the future, he had no uncertainty about whether his currency would be an acceptable means of payment for his trading partner. Since he could buy the foreign currency needed to pay his foreign supplier in unlimited amounts at a known price, his own currency could be considered as money with the status of an international means of payments. Thus, the system of convertibility, as it emerged after 1958, was the closest to a system of just one international money that one could envision.

Thus, there can be little doubt that the international monetary system which evolved after 1958 brought important benefits to the world. In a similar way the EMS provided public good benefits for its members. Why then did these systems only last for a little more than a decade? What kind of flaws did these systems have? These are the questions to which we now draw attention.

At the most general level the problem of fixed exchange rate systems can be formulated as follows. When a country commits itself to fix its exchange rate (i.e. to keep it within a specified band), it makes a promise: it pledges to keep the exchange rate fixed today and in the future. The problem of every promise, however, is that doubts may arise as to whether it will be kept. In other words, all promises lead to problems of credibility. This is, in a nutshell, the essential problem of fixed exchange rate systems.

The next question then is why countries would want to go back on a promise they made in the past. (Presumably, when they pledged to fix the exchange rate they must have considered that it was in their national interest to do so.) The answer is that there may arise circumstances in which the fixed exchange rate arrangement ceases to be seen as serving the national interest of the country. In that case the country will have an interest to renege on its promise. Economic agents will suspect this, and will take their precautions by selling (buying) the currencies involved. We have a speculative crisis. Much of this chapter will consist in identifying the conditions and the circumstances under which this credibility problem arises.

We will identify two problems of the fixed exchange rate system that lead to the credibility problem we have just identified. We call them the (n − 1) problem and the adjustment problem.

2. The (n − 1) problem

Every agreement to fix the exchange rates between two or more currencies necessitates rules which will govern the creation of money (liquidity) in this system of many countries. The issue has its origin in what is called the (n − 1) problem. In a system of n countries there are only n − 1 independent exchange rates. (If you do not understand this, take the case of two countries: they have only one exchange rate to care about.) Therefore only n − 1 countries have to use their monetary policies so as to maintain all the exchange rates fixed. There will be one monetary authority which is free to set its monetary policy independently from the exchange rate constraint. Put differently, the system has one degree of freedom. In a sense this is good news because it allows the countries in the system to use that degree of freedom to pursue some joint objective (e.g. stimulating the economy, or alternatively reducing inflation). The bad news, however, is that this degree of freedom is likely to be a source of conflict between the members of the system.

Let us illustrate the problem by a simple two-country model of the money markets. We assume a traditional *money demand function* in two countries, called A and B:

$$P_A L_A(Y_A, r_A) \tag{3.1}$$

and

$$P_B L_B(Y_B, r_B) \tag{3.2}$$

where P_A and P_B are the price levels in countries A and B; L_A and L_B are the liquidity preference functions in countries A and B; Y_A and Y_B are the levels of real income in countries A and B; and r_A and r_B are the levels of the (nominal) interest rate in A and B. Real income has a positive effect on the demand for money; the interest rate has a negative effect.

Money market equilibrium implies that the demand equals the supply of money in both countries, i.e.

$$P_A L_A(Y_A, r_A) = M_A \tag{3.3}$$

and

$$P_B L_B(Y_B, r_B) = M_B \tag{3.4}$$

where M_A and M_B are the supply of money in countries A and B.

Let us assume that the money markets of the two countries are linked together by the fact that capital is freely mobile between the two countries. In other words, there is full convertibility of the two currencies, both for current and capital account transactions. This allows us to use the *interest parity theory*. In Box 3.1 we develop this theory in more detail than we do here. Here we just use one version of this theory, the 'open' interest parity:

$$r_A = r_B + \mu \tag{3.5}$$

where μ is the *expected* rate of devaluation of the currency of country A (revaluation of currency B). This equation has a very simple interpretation. When the currency of country A is expected to devalue, μ becomes positive, and the interest rate of country A has to increase relative to the interest rate of country B. This is so because wealth owners will only be willing to hold A assets if they are compensated for the expected future decline in the value of the A currency by a higher interest return on A assets. Thus, this theory tells us that countries with weak currencies, i.e. currencies that are expected to depreciate, have a high interest rate. The latter is necessary to compensate for the expected loss from holding this currency.

Let us now apply this model to the case where the exchange rate between the two currencies is fixed. In addition, let us assume that economic agents are confident that the exchange rate will not change in the future. Thus, we assume that the commitment to a fixed exchange rate between currencies A and B is credible. It then follows that μ, the expected rate of devaluation of currency A, is zero. As a result, the interest rates will have to be equal in the two countries. (Later in this chapter we study how a credibility crisis affects the system.)

The model is represented graphically in Fig. 3.1. On the vertical axis we set out the interest rates, on the horizontal axis the demand and the supply of money. The money demand function is represented by the downward sloping

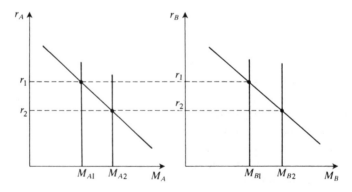

FIG. 3.1. The n − 1 problem in a two-country monetary model

line, because we make the usual assumption that the demand for money is negatively related to the interest rate.

It is clear from Fig. 3.1 that there are many levels of interest rates that will satisfy the fixed exchange rate commitment. By the same token there are many levels of the money supply in both countries which satisfy this commitment. In Fig. 3.1 we represent two of the many possibilities. The interest rate can be r_1 and the money supplies M_{A1} and M_{B1}, respectively. Or the interest rate can be r_2 and the money stocks M_{A2} and M_{B2}. Both satisfy the same exchange rate commitment. One can say that the fixed exchange rate commitment is compatible with any *level* of interest rate and money stocks.

Thus, there is a fundamental indeterminacy in the system, which follows from the n − 1 problem. In order to solve this problem, these two countries will have to agree (implicitly or explicitly) on the way monetary policies are to be conducted so as to fix one particular level of the interest rate. This problem has also been called the problem of providing a 'nominal anchor' in the system. That is, there must be some mechanism which pins down the nominal money stock and the interest rate in the system. There are many ways to do this, each of which, however, is not without new problems. Problems and conflicts will arise when the consensus about the appropriate level of the money stock breaks down. We analyse these problems in the context of the Bretton Woods system in the next section. Later we turn our attention to the EMS.

Box 3.1. The Interest Parity Theory

The interest parity theory starts from the proposition that two assets with the same risk characteristics should have the same return. If this were not the case, economic agents would arbitrage between the two assets until the rates of return were equalized. Put differently, if one asset has a higher rate of return than another asset with the same risk, agents will sell the latter in order to acquire the former. They will continue to do this until the rates of return become equal. Let us apply this fundamental insight to the foreign exchange markets. Suppose residents of a country have the choice of holding a domestic interest earning asset and a foreign interest earning asset. Let us call both of them one-year time deposits.

An investment of one dollar in a domestic time deposit will be worth the following amount, after one year:

$$1 + r_t \tag{3.6}$$

where r is the interest rate in period t on the domestic time deposit.

The investment in a foreign time deposit carries an exchange risk. The domestic resident can, however, transform this investment into one with the same risk as the domestic investment by selling the future value of his foreign investment in the forward market. The value of this risk adjusted investment in a foreign time deposit after one year then becomes:

$$(1 + r_{ft}) \frac{F_t}{S_t} \tag{3.7}$$

where r_{ft} is the foreign interest rate, F_t is the forward exchange rate and S_t is the spot exchange rate in period t. (Exchange rates are defined as the amounts of foreign currency per unit of the domestic currency.)

In order to see how arbitrage works, suppose that the foreign return (equation (3.7)) exceeds the domestic return. Then residents will buy foreign exchange spot (in order to invest in a foreign time deposit) and sell the same amount (plus the interest return) in the forward market at the price F_t. This arbitrage activity ensures that the spot rate is bid up and the forward rate is pushed downwards. This will continue until the (risk adjusted) return on the foreign investment is equalized with the domestic return.[1] We obtain the interest parity theorem:

$$1 + r_t = (1 + r_{ft})\frac{F_t}{S_t}. \tag{3.8}$$

This interest parity theorem is also often written as follows:[2]

$$r_t - r_{ft} = (F_t - S_t)/S_t. \tag{3.9}$$

This version of the interest parity theorem says that the interest differential is equal to the forward premium (discount). For example, if the interest differential favours the domestic currency, this must be compensated by a forward premium, making it attractive to buy foreign currency spot and sell it forward.

The interest parity theorem embodied in equation (3.8) (or alternatively equation (3.9)) is also called the *closed* interest parity. There is considerable evidence that this theorem holds very well empirically.[3]

The *open* interest parity goes one step further. It introduces a theory of how the forward exchange rate is determined. In efficient markets the price reflects the state of expectations of economic agents about the future. Thus, if the forward market is efficient it must reflect the prevailing expectations about the future spot rate. Let us write this hypothesis as follows:

$$F_t = E_t(S_{t+1}) \tag{3.10}$$

where $E_t(S_{t+1})$ is the expectation held by economic agents in period t about the next period spot rate (S_{t+1}). In order to see why the equality must hold, let us assume that the forward rate (which is a known variable) exceeds the expected future spot rate. In this case, speculators will expect to make a profit by selling foreign exchange in the forward market. For they expect that the future spot rate will be lower so that when their forward contract expires, they will be able to buy foreign exchange cheaply in the spot market.

Substituting (3.10) into (3.8) yields the *open* interest parity:

$$1 + r_t = (1 + r_{ft})\frac{E_t(S_{t+1})}{S_t}. \tag{3.11}$$

---

[1] This process of arbitrage is very quick. In fact, it works so well that arbitrageurs do not really move funds to establish the interest parity. Once the interest rate and one of the exchange rates (e.g. the spot rate) are known, the forward rate is established using the formula.

[2] This second version of the interest parity theorem is only approximately correct. One obtains it by subtracting $(1 + r_{ft})$ from both sides of equation (3.8). Rearranging then yields $(r_t - r_{ft})/(1 + r_{ft}) = (F_t - S_t)/S_t$, which is approximately equal to (3.9) if the level of the foreign interest rate is not too high.

[3] See Levich (1985) for empirical evidence.

We can rewrite this equation as follows:

$$\frac{1 + r_t}{1 + r_{ft}} = \frac{E_t(S_{t+1})}{S_t}. \tag{3.12}$$

This equation has a very fundamental interpretation. It says that when the domestic currency is expected to depreciate in the future ($E_t(S_{t+1}) > S_t$), the domestic interest rate must exceed the foreign interest rate. Such an interest differential is needed to compensate economic agents for the expected capital loss from holding domestic assets. (It is clear that the opposite reasoning holds when the domestic currency is expected to appreciate in the future.)

The *open* interest parity as embodied in equation (3.12) only holds if the domestic and foreign investments have the same risk characteristics. This, however, is generally not the case. This can be seen from the fact that the return on the domestic asset (the left-hand side in equation (3.11)) is known with certainty to the domestic investor, whereas the foreign return (the right-hand side in equation (3.11)) is unknown, since the future spot rate is unknown. In order for residents to hold foreign assets, an additional risk premium may be required. This risk premium is nothing but the excess return on the foreign asset needed to compensate investors for the higher risk involved. We then have

$$(1 + r_t)(1 + \Pi_t) = (1 + r_{ft})\frac{E_t(S_{t+1})}{S_t} \tag{3.13}$$

where Π_t is the risk premium in period t. It can be positive or negative. The latter follows from the fact that for the non-resident the domestic asset is the more risky one. Only if economic agents are risk neutral will the risk premium be zero.

There is now considerable evidence that the simple open interest parity theorem embodied in equation (3.11) is not verified empirically, and that risk premiums are important.[4] As a result, the formulation of the theory as in equation (3.13) is a better approximation of reality. Unfortunately, the empirical studies we have seem to indicate that the risk premium is extremely volatile. Despite many attempts to model the risk premium, it has appeared to be impossible to do so in a satisfactory way. As a result, we lack a theory which is able to explain which factors lead to changes in the observed risk premiums. We will return to this problem in a later chapter.

The open interest parity equation (3.11) can also be rewritten in a simplified (and approximate form) as follows (note that we have dropped the subscript t):

$$r = r_f + \mu \tag{3.14}$$

where $\mu = (E_t(S_{t+1}) - S_t)/S_t$, i.e. the expected rate of change of the exchange rate. If μ is positive/negative, agents expect a depreciation/appreciation of the domestic currency. This is the formulation used in the main text.

---

[4] There is a very large literature on the issue whether the forward premium is an unbiased estimate of future exchange rate changes (see Levich (1985) for a survey). A consensus seems to emerge that the forward premium is a biased predictor of future exchange rate changes, mainly because of risk premiums. See Fama (1984), Frankel (1986), Engel (1995). We will return to this issue in greater detail in Chapter 7.

Finally, the open interest parity equation with a risk premium (equation (3.13)) becomes in a simplified form:

$$r = r_f + \mu - \Pi. \tag{3.15}$$

Equation (3.15) makes clear that interest differentials may arise not only because of expected depreciations or appreciations but also because of the existence of risk premiums.

2.1. The n – 1 problem in the Bretton Woods system

The Bretton Woods system based on the gold exchange standard provided a rule governing the creation of the world money stock. If it worked properly, it forced discipline on the centre country, the US, by the fact that the central banks of the other countries threatened to convert their dollar holdings into gold, if the US over-issued dollars. How well did this mechanism work?

The US economic policies of the 1960s were increasingly influenced by the then prevailing ideas that the government had a responsibility for generating sufficient growth so as to maintain a situation of full employment. These policies led to an expansionary bias in the conduct of monetary and fiscal policies. Figs 3.2 and 3.3 illustrate this. Fig. 3.2 shows the US budget deficits from 1960 to 1972. Budget deficits had a tendency to increase over the decade. The year 1969 was a brief interlude, during which a strong budgetary contraction was

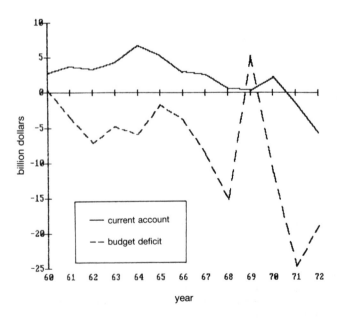

FIG. 3.2. Current account and budget deficits of the US

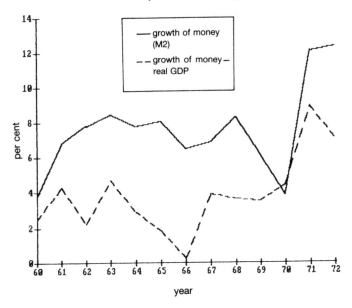

FIG. **3.3.** Growth of money (M2) in the US

engineered. This lasted only one year. It should be noted that the deterioration of the budgetary situation also had something to do with the military build-up in Vietnam and the difficulties of financing these extra expenditures through increased taxation.

Fig. 3.3 shows the growth rates of the money stock (M2), during the same period. If we subtract from this growth rate the growth rate of real GDP, we obtain a proxy for the money creation in excess of the need to finance transactions in a growing economy. Such excess money creation normally leads over time to price increases.[5] Fig. 3.4 which shows the rate of inflation in the US during the 1960s, illustrates its upward 'creep' during that period.

When the US started this trend of fiscal and monetary expansion, it transmitted this expansion to the rest of the world whose currencies were pegged to the dollar. By maintaining a fixed exchange rate with the dollar, these other countries were forced to import more inflation. The monetary authorities of countries like Germany, Japan, Switzerland, now had the choice of accepting these inflationary impulses or resisting them. Given the anti-inflationary policy preferences of these countries they resisted them. At first, they tried to resist them while keeping a fixed dollar exchange rate. For example, capital control measures were imposed in Germany and in Switzerland in order to stem the tide. In addition, the authorities attempted to sterilize their interventions, i.e. they tried to prevent

---

[5] We assume here that changes in velocity do not compensate these movements in the money stock. In the short run, this is quite often the case. Over the whole period 1960–72, however, velocity increased on average by less than 0.5% per year. Thus, most of the excess money creation spilled over into higher prices.

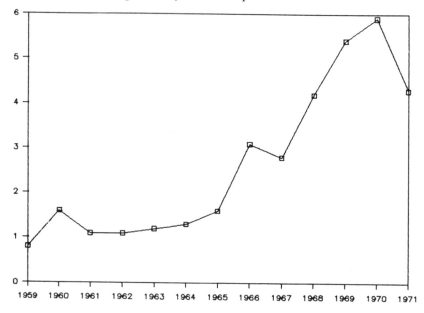

FIG. 3.4. Inflation in the US (in per cent)

the interventions in the foreign exchange markets from affecting the domestic money markets. These measures, however, turned out to be quite ineffective.[6]

An acute credibility problem arose. It became evident to speculators that the German, Swiss, and Japanese authorities were concerned about domestic inflation, and that they therefore would find it in their interest to use the only instrument capable of preventing the US-induced inflation from being imported, i.e. a revaluation of the mark, the Swiss franc and the yen. This destroyed the credibility of the fixed exchange rate commitment and led to massive speculative purchases of these currencies. It also forced the authorities to accumulate dollars in unprecedented amounts.

In Figs 3.5 and 3.6 we show the increase in the stock of international reserves of Germany, Japan, and the other industrialized countries during the second half of the 1960s and the early 1970s.[7] It can be seen that especially during the period 1970–3 the build-up of dollar reserves was truly massive. It also forced the authorities to let the domestic money stock increase substantially, thereby fuelling domestic inflation.

Why did countries like Germany, Switzerland, and Japan not convert their

---

[6] See Hewson and Sakakibara (1975), who show that most of these capital controls were circumvented, and had a low effectiveness in stemming the tide of speculative movements. See also Herring and Marston (1977) on the size of the sterilization policies in Germany. It appears from this study that the German authorities were unable to completely sterilize the monetary effects of their interventions in the foreign exchange market.

[7] These foreign exchange reserves consist for the most part of dollar reserves.

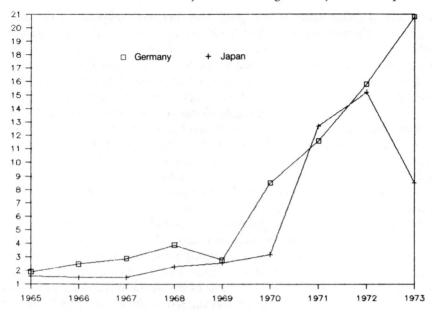

FIG. 3.5. Foreign exchange, Germany and Japan (billion SDR)

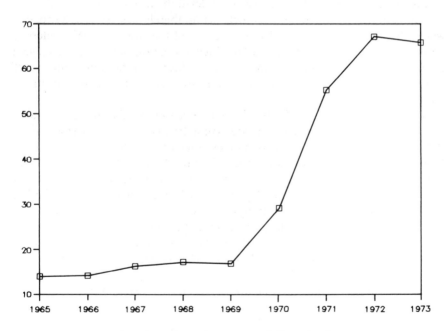

FIG. 3.6. Foreign exchange, industrial countries (billion SDR)

accumulated dollar holdings into gold? This they were supposed to do, so as to give a disciplinary signal to the US authorities. The fact is that they did very little of this. Only France engaged in substantial conversions. The reason why the major industrial countries failed to use their disciplinary device had more to do with politics than with economics. Germany and Japan were politically and militarily too dependent on the US during the 1960s to afford a confrontation with that country. As a result, the gold–dollar standard feature of the Bretton Woods system never worked well. Although the dollar was legally convertible into gold, *de facto* it was not. Gradually, the system evolved into a pure dollar standard. The source of the international creation of money became the dollar with no real link to gold.[8] This switch to a dollar standard at the end of the 1960s, did not, however, eliminate the need to devise rules for the creation of money in the system. How did these rules work?

The dollar standard which appeared at the end of the 1960s implied that the world money stock would be determined uniquely by US monetary policies. The way this system worked can be illustrated in the context of the two-country model of the money markets that we used earlier (see Fig. 3.1). Let us call country A the US, and country B the rest of the world. If the US fixes its own money stock at the level M_{A2}, this forces the rest of the world to fix its money stock at M_{B2}. The rest of the world has no freedom to determine any other level of the money stock than the one represented by M_{B2} in Fig. 3.1.

It is useful to analyse in somewhat more detail the mechanics involved in the determination of the world money stock. Let us, therefore, start from a situation where (because of a fear of inflation) the rest of the world (ROW) prefers to reduce its money stock from M_{B2} to M_{B1}. Such a situation would lead to a higher interest rate in ROW, and therefore, would induce a capital flow from the US to the rest of the world, forcing the authorities of ROW to buy dollars and to sell their own currency.

What are the monetary effects of this intervention in the foreign exchange markets? In principle, these effects are symmetric, i.e. the money stock of the ROW inevitably increases, *and* the money stock of the US declines. The latter follows from the fact that the authorities of the ROW buy dollars, i.e. take dollars out of circulation. As a result, the intervention by the authorities of the ROW reduces the US money stock. In Fig. 3.1 the M_A line tends to shift to the left.

This is, however, not the way things worked in practice. The Federal Reserve took care (and still does today) to sterilize the contractionary effects of the interventions by the authorities of the ROW. The Fed can do this by an open market operation, involving a purchase of US Treasury Securities in the market. This operation restores the US money stock to its level prior to the intervention by the authorities of the ROW, i.e. to M_{A2} in Fig. 3.1.[9] The upshot of all this is

---

[8] Despres, Kindleberger, and Salant (1966) were among the first economists to argue that the world had switched to a dollar standard. See also Krause (1970), and Haberler and Willett (1968).

[9] There is another institutional feature which leads to this automatic sterilization of the effects of interventions by the ROW on the US money stock. When the ROW buys dollars in the foreign exchange market, it will want to invest these in interest earning assets. These are mostly

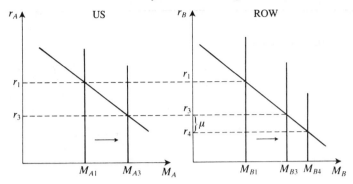

FIG. 3.7. A US monetary expansion in the dollar standard system

that the ROW is forced to allow its money stock to adjust to whatever level is determined by the US. Thus, in this dollar standard system, the US monetary policies determine the monetary policies in the rest of the world.

This asymmetric system of regulating the world money stock could in principle work well (apart from the political problems of hurt national pride it creates in some countries.)[10] It was, however, very vulnerable to the credibility problems when the US engaged in inflationary policies.

In order to make this point clear, suppose that the US engages in an expansion of the money stock (as they did in practice). This must inevitably lead to an expansion in the money stock of the ROW. This is illustrated in Fig. 3.7. The US expansion from M_{A1} to M_{A3} leads to an expansion of the money stock in the ROW from M_{B1} to M_{B3}. This in turn will induce inflationary pressures in the ROW.

If the authorities of the ROW, however, have a domestic price target, they will have an incentive to revalue the currency. As a result, a credibility problem arises. Speculators will start doubting the resolve of the authorities to keep the exchange rate fixed. A speculative crisis is inevitable. We can represent this speculative crisis in our two-country model by noting that speculators will now expect a future revaluation of the currency of the ROW. Thus, in the interest parity condition (equation (3.5)) μ becomes positive (the dollar is expected to devalue).

A positive difference is introduced between the US interest rate and the ROW interest rate. The latter will have to decline relative to the US rate to compensate for the expected capital gain from holding ROW interest earning assets. The implications are represented in Fig. 3.7. Since in this asymmetric system, US monetary policies are unaffected by what happens in the rest of the world, the US interest rate is unaffected also. Thus, the US maintains its money stock at

US Treasury Securities. Thus, the authorities of ROW will buy US Treasury Securities in the open market (through the intermediary of the Fed), thereby increasing the US money stock in circulation. For more detail see Balbach (1978).

[10] General de Gaulle spoke of this asymmetric system as involving an 'exorbitant privilege' for the US.

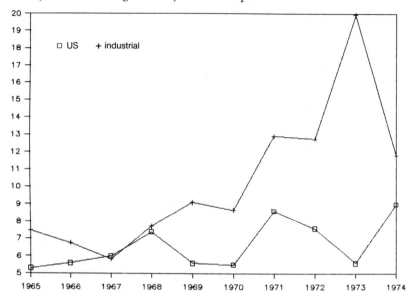

FIG. 3.8. Growth of money base (in per cent)

the level M_{A3} and its interest rate at r_3. In the ROW, however, a decline of the interest rate from r_3 to r_4, and a further increase in the money stock (from M_{B3} to M_{B4}) becomes necessary. The latter is brought about by the speculative purchases of the ROW currency by private speculators, forcing the authorities to supply the domestic currency.

We conclude that the conflict between the US and the other major countries about the appropriate monetary policy for the system as a whole destabilized the system. The speculative crisis which followed also led to an increase in the world money stock. This feature of the system became quite important in the early 1970s when chronic and large speculative crises led to massive increases in the world money stock. We show this in Figs 3.8 and 3.9.

The most striking aspect of these figures is the fact that the growth rates of the monetary aggregates of the US were relatively stable throughout the speculative turmoil of the second half of the 1960s and the first years of the 1970s. At the same time, however, the evidence of Figs 3.8 and 3.9 illustrates the large fluctuations of these growth rates in the rest of the industrialized world, especially during the very end of the fixed exchange rate regime (1970–3), when very large speculative crises, involving the dollar, arose. Clearly these crises led to a destabilization of the world money supply process.[11]

In the end it became evident that the tide could only be turned by stopping the interventions in the foreign exchange markets, and by allowing the dollar price to fluctuate freely. In 1971, under the Smithsonian Agreement, the dollar was devalued against the major currencies. This agreement, which was hailed

[11] For an in-depth discussion of this subject see McKinnon (1982).

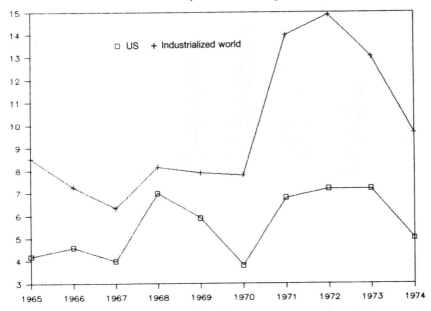

Fɪɢ. **3.9.** Growth of money stock (M1) (in per cent)
Source: IMF, *International Financial Statistics*

by President Nixon as the greatest in history, lasted less than two years. The confidence in the new set of official dollar exchange rates was short-lived. In 1973 the system of fixed exchange rates among the major currencies finally collapsed, when the monetary authorities of Germany, Japan, the UK, and a few other industrial countries decided to stop committing themselves to support a fixed dollar price for their currencies. A new era in international monetary relations had started.

2.2. The n − 1 problem in the EMS

As mentioned earlier the EMS was initially a very flexible system. Up to the middle of the 1980s the member countries devalued and revalued frequently. Moreover, the size of these realignments was typically small. As a result, after a realignment the lower limit of the new band of fluctuation was typically below the upper limit of the old band, so that the market exchange rate would barely move. This also implied that speculators would typically not make large speculative gains.

The system became much more rigid after the mid-1980s, when the major EMS member countries made it clear that they wanted to keep the central rates fixed. The EMS evolved into a truly fixed exchange rate regime. The n − 1 problem could start to have its effects.

Although the EMS was supposed to be symmetrical in its operations, it

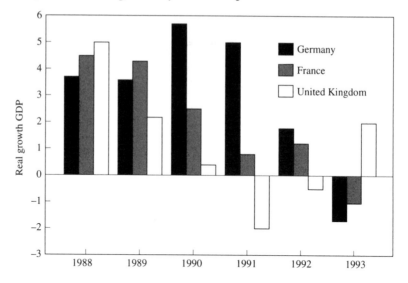

Fɪɢ. **3.10.** Real growth GDP
Source: European Commission, *European Economy*

gradually evolved into an asymmetric system very much like the dollar standard during the Bretton Woods era. The country emerging as the centre country of the system was Germany. There were essentially two reasons for this. First, Germany was the largest and economically most powerful member. Second, and more importantly, Germany had also acquired a strong reputation for low inflation. As a result, many EMS members struggling with high inflation found it attractive to peg their exchange rate to the DM and to announce this as part of their anti-inflationary strategy. In so doing they hoped to profit from the favourable German reputation so that the cost of disinflation would be reduced.[12] (In the next chapter we evaluate these strategies). As long as these countries aimed at reducing inflation they were quite happy to follow the German lead. Countries willingly accepted the German leadership position in the system.

Conflicts arose in 1992–3, however, when inflation had ceased to be a problem in countries like France, the UK, and Italy. A new problem emerged. This was the recession of 1991–3 which was particularly severe in these countries. Germany on the other hand had just experienced its unification. This had created a booming economy and inflationary pressures. Figs 3.10 and 3.11 show the differences. In Fig. 3.10 we show the growth rates of GDP in France, the UK, and Germany. It can be seen that in 1991 France and the UK had already moved into a serious recession while Germany still experienced a healthy boom. On the inflation front the reverse was true (see Fig. 3.11). Germany saw its inflation

---

[12] There is a large literature on exchange rate pegging as an instrument to fight inflation. See Giavazzi and Pagano (1988), Giavazzi and Giovannini (1989), De Grauwe (1990).

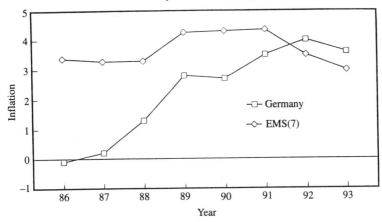

Fig. 3.11. Inflation in Germany and EMS
Source: European Commission, *European Economy*

rate increase while the other EMS countries experienced a decline in their inflation rates, which even dropped below the German level in 1991.

These differences in economic conditions set the stage for the coming conflict. Germany insisted on pursuing an anti-inflationary policy. The other countries like the UK and France were very reluctant to do so. As long as they kept the exchange rate peg with Germany they would be forced to follow Germany in its monetary restriction, despite the fact that their problem was one of too much deflation not one of too much inflation. These problems and the merit of continuing to fix the exchange rate with the DM were widely discussed in countries like France and the UK. Well-known academic economists, and also politicians, came out against such a policy. This created doubts in the minds of speculators concerning the resolve of the governments in these countries to maintain a fixed exchange rate with the DM.

This $n - 1$ problem that arose in the beginning of the 1990s can be illustrated using the two-country monetary model of the previous section. We call the two countries France and Germany. Suppose that France is hit by a negative output shock, while Germany is not. (This is not really what happened. All we want to analyse is an asymmetric development of output in the two countries.) Since output appears in the money demand function, this negative output shock shifts the money demand function in France to the left. We show the result in Fig. 3.12.

As long as France keeps its exchange rate fixed with Germany the decline in output forces France to reduce its money stock. The mechanics that leads to this result is as follows. The decline in output reduces the demand for money in France. Capital flows from France to Germany. The Banque de France must intervene and buys FF against DM in the foreign exchange market, thereby reducing the French money stock (from M_{B1} to M_{B2}). Thus France is forced to engage in monetary deflation during a recession. This is likely to exacerbate the recession in France.

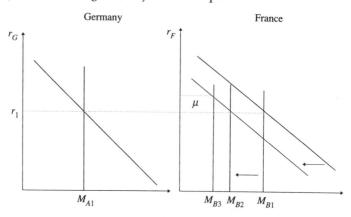

FIG. 3.12. A decline of output in France

Note that the previous result is due to the fact that the EMS works in an asymmetric way. That is, Germany fixes its money stock and refuses to compromise on this. In a symmetric working of the system this would not have been the case. To see this, take the situation after the intervention of the Banque de France. This intervention also increases the German money stock (which in the asymmetric working of the EMS is offset by the Bundesbank by so-called sterilization policies). As a result, if the EMS had worked in a symmetric way the problem of France would have been alleviated by the monetary expansion in Germany, which would have led to a lowering of the interest rate in the system as a whole. Germany, however, refused to follow a looser monetary policy given that its overriding objective was to reduce inflation.

The problem of monetary deflation in an asymmetric working of the EMS was exacerbated by the speculative crises that erupted during 1992–3. As speculators expected a revaluation of the DM, the interest rates in the other countries were pushed even higher, adding to the monetary deflation. This can also be shown in the following way. Rewrite the interest parity condition as follows:

$$r_G = r_F + \mu$$

where r_G and r_F are the German and French interest rates, μ is the expected rate of devaluation of the DM. When the DM is expected to revalue, μ is a negative number. Thus the expected revaluation of the mark requires either an increase in the French interest rate or a decline in the German one, or a combination of both. The asymmetric workings of the EMS ensured that it was the French interest rate that increased. We show this outcome in Fig. 3.12. The negative μ now drives up the French interest rate. The German authorities keep the money supply unchanged so that the German interest rate also remains unchanged. This forces the French authorities to reduce their money supply even more (to M_{B3}).

The monetary deflation during the crisis of 1992–3 was quite substantial. We show evidence of this in Fig. 3.13 which gives the growth rates of the money

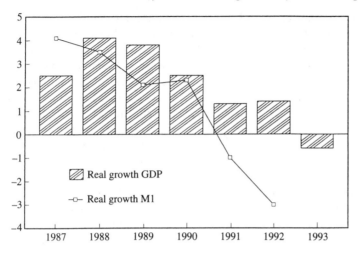

Fɪɢ. **3.13.** Growth rate of M1 and real growth of GDP in EMS countries
Source: IMF, International Financial Statistics

stock in EMS countries other than Germany. It can be seen that during the recession of 1991–3 the real growth rates of money actually became negative in EMS countries outside Germany. This was not the case in Germany itself, where real growth rates of money continued to be positive. Thus, we observe a phenomenon which is quite similar to the one observed at the end of the Bretton Woods system. At that time speculation against the dollar led to an explosion of money in the rest of the system. At the end of the EMS era the flight into marks led to a large monetary contraction in the rest of the system. In both cases the movement out of the key currency (the dollar during 1971–3) and into the key currency (the mark in 1992–3) destabilized the money supply process in the rest of the system. In the first case this led to inflationary pressures, in the second one to deflationary pressures.

The conflict that arose between the UK and France on the one hand and Germany on the other hand about the appropriate stance of monetary policy in the system led to a classic credibility problem. Speculators suspected that the authorities of these countries might stop pegging their currencies to the DM in the future. Large speculative movements erupted in September 1992 and later during 1993. The pound sterling left the system in September 1992. In August 1993, speculation was so intense that the EMS collapsed. The margins of fluctuation were raised to 30 per cent (2 × 15 per cent). The fixed exchange rate experiment of the EMS was all but buried. Only the Netherlands continued to maintain the old band of fluctuation. After a few months some of the smaller members of the EMS like Belgium also announced that they would continue the peg with the DM. The EMS as a multilateral experiment in fixing exchange rates was a failure.

The lesson one can learn from both the EMS and the Bretton Woods system is that sooner or later these systems run into the n − 1 problem. Some disturbance will make it inevitable that conflicts arise between the major participants in the system. During the 1990s, conflicts arose between Germany on the one hand and France and the UK on the other because of a major recession. The disagreement about the system-wide monetary policy undermined the credibility of the commitment to the fixed exchange rate. In fact it also exacerbated the recession. During the Bretton Woods period the problem was not deflation but inflation. The inflationary policies followed by the US were increasingly seen as unacceptable by the other major participants. The conflict that arose about the appropriate monetary policy in the system undermined the credibility of the fixed exchange rate commitment and led to its collapse. Thus one can conclude that fixed exchange rate regimes between sovereign nations must sooner or later end. As time goes on, some shock will occur leading to disagreement about the appropriate monetary response in the system. This disagreement between the major participants inevitably spills over into the foreign exchange market and destroys the fixed exchange rate arrangement.

The n − 1 problem is the most basic problem leading to credibility issues. There are other problems, however, also leading to credibility issues. These problems have typically not led to a collapse of the system as a whole. They have often induced speculative crises in individual countries and forced these to devalue (or revalue) their currencies. To these problems we now turn.

Box 3.2. The Triffin dilemma

As mentioned earlier, one of the characteristics of the gold exchange standard was the commitment of the US (towards foreign central banks) to guarantee the convertibility of its dollar liabilities into gold. At the end of the 1950s Triffin identified a potential problem of such a system.[13] This has become known as the Triffin dilemma. It can be explained as follows.

In a growing world the demand for money (convertible currencies) to be used in international transactions increases. Each of these convertible currencies, in turn, is guaranteed by a central bank to be convertible in dollars. As a result, the demand for dollars to be held as reserves by these central banks also increases when the world economy grows. This is not in itself a problem. The US can supply these desired dollars by running balance of payments deficits.

The problem, according to Triffin's analysis, arises because there is no reliable mechanism which increases the supply of gold. This supply of gold is guided by exogenous forces, for example, new discoveries, technological developments in mining gold.

Inevitably the US will find itself in an uncomfortable situation. If it satisfies the increased demand for dollar reserves in the world, its dollar liabilities increase. The gold stock, however, does not. As a result, the ratio of dollar liabilities to gold held by the US is bound to increase, leading to a loss of confidence in the ability of the US to guarantee the convertibility of dollars into gold. Making things

---

[13] See Triffin (1960).

worse, foreign central banks, anticipating this liquidity problem of the world central banker, will speed up the collapse of the system by converting dollars into gold.

If, in order to avoid the inevitable collapse, the US resisted the increased demand for dollar reserves, by not allowing its balance of payments to move into deficit, the growth of trade and output in the world would be curtailed. The world would be condemned to deflation due to a lack of dollar reserves. Thus, the famous Triffin dilemma arose. If the US accommodated the increased demand for dollar reserves, a credibility crisis would arise leading to an inevitable collapse. If it resisted this demand, it condemned the world to deflation.

The dilemma seemed formidable and inescapable. And yet the solution, according to Triffin, was as simple as the problem seemed intractable. Just substitute another asset for gold, and let it grow at a rate close to the growth rate of international trade (as a proxy for the increased demand for international reserves). This other asset would have to be one acceptable to the countries participating in the system. In Triffin's view this had to be a liability of the International Monetary Fund.

This diagnosis of the problem of the gold exchange standard has been extremely influential. It has led to numerous discussions and proposals to find an alternative to gold. These proposals ultimately led to the establishment of the Special Drawing Right (SDR) in 1970, which was conceived as a substitute for gold, and which was seen as an instrument to escape the Triffin dilemma.[14]

Doubts about the Triffin analysis   The events that unfolded during the 1960s seem to confirm Triffin's diagnosis of the gold exchange standard. This is shown by Fig. 3.14 which presents the gold–dollar ratio (the liquidity ratio). It can be seen that this ratio declined continuously during the post-war period. This decline accelerated significantly during the second half of the 1960s. At the end of the decade, the gold–dollar ratio had declined so much that the US was forced to suspend the convertibility of dollars into gold in 1971. (At about the same time the major central banks ceased to guarantee the convertibility of their money into dollars at a fixed price.)

A closer look at the data reveals, however, that the Triffin explanation of the demise of the gold exchange standard is incomplete. Fig. 3.15 shows the gold holdings of the US and US dollar liabilities separately. The most striking aspect of these data is that the accelerated decline in the liquidity ratio during the second half of the 1960s came about as a result of a dramatic increase in US dollar liabilities. During the same time the US gold stock continued to decline at the same steady rate as before. What Triffin had predicted, however, was that the declining liquidity ratio of the US would lead to large-scale conversions of dollars into gold by central banks. These conversions would in fact tend to reduce the outstanding dollar liabilities, because when the US was selling gold to the foreign central banks it would at the same time be buying back dollars, thereby reducing the outstanding stock of dollars. This conversion would in fact be deflationary for the world, because it would reduce the total amount of international reserves.[15] The liquidity crisis that Triffin had predicted, and that

---

[14] For a history of these proposals see Solomon (1977).

[15] For further details see Triffin (1960). The reader can find in this book many warnings that the world is facing a shortage of international reserves (see chs 4 and 5), and that world deflation similar to the 1930s is imminent.

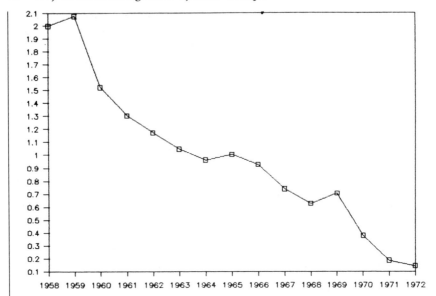

FIG. 3.14. US liquidity ratio
Source: IMF, *International Financial Statistics*

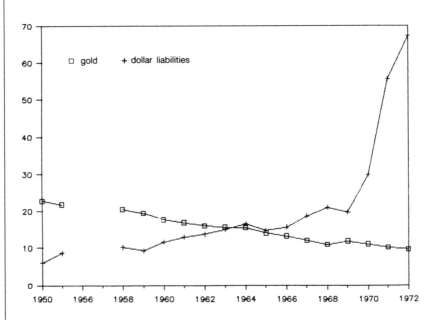

FIG. 3.15. US gold stock and dollar liabilities (in billion dollars)
Source: IMF, *International Financial Statistics*

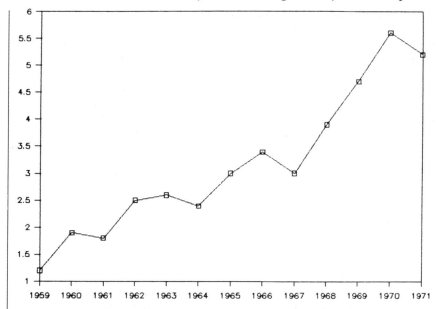

FIG. 3.16. Inflation in industrialized countries (in per cent)
Source: IMF, *International Financial Statistics*

influenced the discussions of international monetary reform so much, was the international version of the traditional bank crises which occurred during the 1930s, when deposit holders ran to the bank to convert their deposits into cash, thereby precipitating a sudden decline in the money stock, and a recession.

The facts are that such a liquidity crisis did not occur during the 1960s. Neither did the international deflation occur, which was predicted by Triffin to be inherent in the gold exchange standard. Instead, the world experienced an increase in inflation throughout the 1960s (see Fig. 3.16).

The reason why the liquidity crisis and the ensuing deflation did not arise is that the gold convertibility of the dollar was effectively (not legally) abolished during the second half of the 1960s. Despite the increase in dollar liabilities and the ensuing decline in the gold/dollar ratio the major central banks did not convert their dollar holdings into gold. As a result, the gold–dollar standard evolved into a dollar standard. The discipline inherent in the gold convertibility of the dollar disappeared. Instead of deflation, inflation became a world-wide problem.

There is another development during the 1960s which is worth mentioning here. Up to 1968 the major central banks intervened in the private gold market to peg the market price to the official price of $35 an ounce. This became increasingly difficult to do. As prices of all commodities were increasing (due to world-wide inflation), the price of gold remained fixed. In other words the relative price of gold continuously declined. (Since the price level in the US increased by 40 per cent during the 1960s, it can be said that the relative price of gold declined by 40 per cent during the same period.) This increased the private demand for gold and reduced the production of gold. At the fixed price of $35 per ounce the excess demand in the private market increased every year. The central banks could not continue to sell in the private market so as to fix the gold price, because this would have led to a complete depletion of their gold stock.[16] This price fixing was discontinued in 1968. The private price of gold started a sharp upward climb. With the uncoupling of the private and the official price of gold the convertibility of the dollar into gold became a fiction. It can be said that the gold exchange standard ended *de facto* in 1968. It would take another three years for the system to end *de jure*, when on 15 August 1971, President Nixon ended the American commitment to sell gold at a fixed price to foreign central banks.

This is quite a different story from the Triffin dilemma. Although the problem identified by Triffin was a real one, it can be said that when the gold exchange standard collapsed, the Triffin problem was well under way to being solved. The decision made in Rio de Janeiro in 1968 to start creating SDRs from 1970 onwards, was the first step towards a resolution of the Triffin dilemma. The creation of SDRs was intended to supplement the lagging supply of gold, and would have been sufficient to maintain a high enough liquidity ratio.

Thus the international community managed to take significant steps towards resolving the problems associated with a lagging supply of gold. However, in trying to avert the deflationary consequences of this gold shortage, it lost sight of another threat to the gold–dollar standard. This threat came from the creeping inflation which was set in motion during the 1960s and which drove the official gold–dollar price away from its market value. In the end it led to an expulsion of gold out of the international monetary circuit.

3. The adjustment problem

3.1. Introduction

At the most general level this problem can be explained as follows. Suppose a country with a fixed exchange rate is hit by a shock which produces a balance of payments deficit. This country will have to adjust so as to eliminate the deficit (a country cannot have a balance of payments deficit indefinitely). Given that the exchange rate is fixed, the only way to eliminate the balance of payments deficit is to reduce aggregate demand. (Note that this also corresponds to the 'rules of the game' of a fixed exchange rate system.) This adjustment process is generally painful because it leads to lower output and employment. The perception that these policies lead to undesirable costs for the domestic economy and that the use of an additional instrument, the exchange rate, could reduce these costs, creates an incentive to use the exchange rate. This in turn leads to a weakening of the commitment towards a fixed exchange rate.

---

[16] Jurg Niehans has claimed that this was a manifestation of Gresham's law: bad money (the dollar) drove out good money (gold) from the monetary circuit. See Niehans (1978).

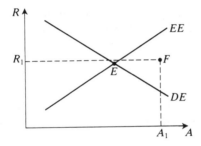

FIG. 3.17. The Swan diagram and the adjustment problem

Put differently, due to exogenous disturbances (for example a domestic inflationary shock) the official exchange rate of the country ceases to be an equilibrium exchange rate. Private agents realize that it is not in the interest of the authorities to maintain their commitment to an unrealistic exchange rate, and therefore start to speculate that the exchange rate will be changed.

Why do fixed exchange rate systems lack an acceptable mechanism to equilibrate the balance of payments without changes in the exchange rates? This is the question we now have to analyse. In order to do so we have to introduce some more theory.

3.2. The adjustment problem: the theory

An elegant way to present the adjustment problem is by way of the 'Swan-diagram'. This instrument of analysis was developed by an Australian econom-ist during the 1960s, and remains useful today.[17] The diagram is represented in Fig. 3.17.

On the vertical axis the real exchange rate (R) is set out. It is defined as follows

$$R = SP^*/P \qquad (3.16)$$

where S is the nominal exchange rate, P is the domestic price level, and P^* is the foreign price level. R can also be interpreted as a measure of competitiveness. An increase in R which arises, for example, as a result of a devaluation (i.e. an increase in S), or a decline in the domestic price level P, makes the domestic economy more competitive. As a result, exports will be stimulated, and imports will be discouraged (*ceteris paribus*). This, in turn tends to improve the current account of the balance of payments.

On the horizontal axis, we set out the total level of spending in the economy. This is often called 'absorption'. The relation between absorption and output is given by the well-known macroeconomic equilibrium condition:

$$Y = C + I + G + X - M \qquad (3.17)$$

[17] See Swan (1963).

where Y is the supply of output, C is private spending, I is private investment, G is government spending, X is the level of exports, and M is the level of imports. All variables are expressed in real terms.

Equation (3.17) can also be rewritten as

$$Y - A = X - M \tag{3.18}$$

where A is the level of absorption ($A = C + I + G$). This equation makes clear that when absorption exceeds output, imports exceed exports, i.e. the current account shows a deficit.

In Fig. 3.17 two equilibrium conditions are defined. One is called EE (for external equilibrium) and represents the combinations of real exchange rate and absorption levels for which the current account of the balance of payments is in equilibrium. It is a positively sloped line for the following reason. When the real exchange rate increases (competitiveness improves), the current account improves. In order to maintain current account balance, the level of absorption must increase (so that imports can increase).

All points below the EE line correspond to situations in which the current account shows a deficit. This can be seen as follows. Take point F. At the real exchange rate R_1 the level of absorption A_1 is too high: there will be too much spending on imports, and the current account shows a deficit. Similar reasoning leads to the conclusion that all the points above the EE line represent surpluses in the current account of the balance of payments. It, therefore also implies that as long as a country remains located above/below EE, it reduces (increases) its net debtor position relative to the rest of the world.

The DE line represents the combinations of real exchange rate and absorption for which there is *domestic* equilibrium. The latter is defined here as a level of unemployment corresponding to the natural rate.[18] A level of unemployment below the natural rate leads to inflationary pressures, while a level above the natural rate leads to a downward pressure on the price level.

The DE line is negatively sloped for the following reason. Suppose we start from an initial domestic equilibrium. Let the real exchange rate increase. This will tend to increase exports and output and, as a result, will reduce the unemployment rate below the natural rate, and will trigger inflationary pressures. In order to maintain domestic equilibrium the level of absorption must, therefore, decline.

Points to the right of the DE line correspond to situations of inflationary pressure in the economy. Points to the left of the DE line correspond to unemployment which exceeds the natural rate. The Swan diagram, therefore, also allows us to characterize four types of disequilibria (unemployment–trade deficit; unemployment–trade surplus; inflation–trade deficit; inflation–trade surplus).

Full equilibrium, i.e. external and domestic equilibrium is achieved at point E, where the EE and the DE line intersect. In E we have a combination of real

---

[18] The idea of a natural rate of unemployment was introduced by Friedman (1968). It is often given the interpretation of a level of unemployment which does not lead to an accelerating rate of inflation.

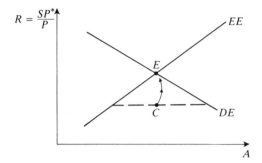

FIG. 3.18. Domestic inflationary shock

exchange rate and absorption which makes equilibrium in the current account and in the domestic goods market possible.

Let us now analyse the effects of disturbances which move the economy away from the equilibrium point E. We will analyse two such disturbances, one is a domestic inflationary shock, the other is an improvement in the terms of trade.

3.3. A domestic inflationary shock

Let us consider an economy which is hit by a domestic inflationary shock. Such a disturbance may be due to a wage explosion, such as the one which occurred in France after the riots of May 1968. The effect of such a shock is to reduce the real exchange rate ($R = SP^*/P$ with P increasing). Put differently, the competitiveness of the domestic economy declines. As a result, exports decline and domestic output is negatively affected.

We represent the effects of this disturbance in Fig. 3.18. Initially the economy is at E. The domestic inflationary shock drives R down, so that the economy moves to a point like C, where the current account shows a deficit, and where unemployment has increased above the natural rate. The question which now arises is the following. Does there exist an automatic adjustment mechanism which will ensure that the economy moves back to the initial equilibrium point E? It is clear that such an adjustment must involve a decline in the domestic price level. This follows from the fact that the exchange rate is fixed, and that the foreign price level should be considered exogenous. Thus, the only way for the economy to move upwards again in Fig. 3.18 is by a decline in P, which raises the competitiveness variable (R).

In a world of price and wage flexibility, there are essentially two mechanisms that will make such an adjustment possible. First, the increase in the unemployment level reduces the wage level. This, in turn, makes it possible for the price of the domestic output to decline. Second, the current account deficit forces the monetary authorities to intervene in the foreign exchange market and to sell foreign currency against the domestic one. As a result, the money stock declines and the domestic interest rate increases. The effect of this mechanism is deflationary: it reduces absorption and decreases the price level. Note that this second adjustment mechanism presupposes that the authorities allow the 'rules of the game' of the fixed exchange rate system to operate, i.e. they allow the deficit in the current account to affect the money market.

The effect of these two channels, through which the automatic adjustment operates, is to improve competitiveness, to reduce unemployment and to improve the current account of the balance of payments. In Fig. 3.18 the economy moves upward again along the arrow starting from point C.

It should be stressed that there are many different paths which the economy can follow during the adjustment period. The arrow represented in Fig. 3.18 is only one of the many dynamic processes. What exactly this adjustment path will look like depends, among other things, on the speed with which wages and prices adjust. The important point is that in a world of wage and price flexibility, there exists an automatic system leading to an equilibration of the current account and a reduction in unemployment.

What happens in a world of wage and price rigidity? The question is important since in the real world it is likely that the degree of wage and price flexibility may be so small that the adjustment mechanism just described does not operate at all, or at a speed too slow to be acceptable to policy-makers.

Let us return to Fig. 3.18. After the initial shock the economy is at point C. Let us now assume complete downward wage and price rigidity. It is immediately clear that nothing will push the real exchange rate upwards: the exchange rate is fixed, the domestic price level is rigid, and the foreign price level is exogenous. The economy is stuck on a horizontal line represented by the dotted line through C.

The famous dilemma situation analysed by Meade (1951) now appears. If the policy-makers aim at reducing the unemployment level, they can stimulate the economy by more spending (or less taxation). Absorption increases, and the economy moves to the right along the horizontal line closer to the domestic equilibrium. This movement, however, occurs at a price. The economy now moves away from the external equilibrium line: the current account deficit increases, and the net foreign debt increases at an accelerating rate. If, on the other hand, the authorities aim at equilibrating the current account, they will have to reduce spending (increase taxes), so that absorption can decline. The economy moves to the left along the horizontal line. The policy-makers face a dilemma, and will have to make a choice.[19]

We have now arrived at the essence of the adjustment problem of the fixed exchange rate system in a world of wage and price rigidity. Whatever the

[19] This famous dilemma situation was analysed by Tinbergen (1952) in his theory of economic policy. The source of the dilemma is that in this world of wage and price rigidity, the policy-makers pursue two targets with only one instrument. In order to solve the dilemma, a second instrument must be made available. This can only be the exchange rate. By changing the exchange rate, in this case by increasing it, the economy can be lifted out of the low competitiveness trap it is in, so that it can move upwards.

authorities choose, a devaluation is inevitable. If the authorities choose to pursue a domestic equilibrium objective, the economy will accumulate current account deficits which are not sustainable. The reason for this is that a continuous deficit implies a continuously declining stock of international reserves. Since the latter are finite there comes a point when this stock is depleted and the authorities are unable to intervene in the foreign exchange market. At that point they must let the exchange rate increase. In fact the crisis will typically occur prior to the depletion of the stock of international reserves, as speculators, anticipating the future depletion, start an 'attack' on the currency.[20]

If, on the other hand, the authorities choose to follow the 'rules of the game', they will have to deflate total spending to restore the external equilibrium. The increasing unemployment resulting from this policy choice, however, is perceived as suboptimal by policy-makers who care about unemployment. They will therefore have an incentive to use the exchange rate (a devaluation) as an additional instrument to achieve a better balance between the domestic and external equilibrium, and to lift the economy out of its low competitiveness trap. The realization that this policy option is available, and that the policy-makers have a strong incentive to use it, will be sufficient for speculators to test the authorities' resolve for the fixed exchange rate. A speculative crisis will emerge which will force the hand of the authorities.

Put in more modern language: the commitment to a fixed exchange rate quickly loses credibility when the economy is trapped on the line through *C*. Only if we can ensure that the authorities give no weight at all to unemployment in their objective function (so that they will not hesitate to move the economy to the left in Fig. 3.18), is the fixed exchange rate commitment credible. There are few countries in the world where authorities with such an objective function can stay in power very long.

In the preceding analysis we have contrasted two polar cases, one of wage and price flexibility and one of wage and price rigidity. In the real world we are in a mixed situation. It also follows that there will usually be some flexibility allowing countries to lift themselves out of the trap we have illustrated in Fig. 3.18. In addition, as was pointed out by Mundell, there are other forms of flexibility, in particular mobility of labour, which may alleviate the dilemma situation, and which may make the fixed exchange rate system credible.[21] In the context of Fig. 3.18, this would involve an emigration of unemployed labour. As a result, the country can achieve its external equilibrium target without increasing unemployment.

This being said, it remains true that for many countries the degree of flexibility (including labour mobility) is too small to avoid a situation of protracted disequilibrium as illustrated in Fig. 3.18. In those countries the commitment towards the fixed exchange rate will be eroded, once the country suffers from the domestic inflationary shock.

[20] Formal models of such speculative attacks and their timing have been proposed by Krugman (1979). We study these in the next chapter.

[21] See Mundell (1961). This is the famous theory of optimal currency areas.

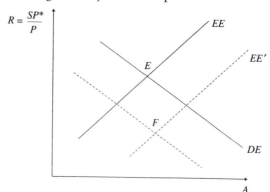

FIG. 3.19. Improvement in the terms of trade

3.4. An improvement in the terms of trade

In this section we analyse a different shock. Suppose a country experiences an improvement in its terms of trade. This may be the result, for example, of an increase in the foreign demand for its domestic output (say oil in a country like Mexico or Norway).

Let us start from the Swann diagram again (Fig. 3.19). As a result of the improvement in the terms of trade both the *EE* and the *DE* schedules shift. The *EE* schedule shifts downwards because the improvement in the terms of trade creates a current account surplus. In order to return to current account equilibrium the real exchange rate must decline (a real appreciation is necessary). Thus, we now need a lower *R* to maintain external equilibrium. The *DE* schedule shifts to the left for the following reason. The increased foreign demand for domestic output creates domestic inflationary pressures. In order to eliminate these, and to maintain internal equilibrium, the level of absorption must decline. As a result of these two shifts the new equilibrium point moves from *E* to *F*.

Thus, the economy must now move from *E* to *F*. We can immediately see that if the country maintains a fixed exchange rate, there is only one way through which this movement can come about. This is through an increase in the domestic price level. As a result, a country which experiences an improvement in its terms of trade and which maintains a fixed exchange rate will have to allow a process of domestic inflation.

There is, however, another adjustment path possible. The country could also allow an appreciation of its currency (a decline in *S*). This would produce the same required decline in the real exchange rate *R* as the one obtained with domestic inflation. We now come to the credibility problem of the fixed exchange rate. If the authorities of the country involved are known to be very averse to inflation, speculators may start having doubts about their commitment to keeping the exchange rate fixed. The speculators know that these inflation-hating authorities prefer an appreciation of the currency to domestic inflation.

They may therefore speculate that the authorities will revalue the currency. A speculative crisis will be set in motion. Only if the authorities do not care about the higher inflation (and if they can convince speculators of this) can the credibility problem be avoided.

In the previous sections we have described the adjustment problem of the fixed exchange rate system. We have argued that when the authorities pursue targets other than external equilibrium, the fixed exchange rate will suffer from a credibility problem. This credibility problem arises because exogenous shocks lead to external disequilibria which can only be corrected by allowing large domestic disequilibria to occur. In a sense one can say that the official exchange rate ceases to be an equilibrium rate. This will give a strong incentive to the authorities to correct the disequilibria by changing the exchange rate. As a result, speculative crises will be difficult to contain.

The nature of the adjustment problem is different from the n – 1 problem discussed earlier in the following sense. First, the adjustment problem can typically be limited to one country. As a result, it will not jeopardize the system as a whole. The country involved will devalue or revalue its currency, or it may decide to leave the system. Second, the adjustment problem arises because of a conflict between the domestic and external objectives of the authorities of a country. The n – 1 problem is the result of a conflict between the authorities of different countries. Conflicts between different countries are usually more likely to undermine the stability of the system as a whole. Third, adjustment problems typically show up in the evolution of basic economic variables (current account, price trends, etc.). This is often not the case in the n – 1 problem. In 1993, for example, France had a better current account and lower inflation than Germany. And yet speculators sold FF. They did it because they were afraid that the future French government would stop pegging to the DM and thereby be forced to deflate the economy.

It should be stressed that the adjustment and the n – 1 problem are often interrelated. Take the example of the EMS crisis in 1992–3. Some economists have argued that what started it all is a domestic German adjustment problem resulting from German unification.[22] The latter required a real appreciation of the German mark (very much as in our example of an improvement in the terms of trade). Since the other countries in the system pegged to the German mark, this real appreciation could only come about by an increase in the German price level or a decline in the price level in the other EMS countries. Germany refused the first solution. As a result deflation was forced on the other countries. The EMS collapsed because the cost for these other countries was perceived to be too large. Thus, what started it all was an adjustment problem in one country. This country happened to be the most important one in the system, so that the problem quickly degenerated into a conflict between the major members of the system.

In the following sections we illustrate this adjustment and credibility problem

---

[22] See e.g. Portes (1993), and Eichengreen and Wyplosz (1993).

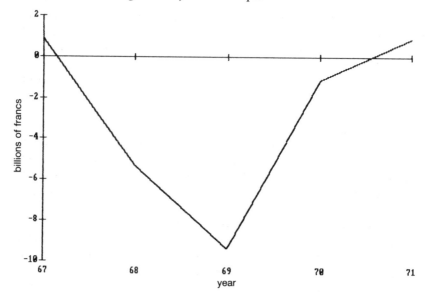

FIG. 3.20. France's current account

by a number of case-studies for individual countries during the 1960s and the 1980s.

3.5. Case-study: France during 1968–9

A first interesting case is France during 1968–9. In May 1968, a near-revolutionary situation existed that threatened the survival of the Gaullist government. In order to contain the threat, the government granted large wage increases during the so-called 'Accord de Grenelle'. The effect on the external balance was swift. As a result of the increase in disposable income the demand for imports accelerated. In addition, due to the wage increases the competitive position of France deteriorated. All these phenomena led to a quick deterioration of the current account from a surplus in 1967 to a deficit of close to FF 10 billion in 1969. Fig. 3.20 illustrates this sharp decline in the current account of the balance of payments.

It is clear that with a sufficient dose of deflationary policies this disequilibrium could have been turned around. In terms of the analysis implicit in Fig. 3.18, the French authorities could have reduced government spending to equilibrate the current account. Speculators, however, guessed correctly that the French authorities would prefer to devalue than to allow the French economy to go through a recession to equilibrate the current account. In other words, they anticipated that the official exchange rate which was not consistent with equilibrium, would be changed.

As a result of such expectations, large speculative runs against the franc were set in motion. Whereas at the end of 1967, the French central bank held a stock

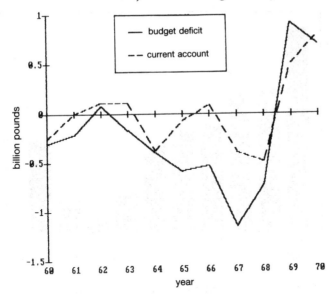

Fɪɢ. 3.21. Government budget and current account in the UK
Source: IMF, *International Financial Statistics*

of international reserves of $1.8 billion, it lost the largest part of this stock during 1968. At the end of 1968 only $0.3 billion was left in the vaults of the Banque de France. Although President de Gaulle at first declared he would never devalue the franc, his successor Pompidou, who came to power in 1969, devalued the franc. Together with fiscal and monetary restraint this led to a swift equilibrium in the current account.

3.6. Case-study: The United Kingdom during the 1960s

A second important example of a country suffering from adjustment problems during the 1960s was the United Kingdom. As a result of relatively expansionary fiscal policies, the government budget turned to large deficits during the middle of the decade. This also had the effect of increasing imports and led to the deterioration of the current account. Fig. 3.21 shows the current account of the UK during the period 1960–70, together with the government budget balance. It can be seen that from 1962 to 1967, the government budget deficit became larger and larger. As a result, during 1963–5 and later during 1967 the current account deteriorated significantly.

A first speculative crisis erupted during 1964. Speculators judged that an equilibrium would not come about without a devaluation of the pound sterling and started selling sterling in the foreign exchange market. The Labour government at first resisted this pressure, and decided not to devalue the currency. In order to stem the tide, monetary policy was tightened and an import surcharge

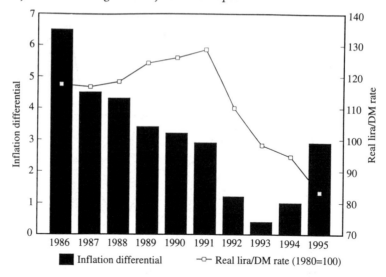

FIG. 3.22. Inflation differential between Italy and Germany

Source: European Commission, *European Economy*, and J P Morgan

on manufactures was imposed. This led to a short-lived improvement in the current account. In a sense it can be said that during that period, the British authorities tried to convince speculators that they meant to stick to the rules of the game of the fixed exchange rate system.

In 1967 the current account deteriorated again. Speculative sales of sterling intensified and led to large losses of international reserves of the Bank of England. Finally, the government gave in and devalued the pound sterling. Together with a programme of fiscal contraction this led to a spectacular improvement in the current account in 1968–70.

3.7. Case-study: Italy during 1987–92

As was indicated earlier, the EMS evolved into a system of rigidly fixed exchange rates after 1987. From that date onwards the regular small realignments disappeared. In Italy, however, inflation continued to be higher than in Germany year after year. We show the evidence in Fig. 3.22. We observe that the inflation differential declined but remained positive. Since the lira remained fixed after 1987 these positive inflation differentials cumulated so as to produce an increasing divergence in the Italian price level relative to the German one (and the other EMS members). As a result, the Italian lira became increasingly overvalued producing increasing problems of competitiveness for Italian industry. We show the evolution of the real exchange rate of the lira in Fig. 3.23 and observe the increasing real appreciation of the lira. The increasing overvaluation of the lira also led to mounting current account deficits (also shown in Fig. 3.23). The situation became unsustainable and led speculators to guess that the Italian

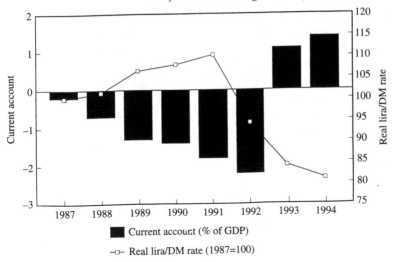

Fɪɢ. 3.23. Real lira/DM rate and the Italian current account
Source: European Commission, *European Economy,* 1995

authorities would devalue the lira. This happened in September 1992. In fact Italy dropped out of the EMS altogether and the lira started a steep decline.

4. Conclusion

The experience with fixed exchange rates during the post-war period can teach us some important lessons. First, the fixed exchange rate system, as it worked during that period, had some great advantages. When it worked properly, i.e. when there was confidence that these official exchange rates would be maintained, it provided all the benefits of using a single money in international transactions. Economic agents of a country whose currency was freely convertible into foreign currencies at a fixed price enjoyed the certainty that they would be able to settle their affairs in their own currency. This brought benefits to international trade and to the economy in general.

A second lesson we learned from this fixed exchange rate experience is not so positive. Fixed exchange rate regimes are extremely fragile. They are based on the credibility of promises made by monetary authorities to keep their exchange rates fixed now and in the future. Inevitably these promises will be put in doubt. We identified two reasons for this. The first one is the most fundamental one. A fixed exchange rate system necessitates a consensus among the major participants about the stance of monetary policy for the system as a whole (we have called this the n − 1 problem). Inevitably, as time goes on, conflicts between the major participants will arise. At the end of the 1960s conflicts arose because the major European countries and Japan felt that the US was pursuing too inflationary policies. Speculators observed this conflict and anticipated that countries like Germany and Japan would loose their commitment to pegging their currencies to the dollar (and thereby importing inflation). In the early 1990s conflicts arose within the EMS because countries like France and the UK felt that the monetary policies pursued by Germany (the leading country in the EMS) were too deflationary. This conflict was perceived by speculators as weakening the commitment to fixed exchange rates. The speculative crises that erupted brought down the system.

The second problem we identified we called the adjustment problem. Sooner or later individual participants will find that their exchange rate commitment conflicts with domestic economic objectives. For example, the economy may be shocked into a disequilibrium in the current account. When this happens, quite often an adjustment of the exchange rate will be welfare improving (in terms of the stabilization of output, employment, and prices), compared to an adjustment which excludes a devaluation (or revaluation) of the currency. Speculators observing this conflict between domestic economic objectives and the fixed exchange rate arrangement will start doubting that the authorities will maintain their commitment.

The problem faced by fixed exchange rate regimes can also be placed in the context of the time consistency of economic policies. When the authorities commit themselves to a fixed exchange rate, economic agents know that this policy rule will not be optimal at all future periods. The realization of this time inconsistency of a fixed exchange rate rule, makes the announcement of such a rule by the authorities not credible. Economic agents know that in future periods it will be optimal to change the rule. They realize that there are situations in which the authorities will prefer exchange rate adjustments to keeping the exchange rate fixed. This state of affairs makes the system very vulnerable to speculative runs.

This problem can only be solved if monetary authorities change their policy preferences. Barring explicit co-operative arrangements, the authorities of the participating countries must be willing to accept the outcome of monetary policy choices made by the leading country in the system. In addition, they have to completely subordinate their monetary policies to the maintenance of external equilibrium at a fixed exchange rate. Few sovereign countries are willing to do so. As a result, fixed exchange rate arrangements do not last, and will always collapse.

The essence of the problem of fixed exchange rates therefore is that the commitment to fixed exchange rates is not binding enough, leading to inevitable problems of credibility. There are only two solutions to this problem. One is that countries make the commitment to fixed exchange rates truly binding. This can only be achieved by the creation of a monetary union in which one currency replaces the individual currencies and is managed by one central bank. A group of countries is trying to do this in Europe during the 1990s. The other solution is to eliminate fixed exchange rate commitments and to allow for more flexible arrangements. This is the solution that was chosen by the major industrial countries in the world during the 1970s. The question arises as to whether the degree of flexibility that has been achieved since then has not become excessive. This is the theme of Chapter 5.

4

MODELLING THE COLLAPSE OF FIXED EXCHANGE RATE SYSTEMS

In the previous chapter we analysed why fixed exchange rate systems tend to disappear. We used a relatively informal approach to analyse this question. In this chapter we analyse this issue further using more formal (but still simple) models.

Since the end of the 1970s economists have introduced issues of credibility explicitly into their models. The use of these models will allow us to deal explicitly with credibility instead of talking about it (as we did in the previous chapter) and to go one step further so as to identify more rigorously the factors that influence credibility. In addition, some of these models will also make it possible to analyse the timing of the collapse explicitly.

We will study three models in this chapter. One is the celebrated Barro–Gordon model that will be extended to an open economy. A second model is the one developed by Krugman to describe the timing of the collapse of a fixed exchange rate system. A third model, developed by Obstfeld, describes the self-fulfilling nature of speculation. We will end by studying models that make predictions about the behaviour of the exchange rate within the band (so-called target zone models).

1. Credibility of fixed exchange rates: a formal analysis

In this section we develop a model that analyses in a more formal way the credibility problem of fixed exchange rates. The model is based on the Barro–Gordon analysis that we extend to an open economy. Here we use a graphical exposition. In an appendix we derive the solution of the model algebraically.

Let us start from the standard Phillips curve which takes into account the role of inflationary expectations. We specify this Phillips curve as follows:

$$U = U_N + a(\dot{p}^e - \dot{p}) \tag{4.1}$$

where U is the unemployment rate, U_N is the natural unemployment rate, $\dot{p}$ is the observed rate of inflation, and $\dot{p}^e$ is the expected rate of inflation.

Equation (4.1) expresses the idea that only unexpected inflation affects the

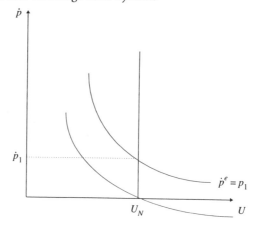

FIG. 4.1. The Phillips curve and the natural rate of unemployment

unemployment rate. Thus, when the observed inflation rate, $\dot{p}$, is higher than the expected rate of inflation, $\dot{p}^e$, the unemployment rate declines below its natural level.

We will also use the rational expectations assumption. This implies that economic agents use all relevant information to forecast the rate of inflation, and that they cannot be systematically wrong in making these forecasts. Thus, on average $\dot{p} = \dot{p}^e$, so that on average $U = U_N$.

We represent the Phillips curve in Fig. 4.1. The vertical line represents the 'long-term' vertical Phillips curve. It is the collection of all points for which $\dot{p} = \dot{p}^e$. This vertical line defines the natural rate of unemployment, U_N, which is also called the NAIRU (the non-accelerating-inflation rate of unemployment). The second step in the analysis consists in introducing the preferences of the monetary authorities. The latter are assumed to care about both inflation and unemployment.

We represent these preferences in Fig. 4.2 in the form of a map of indifference curves of the authorities. We have drawn the indifference curves concave, expressing the idea that as the inflation rate declines, the authorities become less willing to let unemployment increase in order to reduce the inflation rate. Put differently, as the inflation rate declines the authorities tend to attach more weight to unemployment. Note also that the indifference curves closer to the origin represent a lower loss of welfare, and are thus preferred to those farther away from the origin.

The slope of these indifference curves expresses the relative importance the authorities attach to combating inflation or unemployment. In general, authorities who care a lot about unemployment ('wet' governments) have steep indifference curves, i.e. in order to reduce the rate of unemployment by one percentage point, they are willing to accept a lot of additional inflation.

On the other hand, 'hard-nosed' monetary authorities are willing to let the

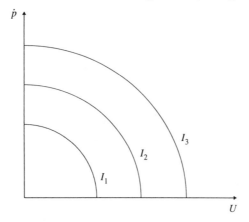

FIG. 4.2. The preferences of the authorities

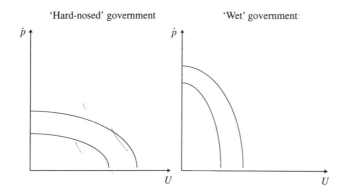

FIG. 4.3. The preferences of the authorities

unemployment rate increase a lot in order to reduce the inflation rate by one percentage point. They have flat indifference curves. In the limit, authorities who care only about inflation have horizontal indifference curves. We represent two of these cases in Fig. 4.3.

We can now bring together the preferences of the authorities and the Phillips curves to determine the equilibrium of the model. We do this in Fig. 4.4.

In order to find out where the equilibrium will be located, assume for a moment that the government announces that it will follow a monetary policy rule of keeping the inflation rate equal to zero. Suppose also that economic agents believe this announcement. They therefore set their expectations for inflation equal to zero. If the government implements this rule we move to point A.

It is now clear that the government can do better than point A. It could cheat and increase the rate of inflation unexpectedly. Thus, suppose that, after having announced a zero inflation, the authorities increase the inflation rate unexpectedly. This would bring the economy to point B, which is located on a

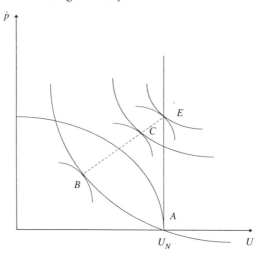

FIG. 4.4. The equilibrium inflation rate

lower indifference curve. One can say that the government has an incentive to renege on its promise to maintain a zero inflation rate.

Will the government succumb to this temptation to engineer a surprise inflation? Not necessarily. The government also knows that economic agents are likely to react by increasing their expectations of inflation. Thus, next period, the Phillips curve is likely to shift upwards if the government decides to increase the rate of inflation unexpectedly. The government should therefore evaluate the short-term gain from cheating against the future losses that result from the fact that the Phillips curve shifts upwards.

But suppose now that the government consists of short-sighted politicians who give a low weight to future losses, and that it decides to cheat. We then move to point B. This, however, will trigger a shift of the Phillips curve upwards. Given these new expectations, it will be optimal for the authorities to move to point C. This will go on until we reach point E. This point has the following characteristics. First, it is on the vertical Phillips curve, so that agents' expectations are realized. They have therefore no further incentives to change their expectations. Second, at E the authorities have no incentive to surprise economic agents with more inflation. A movement upwards along the Phillips curve going through E would lead to a higher indifference curve, and therefore to a loss of welfare.

Point E can also be interpreted as the equilibrium that will be achieved in a rational expectations world when the authorities follow a discretionary policy, i.e. when they set the rate of inflation optimally each period given the prevailing expectations.

It is clear that this equilibrium is not very attractive. It is, however, the only

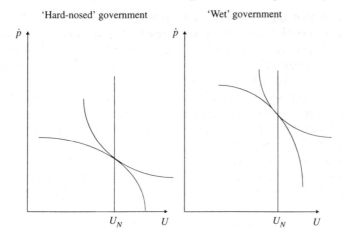

FIG. **4.5**. Equilibrium with 'hard-nosed' and 'wet' governments

equilibrium that can be sustained, given that the authorities are sufficiently short-sighted, and that the private sector knows this. The zero inflation rule (or any other constant inflation rule below the level achieved at E) has no credibility in a world of rational economic agents. A zero inflation rule, although desirable, will not come about automatically.[1]

It should be stressed that this model is a static one. If the policy game is repeated many times, the government will have an incentive to acquire a reputation of low inflation. Such a reputation will make it possible to reach a lower inflation. One way the static assumption can be rationalized is by considering that in many countries political institutions favour short-term objectives for politicians. For example, the next election is never far away, leading to uncertainty whether the present rulers will still be in place next period. Thus, what is implicitly assumed in this model is that the political decision process is inefficient leading politicians to give a strong weight to the short-term gains of inflationary policies. The politicians as individuals are certainly as rational as private agents; the political decision process however may force them to give undue weight to the very short-term results of their policies.

The Barro–Gordon model makes clear that the preferences of the authorities matter a great deal in determining the location of the discretionary equilibrium, and therefore the equilibrium level of inflation. We show this in Fig. 4.5 where we present the cases of the 'wet' (steep indifference curves) and the 'hard-nosed' (flat indifference curves) governments. Assuming that the Phillips curves have the same slopes, Fig. 4.5 shows that in a country with a 'wet' government, the equilibrium inflation will be higher than in a country with a 'hard-nosed' government.

---

[1] In the jargon of the economic literature it is said that the policy rule of zero inflation is 'time inconsistent', i.e. the authorities face the problem each period that a better short-term outcome is possible. The zero inflation rule is incentive-incompatible.

Note also that the only way a zero rate of inflation rule can be credible is when the authorities show no concern whatsoever for unemployment. In that case the indifference curves are horizontal. The authorities will choose the lowest possible horizontal indifference curve in each period. The inflation equilibrium will then be achieved at point *A* (see Fig. 4.4).[2]

In the previous sections we showed how a government, which is known to care about inflation and unemployment, will not credibly be able to announce a zero inflation rate. It is therefore stuck in a suboptimal equilibrium with an inflation rate that is too high.

This analysis can be extended to open economies. Let us now assume that there are two countries. We call the first country Germany, and assume its government is 'hard-nosed'. The second country is called Italy, where the government is 'wet'.

In this extension of the model to open economies we will use an important theory, i.e. the *purchasing power parity* (PPP) theory. There is a large literature developing the conditions under which PPP holds. In the next chapter we will go more deeply into issues concerning PPP. Here we just postulate that the theory holds. In its simplest form it can be written as follows:

$$S = kP_I/P_G \tag{4.2}$$

where S is the equilibrium price of the German mark in units of lira, P_I is the price level in Italy and P_G the price level in Germany; k is a factor of proportionality which we assume to be constant here.[3]

The intuition behind equation (4.2) is that an increase in the Italian price level relative to the German one leads to a loss of competitiveness for the Italian economy. As a result, exports decline and imports increase. In order to maintain external equilibrium the exchange rate must increase (the lira must devalue). We can also rewrite (4.2) in rates of change, i.e.

$$\dot{S} = \dot{P}_I - \dot{P}_G \tag{4.3}$$

where the points above variables indicate that we take percentage changes.[4] The equation now says that if inflation in Italy is say 10 per cent whereas it is 5 per cent in Germany then the lira must depreciate by 5 per cent a year against the mark.

We show the inflation outcome in Fig. 4.6. Italy has a higher equilibrium rate of inflation than Germany. Its currency will therefore have to depreciate continuously.

We can now use this model to analyse the credibility problem of fixed exchange rates. Suppose that Germany and Italy decide to fix their exchange rate. Is this a credible arrangement? Fixing the exchange rate in this model

---

[2] Rogoff (1985) has suggested that the best thing that could happen to a country is that its monetary policy be run by an orthodox central banker.

[3] Note that if we redefine k as the real exchange rate, R, we have the same equation (3.1) as in the previous chapter. Thus, PPP implies that the real exchange rate is constant.

[4] Technically we first take the log of equation (4.2) and then time derivatives.

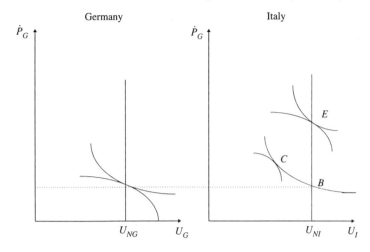

FIG. 4.6. Inflation equilibrium in a two-country model

amounts to announcing that the rates of inflation in the two countries shall be equal. This can be seen from the purchasing power parity condition (4.3). Setting $\dot{S}$ equal to zero is equivalent to equalizing the rates of inflation.

A first problem immediately arises. Which common inflation rate will be selected? There are several possibilities here: shall it be the inflation rate of Germany, or the one of Italy, or an inflation rate between the two? We have the same n − 1 problem we discussed earlier. Let us assume that this problem is solved by selecting the low inflation rate of Germany. We can immediately see that this is a natural outcome in this game. For Germany is unlikely to make an agreement with Italy selecting a high inflation rate which will make it worse off. Similarly, Italy is likely to find it attractive to peg its currency to the low inflation country. In so doing it hopes to profit from Germany's reputation and to move its inflation equilibrium point lower along the vertical Phillips curve. In other words, Germany is almost inevitably going to be selected as the leader of the system.

We now come to our question. Can this arrangement be made credible? The answer is unambiguously negative. This can be seen as follows. Italy announces that it will target its inflation rate to the level given by point B. Private agents, however, realize that the authorities have an incentive to go to point C, i.e. to create a surprise inflation by a surprise devaluation. As the model stands (a static game), the fixed exchange rate regime can never be made credible. A necessary condition for this fixed exchange rate arrangement is that the authorities of the two countries should have the same preferences regarding inflation and unemployment. (We return to this problem to analyse what happens when uncertainty exists about the preferences of the authorities.)

Let us now assume that the previous problem is solved: both countries have exactly the same preferences, and economic agents are aware of this. Does this

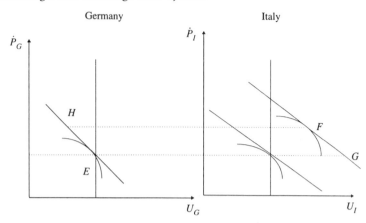

FIG. 4.7. Inflation equilibrium in Germany and Italy

solve the credibility problem? The answer is no. Even though it is necessary that preferences be the same, this is not sufficient. Let us show this as follows. Germany and Italy have the same preferences as shown in Fig. 4.7. As a result, their inflation equilibrium is the same (we also assume the same natural unemployment rate and the same short-term and linear Phillips curves in the two countries). We now assume that an asymmetric shock occurs: Italy experiences a shock which shifts its short-term Phillips curve to the right. No shock occurs in Germany. We now observe the following. Germany wants to stay at point E. Italy however has an incentive to move to F; i.e. given its preferences (which are the same as in Germany), Italy wants to accommodate the shock by some monetary stimulus so as to reduce the short-term consequences of the shock. If Germany is the leader, this will not be possible. Italy will be forced to go to point G. As a result no accommodation is possible, and all the shock is absorbed by an increase in unemployment. Italy is made worse off. This will certainly lead to conflicts between Germany and Italy concerning the appropriate monetary policy. Italy will ask Germany to be more accommodating. If Germany refuses, the conflict will lead to a loss of confidence in the fixity of the exchange rate. Agents realize that Italy has an incentive to let the exchange rate go so as to move to point F and to improve welfare. A speculative crisis is the likely outcome.

What if Italy is leader? The leadership arrangement does not affect the previous result. If Italy is the leader, it will accommodate the shock by allowing its inflation rate to increase. This will force Germany to follow and to move to point H. This reduces welfare in Germany which now has to accept a suboptimal combination of inflation and unemployment. Germany will have an incentive to allow its exchange rate to appreciate. A speculative crisis becomes likely.

It should be stressed that the shock we are analysing in Fig. 4.7 is a temporary one. If it were permanent it would also affect the natural rate of unemployment. We can generalize the result of Fig. 4.7 as follows. When shocks in the short-term Phillips curve are not perfectly correlated, these shocks will lead to conflicts between Germany and Italy about the appropriate policy response. These countries (especially the follower) will have a strong incentive to switch to a more flexible exchange rate arrangement. Thus, for Germany and Italy to form a credible fixed exchange rate arrangement it is necessary that shocks are highly correlated (in addition to the requirement that they should have the same preferences).

If shocks are not perfectly correlated then we must impose stronger conditions on the preferences of one of the countries in order to make this fixed exchange rate arrangement credible. To see this, suppose that Germany is the leader and Italy is subjected to the shock as shown in Fig. 4.7. Italy can only make the fixed exchange rate arrangement credible if it stops pursuing independent inflation and unemployment objectives: in other words, if the indifference curves disappear. Italy can only have one objective, i.e. fixing the exchange rate, which amounts to accepting whatever inflation rate is decided by Germany. If the authorities of Italy can convince private agents that this is their only objective, the fixed exchange rate arrangement can be made credible. Few countries manage to do this. There are, however, countries that come close to this. One example is the Netherlands since the early 1980s. This country has been able to credibly link its currency to the DM. It even weathered the storm of 1992–3. The reason for this success is that the Dutch monetary authorities have made it clear that their only monetary policy objective is the fixity of the guilder/DM rate. All other objectives have been subordinated to that one goal. Few countries, however, have been able, or willing, to do the same. The reason is that this success has been bought by a complete transfer of monetary sovereignty to a foreign nation. In a sense it can be said that the Dutch central bank has become the equivalent of a German Landeszentralbank (regional central bank). Few countries are willing to go that far.

2. Disinflation by pegging to low inflation currency

In the previous section, taking the case of Italy and Germany as an illustration, we identified the problem of a high inflation country which decides to fix its exchange rate to a low inflation currency. We argued that this would only be possible if Italy had the same preferences as Germany. Suppose now that the authorities of Italy want to peg to the German mark and that in order to make this credible they decide to change their preferences. They take on the preferences of Germany. The problem will now be the following. Private agents in Italy are unsure about the seriousness of this 'conversion'. They will therefore want proof that the Italian authorities are serious about this. How can they get such proof? We reveal the answer in Fig. 4.8. The indifference curves $I_1, I_2, \ldots$ are the indifference curves prior to the conversion. $I_1', I_2' \ldots$ are the indifference curves reflecting the changed preferences. Private agents, however, do not know for certain that these are the new indifference curves. They get proof if

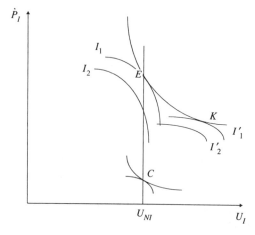

FIG. 4.8. The cost of disinflation

the Italian authorities allow unemployment to increase to point K (where a new indifference curve is tangential to the short-term Phillips curve through the initial equilibrium point E). At that moment private agents observe that the authorities have changed their preferences. They will then be willing to reduce their expectations of inflation, so that the short-term Phillips curve can move downwards. We conclude that the process of disinflation will be a painful one, and that this is necessary to establish the credibility of the fixed exchange rate arrangement.

There are a number of reasons why this process of disinflation may not be successful in establishing the low inflation equilibrium necessary to sustain the fixed exchange rate arrangement. The first is the following. In the previous analysis private agents interpret the increase in the unemployment rate as evidence that the authorities have changed their preferences and are willing to accept more (temporary) unemployment. But suppose that the increase in the unemployment rate is the result of an asymmetric shock in the Phillips curve such as we analysed earlier, and that the authorities have not changed their preferences. In that case, the increase in unemployment will weaken the commitment to the fixed exchange rate. Thus, in an uncertain world, the increase in unemployment observed by private agents can be interpreted in two ways. It can be interpreted as evidence that the authorities are committed to reducing inflation. In that case inflationary expectations will decline. Or it can be seen as the result of a shock which will increase the incentive to follow more expansionary policies. Private agents may then think that the authorities are likely to devalue the currency. This uncertainty about the underlying source of the increase in the unemployment rate will make it difficult to establish a low inflation equilibrium.[5]

A second problem has to do with the dynamics of the disinflation process in an open economy. Let us return to Fig. 4.8 and assume that the increase in the unemployment rate is the result of a change in the preferences of the authorities. The country pegs its exchange rate to currency A. However, during the adjustment period when the country moves from E to K to C, inflation continues to be higher than in Germany (although it converges to the inflation in Germany). Thus, during this transition the price level in Italy will diverge from the price level of Germany. This will create problems of competitiveness for Italy's industry: output is likely to be negatively affected, and the current account will deteriorate. In other words, Italy will exhibit all the phenomena associated with an overvalued currency. If the transition process takes too long (because the authorities have weak credibility) this overvaluation may become unsustainable. A speculative crisis is set in motion, leading to a devaluation. The adjustment to a low inflation equilibrium fails.

These dynamics have plagued many countries that have attempted to reduce their inflation rate by pegging to a foreign currency. It has been observed in Latin American countries during the 1970s and 1980s (Argentina, Brazil, Chile) and also in EMS countries like Italy and Spain.[6] On the whole one can say that there are more failures than successes in these attempts to reduce inflation by fixing the exchange rate.

3. The Krugman model

The Barro–Gordon model identifies the factors that influence the credibility of fixed exchange rate systems. We can go a step further and ask the question whether theory can be used to predict the timing of the collapse. In fact it can, if we are willing to simplify the model a little bit. Krugman presented a pathbreaking analysis in 1979. The Krugman model has later been extended by many authors (see e.g. Flood and Garber (1984)).[7]

We simplify the model considerably compared to the Barro–Gordon model. Also we analyse the issue in the context of one country (facing the rest of the world). The model consists of the purchasing power parity (PPP) condition and the quantity theory of money.

We now write the PPP relation as follows:

$$S = kP/P* \tag{4.4}$$

where P is the index of domestic prices and $P*$ is the index of foreign prices; k is a factor of proportionality which we assume to be constant here.

Our second theoretical building block is the quantity theory of money. This says that the domestic price level changes in proportion to changes in the money stock. Thus,

---

[6] See our discussion of Italy in the previous chapter when we illustrated the phenomenon of overvaluation during the disinflationary process.

[7] The model we present here is a simplified version of the Krugman model.

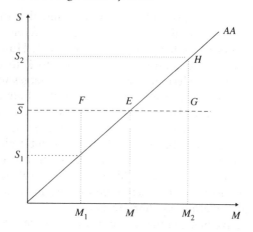

FIG. 4.9. The Krugman model

$$P = mM \tag{4.5}$$

where M is the domestic money stock, and m is the factor of proportionality. The latter depends on the level of output and on the velocity of money. We assume these variables to remain constant. Note that both the PPP and the quantity theories are long-run relationships. Assuming that a similar quantity theory relationship holds for the foreign country we have:

$$P^* = m^*M^*. \tag{4.6}$$

We can now substitute (4.5) and (4.6) into (4.4):

$$S = k(m/m^*)M/M^*. \tag{4.7}$$

This model has a very simple interpretation. It says that the equilibrium exchange rate S changes in proportion to the domestic money stock and changes in inverse proportion to the foreign money stock. Thus, if the domestic money stock increases by say 10 per cent then the exchange rate must also increase by 10 per cent assuming that the foreign money stock remains constant. (Note that all the variables that can affect k, m, and m^* must also remain unchanged.) Alternatively, if the foreign money stock increases by 10 per cent while the domestic money stock remains unchanged the exchange rate must decline by 10 per cent, (i.e. the domestic currency appreciates by 10 per cent).

Equation (4.7) makes clear that in order to keep the exchange rate fixed, the domestic money stock must increase at the same rate as the foreign money stock (assuming of course that k, m, and m^* remain constant).

In Fig. 4.9 we represent equation (4.7) graphically. We set the exchange rate on the vertical axis and the domestic money stock on the horizontal axis. Assuming that M^* does not change we obtain the line AA which describes the equilibrium relationship between the exchange rate and the domestic money stock. When the domestic money stock increases the equilibrium exchange rate increases in the same proportion.

Let us now analyse how a system of fixed exchange rates functions. Suppose the authorities fix the exchange rate at the level $\bar{S}$. We can now immediately see that there is only one domestic money stock, $\bar{M}$, that ensures that the fixed exchange rate $\bar{S}$ is also the equilibrium one. If the authorities choose that money stock, there is no problem with this fixed exchange rate system.

Suppose, however, we start with the money stock M_1, which is below the equilibrium level. As a result, the equilibrium exchange rate S_1 is also below the fixed exchange rate (which the authorities now defend in the market). Put differently, the foreign/domestic currency is too expensive/cheap in the foreign exchange market. This has the following implication. Because the domestic currency is so cheap, exports are stimulated and imports are discouraged. This produces a current account surplus on the balance of payments. Assuming no capital movements this also means that the balance of payments shows a surplus. In other words the monetary authorities accumulate international reserves. We can generalize this point: whenever the fixed exchange rate, $\bar{S}$, exceeds its equilibrium value (determined by the line AA), the monetary authorities accumulate international reserves. Conversely, when the fixed exchange rate is below its equilibrium value (the exchange rate is below the AA line) the stock of international reserves declines. (This follows from the fact that the domestic currency is then too expensive, discouraging exports and stimulating imports.) We can now derive the following result: if the authorities follow the rules of the game the system will be stable. To see this, let us start from M_1. The exchange rate, $\bar{S}$, that the authorities are defending is too high. As a result, the stock of international reserves increases. This leads to an increase in the domestic money stock. We move to the right, thereby reducing the gap between the equilibrium exchange rate and the fixed exchange rate $\bar{S}$. How far do we go? Up to $\bar{M}$. Beyond $\bar{M}$, the equilibrium exchange rate exceeds the fixed exchange rate, creating a dynamic of balance of payments deficits and declining domestic money stock. Thus we conclude that if the authorities follow the rules of the game, i.e. allow the money stock to increase/decrease when the balance of payments shows a surplus/deficit we obtain a stable system converging to the equilibrium point E.

Problems arise when the rules of the game are not followed. Suppose we start again from M_1. Now the authorities decide to increase the domestic money stock at a constant rate independently from the balance of payments position. (They may want to do so for domestic reasons, e.g. to finance government budget deficits.) As the authorities fix the exchange rate we start moving from F in the direction of E. During the movement from F to E the authorities continue to accumulate international reserves (however, at a declining rate). At point E the rate of accumulation stops. Beyond E the authorities start losing international reserves. Let us define point G as the one where the stock of international reserves is depleted.

When will the fixed exchange rate collapse? Let us introduce a rather crucial assumption, i.e. perfect foresight, to answer this question. By perfect foresight we mean that economic agents know the full structure of the model (as represented by equation (4.7) and Fig. 4.9). They can also perfectly forecast future changes in the exogenous variables of the model (like M and M^*). So when will the speculators start the attack on the fixed exchange? A superficial answer would be: when the stock of international reserves is depleted because at that moment the authorities do not have the reserves anymore to defend the fixed exchange rate. In other words when we have reached point G. This, of course, is not the right answer. In order to see this, suppose it were true. Thus, economic agents know that once we reach point G, the authorities will stop defending the fixed exchange rate. As a result, the exchange rate will have to jump from $\bar{S}$ to S_2 (the equilibrium exchange rate in the absence of exchange rate fixing). This leads to a problem. The jump, from $\bar{S}$ to S_2 creates huge profit opportunities for someone starting the speculative attack a fraction of a second before we reach point G. Since all agents are perfectly aware of this (by the assumption of perfect foresight), they will actually buy the foreign currency a fraction of a second earlier thereby precipitating the collapse a fraction of a second before we reach point G. We can now repeat the same reasoning. At the new point of collapse, the exchange rate will still have to jump, creating huge profit opportunities. This leads to the start of the speculative attack a little earlier. We continue this reasoning and arrive at the following startling result. The system collapses when we reach point E. Once we reach point E we can switch to the new flexible exchange rate regime without creating a jump in the exchange rate. This is necessary to avoid profit opportunities which, in this world of perfect foresight, will induce speculators to shift the timing of the attack forward. Thus, the speculative attack and the collapse of the system will occur long before the authorities have run out of international reserves.[8]

In fact, the result is even more startling. The timing of the attack is independent of the stock of international reserves the authorities start with. We could give the authorities a lot of international reserves at the start. As a result, the point G where the stock is depleted would be located further to the right. This would not alter the result that the speculative attack is triggered as soon as we reach point E. Thus, in a sense it can be said that speculators are not fooled by large stocks of international reserves. Their concern is the underlying fundamental variables. If these are out of line with the fixed exchange rate commitment they will start the attack precipitating the collapse of the fixed exchange rate arrangement, irrespective of the stock of international reserves held by the authorities.[9]

---

[8] Note that the collapse cannot come before we reach point E. The reason is that if speculators start buying foreign exchange before E is reached and thereby trigger a collapse, the exchange rate will jump downwards inducing losses for the speculators.

[9] In the real world, the stock of international reserves is likely to matter. In the absence of perfect foresight, speculators may be uncertain about the equilibrium exchange rate. As a result they may use the size and the change in the international reserve stock as signals about the equilibrium exchange rate.

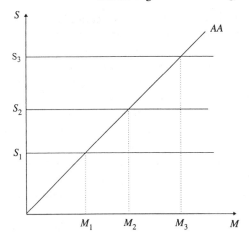

FIG. **4.10.** The Obstfeld model

4. The Obstfeld model

In the Krugman model speculators start a speculative attack because they observe that the authorities do not follow policies consistent with their commitment to keep the exchange rate fixed. Could it be that speculators start an attack even if the authorities follow the right policies (i.e. policies consistent with keeping the exchange rate fixed)? The answer is positive. This was shown by Maurice Obstfeld in an important paper published in 1986. The model used by Obstfeld can be explained in a simplified way using essentially the same theoretical ingredients used in the Krugman model. We represent the model in Fig. 4.10.

Let us assume that the authorities have pegged the exchange rate at the level S_2, and that they fix the money stock at the corresponding level M_2 so as to sustain the fixed exchange rate arrangement. Thus, their monetary policies are perfectly in line with the exchange rate commitment. There should be no problem in keeping the exchange rate fixed. So it seems. In fact the conclusion is wrong. The reason is as follows. In a fixed exchange rate system there are infinitely many combinations of exchange rate and money stock that are consistent with a fixed exchange rate commitment. Thus, in Fig. 4.10, the country could have chosen to fix the exchange rate at the level S_1 and to adjust the money stock accordingly (i.e. to M_1). Alternatively, the choice could have been S_3 and M_3. All these combinations are equilibrium combinations of the exchange rate and the money stock, and allow the authorities to maintain the exchange rate at the chosen level.

In this world of multiple equilibria the following problem arises. Speculators (with perfect foresight) also know that there are multiple equilibria, and that each equilibrium is perfectly feasible. Let us see what this implies. Assume that the authorities have fixed the exchange rate at the level S_2 and the money stock at the level M_2. Speculators know that they could have made a different choice, say S_3 and M_3. A profitable speculative attack could now be as follows. Speculators massively buy foreign exchange at the price S_2 expecting that the authorities switch to the combination S_3–M_3. In that case they will be able to sell the foreign exchange at a higher price and make a fortune. Why would the authorities switch to the new equilibrium? The answer is that the defence of the exchange rate is a costly affair. Interest rates will have to be raised thereby reducing aggregate demand and creating unemployment. If the commitment to the S_2 peg is not perfect (and after all many other pegs are possible) the authorities have an incentive to concede to the speculators and to devalue the currency. This is precisely what speculators expect to happen.

The Obstfeld model nicely illustrates the self-fulfilling nature of speculation. Contrary to what happens in the Krugman model, the authorities follow the right monetary policies. In the Obstfeld model the speculation does not arise because of the fact that the authorities follow monetary policies that are too expansionary. The monetary authorities behave correctly. And yet they are subjected to a brutal attack because the speculators suspect that, when attacked, the authorities will not find it worthwhile to fight. As a result, the speculative attack forces the authorities to a new equilibrium with a higher exchange rate and a higher money stock. In this sense it can be said that speculation is a self-fulfilling prophesy.

The contrast between the Krugman and the Obstfeld models can also be formulated as follows. In the Krugman model an inconsistent monetary policy triggers speculation and the breakdown of the fixed exchange rate arrangement. In the Obstfeld model speculation triggers a change in monetary policy and a breakdown of the fixed exchange rate. More than any other model the Obstfeld model illustrates the fragility of fixed exchange rate systems. Even if today the monetary authorities do all the right things, the slightest doubts about their future commitment to the existing fixed exchange rate may trigger a speculative crisis, leading to a collapse.

This fragility of fixed exchange rate arrangements has certainly been enhanced recently by the trend towards greater capital mobility. This has increased the pool of assets that can be quickly mobilized by speculators to attack a currency. Some economists (e.g. Eichengreen, Tobin, and Wyplosz (1995)) have therefore proposed to reintroduce capital controls to discourage these speculative attacks. We return to the issue of capital controls in Section 6.

The Obstfeld model should not be interpreted to mean that speculators will pick a currency to attack at random. Speculators must have some expectation that the monetary authorities will not be willing to defend their currency (because of the cost involved). Some monetary authorities have acquired a reputation for defending the currency at all cost. Speculators are then likely to decide not to attack these strong-willed authorities.

The Krugman and Obstfeld models are important because they highlight the nature of speculation in fixed exchange rate regimes. It is therefore not without interest to relate these models to our discussion of the n − 1 and the adjustment problems. As argued earlier, the n − 1 problem arises when conflicts about the nature of monetary policies for the system as a whole emerge. This is then also most often the environment in which the Obstfeld analysis of speculative dynamics becomes relevant. Speculators become suspicious about the future commitment of particular countries (e.g. France in 1993) towards the fixed exchange rate, even if today the authorities do all the right things to maintain this fixity. It, therefore, also looks as if the speculators are to blame for the crisis and that the authorities are victims of these speculative attacks 'coming out of the blue'.

The adjustment problem will most often be associated with changes in fundamental variables (inflation, current account, etc.) that raise doubts about the sustainability of the fixed exchange rate system. This is the environment in which the Krugman analysis of speculative dynamics becomes relevant.

5. Target zone models

As mentioned earlier, fixed exchange rate systems are never completely fixed. There is always a band of free fluctuation around the official rate. This raises the question of how the exchange rate behaves within the band. Can economic theory be used to answer this question? The answer has been given by Paul Krugman in a path-breaking contribution.[10] This has led to an explosion of papers and articles refining the initial insight of Krugman (for a survey see Svensson (1994)). The models developed by Krugman and followers are commonly called target zone models.

We can use the same theoretical structure as in the previous sections to highlight the main features of the target zone models. See Fig. 4.11. The AA line, as before, represents the equilibrium relationship between the exchange rate and the money stock. It shows the exchange rates that would prevail in a flexible exchange rate system given the money stock chosen by the authorities. We now add to the model the band of free fluctuation: $\overline{S}$ is the official exchange rate, S_L and S_U are the lower and upper limits of the band within which the exchange rate can fluctuate freely. Once these limits are reached the authorities are committed to keeping the exchange rate within the band.

Let us now assume that the authorities are fully committed to maintain this band unchanged. In order to do so, they announce that they will follow a policy aiming at fixing the money stock at the level given by $\overline{M}$ so as to keep the exchange rate safely within the band. There are, of course, random disturbances in the money supply process so that M will fluctuate randomly around $\overline{M}$. How will the exchange rate behave within this band given the random shocks occurring in the money stock?

---

[10] See Krugman (1991). In fact the paper circulated from 1987 onwards, inspiring a large spin-off of papers prior to its publication.

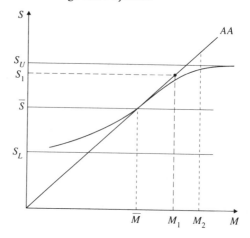

FIG. 4.11. The target zone model

The answer is given in Fig. 4.11. The exchange rate must lie on the S-shaped curve. In order to see why this is so, let us do the following experiment. We start from the initial point when the money stock is exactly equal to $\overline{M}$. The exchange rate is $\overline{S}$. Suppose a random disturbance increases the money stock to M_1. If we were in a flexible exchange rate system the exchange rate would be S_1. Economic agents know that the authorities are fully committed to keeping the exchange rate within the band, and in order to do so they aim at keeping the money stock on average equal to $\overline{M}$. Thus, speculators realize that the future money stock is more likely to decline than to increase (given that it has reached M_1). As a result, the exchange rate is also more likely to decline than to increase (compared to S_1) in the future. Speculators, therefore, will be willing to sell foreign exchange today (expecting a lower price in the future) thereby pushing it down below S_1. We can repeat this argument for many different shocks in the money stock. We find that the exchange rate will be located below the AA line (when the shock is positive) and above the AA line (when the shock is negative).

What happens when the money supply shock is such that the flexible exchange rate solution would bring us outside the band (say to M_2)? At first sight one may think that the exchange rate would then be located on the horizontal upper limit given by S_U. A little thinking shows that this is not possible. If the exchange rate were equal to S_U, speculators would also know with certainty that the future exchange rate would have to decline below S_U. This has to do with the fact that they are fully confident that the authorities will bring back the money stock so as to steer the exchange rate into the band. Since speculators are certain that the exchange rate will decline they are willing to sell when the exchange rate is S_U. As a result, they drive down the exchange rate below S_U. Thus, the exchange rate must be below S_U.

This reasoning leads to the conclusion that the exchange rate will lie on an S-shaped curve as shown in Fig. 4.11. We also conclude that speculation will be stabilizing. In fact, in this model the authorities do not have to intervene in the foreign exchange market when shocks in the money stock push the exchange rate towards the limits of the band. The speculators do it for them. It is clear that this remarkable result only holds because the speculators are fully confident that the authorities will never devalue or revalue the currency. If this confidence is not complete we obtain quite different exchange rate dynamics from the S-shaped curve. (We return to this question in a moment.)

The simple Krugman model, as discussed in the previous section, has been subjected to much empirical testing. In general most empirical studies have been unable to uncover an S-shaped curve in the exchange rate data. In addition, the empirical implications of the model have all been rejected for most fixed exchange rate regimes. The most important empirical implication of the model is that the exchange rate and the domestic interest rate must be inversely related. In order to see this let us use the interest parity condition again:

$$r = r^* + \mu$$

where r is the domestic interest rate, r^* is the foreign interest rate, and μ is the expected future rate of price increase of the foreign currency (expected depreciation of the domestic currency).

We have seen that in the target zone model, an increase in the exchange rate leads to an expectation that the future price of the foreign currency will decline. As a result μ becomes negative. This also implies that the domestic interest rate must decline. Thus, we conclude that in the simple target zone model the movements of the domestic interest rate will be negatively correlated with the movements of the exchange rate in the band. Do we find empirical evidence for this? The answer is that most often the correlation is positive. Thus, as the exchange rate increases and comes closer to the upper limit, domestic interest rates tend to increase, not to decline (for evidence see Svensson (1993 and 1994)). We conclude that the simple target zone model has been soundly rejected by the empirical evidence. What could be the reason for this? The answer has probably to do with the fact that few exchange rate regimes are fully credible (which is the condition for the model to work).

Let us analyse a regime of less than full credibility.[11] Assume that there is a shock in the money stock which drives the exchange rate upwards. Speculators are now uncertain about how to interpret this. Is this shock the result of a random disturbance that the authorities will correct in the future? In that case no problem arises. Or is it the result of a change in policy whereby the authorities have decided to increase the money stock (as in the Krugman model of Section 4.1). In that case doubts will arise about the commitment of the authorities towards the fixed exchange rate. In an uncertain environment, it will be difficult for speculators to know what the source of the shock is. They may very well interpret the upward movement in the exchange rate as a signal of a

---

[11] Bertola and Svensson (1993) were the first to analyse the target zone model when a devaluation risk exists.

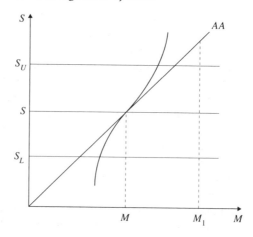

FIG. 4.12. The target zone model with destabilizing expectations

more fundamental change. In that case, the increase in the exchange rate may also become a signal of future troubles. Speculators will then buy the foreign currency instead of selling it. The exchange rate will then lie on an inverted S-curve, as shown in Fig. 4.12. Speculation will be destabilizing.

The empirical evidence seems to indicate that this is what often happens. Movements of the exchange rate within the band often trigger expectations of the kind presented in Fig. 4.12. An increase in the exchange rate within the band then leads to expectations of future increases. As a result, the domestic interest rate most often increases when the exchange rate increases within the band.

The destabilizing effects of exchange rate movements within the band seem to be the rule rather than the exception. This has also often led the monetary authorities to intervene in the foreign exchange market long before the limit of the band is reached so as to limit the movements of the exchange rate within the band. In addition, it has also led some countries to narrow the width of the band. This has been the case for the Netherlands, Belgium, and Austria.

The previous results also imply that, contrary to what has been thought in the past, the existence of a band does not give much additional flexibility to policy-makers. On the contrary, allowing the exchange rate to move around in the band freely can easily trigger speculative attacks, which, when they develop, are very difficult to contain.

6. Capital controls and fixed exchange rates

One of the conclusions of the analysis of the Obstfeld model was that the liberalization of capital movements since the early 1980s had contributed to the problem of self-fulfilling speculative crises. This has led some economists to propose the reintroduction of capital controls to reduce the fragility of fixed exchange rate regimes. Tobin, for example, has proposed to impose a tax of 1 per cent on all capital movements. Eichengreen and Wyplosz have proposed to introduce interest-free deposit requirements by commercial banks for all open positions held in foreign currencies (see Eichengreen, Tobin, and Wyplosz (1995)).

There is no question that the liberalization of capital movements and the trend towards international financial integration have increased the means available for speculation. This has certainly magnified the problem of managing a fixed exchange rate system. As a result, it has speeded up the timing of the collapse of fixed exchange rate systems.

The issues that arise concerning these proposals to reintroduce capital controls are twofold. First, do these capital control measures solve the credibility issues to which fixed exchange rate systems lead? Second, can capital control measures be made effective? Our answer to both these questions will be negative.

Capital controls certainly do not solve the basic problems of credibility of fixed exchange rate systems. When these controls are in place, agents will still ask questions about the commitment of the authorities to keeping the exchange rate fixed. The same factors that lead them to doubt this commitment in the absence of capital controls will lead to similar doubts in a regime of capital controls.[12] The only difference will be that speculation will be more difficult when controls exist.

Can these controls be made watertight so as to avoid a collapse? If so, we should not worry too much about the fact that speculators have lost their confidence in the fixed exchange rate regime. With effective capital controls they would be powerless to act on their beliefs. The fact is that capital controls cannot be made effective enough to avoid a collapse in a world of high trade integration. Speculators have many ways to avoid the controls. They can change the leads and lags in exports and imports. In addition, the new financial instruments that exist today in the form of currency swaps, for example, provide ample opportunities to circumvent the controls. With each imposition of controls private agents would look for other channels, forcing the authorities to extend the control system to other financial activities. Since finance and trade are intertwined, these controls would inevitably have to be extended to international trade. Capital control systems can only work satisfactorily (i.e. be used to sustain fixed exchange rates that are not credible) if trade is also heavily controlled.[13]

The previous discussion is borne out by facts. The Bretton Woods system collapsed, despite the fact that during the 1960s and early 1970s countries like the US and Germany introduced capital controls. When credibility was undermined these controls became increasingly ineffective in sustaining the fixed

---

[12] See Dellas and Stockman (1993) for a formal analysis. In fact these authors show that capital controls can precipitate an attack.

[13] Daniel Gros (1987) has done interesting research on the effectiveness of capital controls. He has shown how these controls tend to lose their effectiveness over time.

exchange rate system. Without doubt these capital controls affected the timing of the collapse and may have postponed it a little. They did not avert the collapse.

7. Conclusion

In this chapter we have discussed some recent economic models that have allowed us to shed additional light on the reasons why fixed exchange rate systems are so fragile. This analysis leads us to reiterate the conclusion reached in Chapter 3: sooner or later this fragility will lead to the collapse of every fixed exchange rate arrangement. This conclusion is also borne out by the facts. Since the collapse of the Bretton Woods system in the early 1970s, the number of countries that have switched to more flexible exchange rate arrangements has increased substantially. Whereas in the early 1980s there were about 30 countries using flexible exchange rate arrangements, this number had increased to almost 90 countries in 1993. Conversely, whereas in the early 1980s approximately 60 countries pegged their exchange rates to an individual currency (mostly the dollar) or in a collective arrangement (like the EMS), the number of countries doing this in 1993 had declined to 45 (see IMF (1995*a*)). This movement towards more flexibility accelerated during the 1980s mainly as a result of the liberalization of capital movements which has brought to the fore the fragility of the fixed exchange rate regime.

   Despite this movement towards more flexibility it remains remarkable that there were still 45 countries maintaining some form of fixed exchange rate in 1993. It must be that floating exchange rate arrangements are also not without problems. To these problems we now turn.

APPENDIX. THE BARRO–GORDON MODEL

The Barro-Gordon model can be written as follows. We start with the Phillips curve:

$$U = U_N + a(\dot{p}^e - \dot{p}) \tag{A1}$$

where U is the unemployment rate and U_N is the natural rate of unemployment; $\dot{p}^e$ is the expected inflation rate and $\dot{p}$ is the observed inflation rate.

The authorities are assumed to minimize the following loss function:

$$L = \dot{p}^2 + b(U - U^*)^2 \tag{A2}$$

where U^* is the target rate of unemployment. It is assumed that

$$U^* = \sigma U_N \tag{A3}$$

where $0 < \sigma < 1$. The rationale that is usually given for this assumption is that there are inefficiencies in the labour market (for example due to tax distortions) leading to increases in the natural unemployment rate. The authorities then target an unemployment rate below the natural rate as a second best policy. b is the weight attached to stabilizing unemployment; $b > 0$.

Substitute (A3) into (A2) and (A2) into (A1):

$$L = \dot{p}^2 + b\{(1 - \sigma)U_N + a(\dot{p}^e - \dot{p})\}^2. \tag{A4}$$

The game played by economic agents and the authorities can now be described as follows. Economic agents set their wages based on their expectations about inflation ($\dot{p}^e$). The authorities then decide upon the optimal inflation, i.e. they minimize the loss function (A4) given private agents' expectations of inflation. This yields the first order condition:

$$\dot{p} - ab\{(1 - \sigma)U_N + a(\dot{p}^e - \dot{p})\} = 0. \tag{A5}$$

Rearranging yields

$$\dot{p} = \frac{ab(1 - \sigma)U_N}{1 + ba^2} + \frac{ba^2\dot{p}^e}{1 + ba^2}. \tag{A6}$$

Next we make a very crucial assumption, i.e. economic agents have rational expectations. They therefore use all available infomation, including the preferences of the authorities. This leads to the conclusion that the inflation rate set by the authorities in equation (A6) is also the one which is rationally expected by economic agents. Therefore, economic agents will set $\dot{p}^e$ equal to the inflation rate found in (A6):

$$\dot{p}^e = \frac{ab(1 - \sigma)U_N}{1 + ba^2} + \frac{ba^2\dot{p}^e}{1 + ba^2}. \tag{A7}$$

Manipulating (A7) yields the following equilibrium inflation rate

$$\dot{p} = \dot{p}^e = ab(1 - \sigma)U_N. \tag{A8}$$

The equilibrium inflation rate depends (among other things) on b, i.e. the weight the authorities attach to unemployment in their loss function. The higher this weight, the higher the equilibrium inflation rate. Note also that the authorities do not affect the unemployment rate in a rational equilibrium because $\dot{p} = \dot{p}^e$ so that $U = U_N$. Finally this solution is also called a discretionary solution because the authorities do not follow a fixed rule, rather they use their discretion to optimize.

We can now substitute the equilibrium inflation rate into the loss function (in this discretionary regime):

$$L_d = \{ab(1 - \sigma)U_N\}^2 + \{b(1 - \sigma)U_N\}^2. \tag{A9}$$

Alternatively the authorities could announce a rule, say a zero inflation rule. If this can be made credible we obtain the loss given by:

$$L_0 = \{b(1 - \sigma)U_N\}^2 \tag{A10}$$

which is unambiguously lower than the loss obtained under discretion. Thus, a zero inflation rule yields higher welfare. However, in a static game this rule is not credible.

5

THE SYSTEM WITHOUT COMMITMENTS

The Bretton Woods system (like all previous and later fixed exchange rate systems) collapsed because the commitments towards convertibility (at a fixed price) were not credible. This lack of credibility led to recurrent crises, during which massive runs on the international reserves of the central banks occurred. As a result, the central banks abolished fixed price convertibility. First, the US monetary authorities closed the gold window in 1971. Later, the central banks of the major industrialized countries closed the foreign exchange window, i.e. they abolished the free convertibility of their currency into dollars *at a fixed price*. From then on, holders of currencies had to convert these currencies in the free market, without the guarantee that this could be done at a fixed price.[1]

Up to this point, the history of *international* money was really mimicking the history of *national* money. As we have seen, in almost all countries the free convertibility (at a fixed price) of the national currency into gold came under pressure, and led the national monetary authorities to abolish fixed-price convertibility. This process had been completed in most countries during the First World War. It is no exaggeration to say that there is a fundamental law which says that commitments towards fixed-price convertibility tend to disappear. As was argued earlier, the basis for the occurrence of this law is the lack of credibility of such a commitment.

Whereas the fundamental tendencies were the same at the international and at the national level, one can also say that from 1971 onwards, the international monetary system stopped copying the trends observed at the national level. At the national level the abolition of fixed-price convertibility frequently led to more coercion. Since fixed-price convertibility had failed to provide the basis for a stable monetary system, the authorities used their coercive power, and forced their residents to use the national money for domestic transactions. Something quite different happened at the international level after 1971. The abolition of fixed-price convertibility did not lead to more controls on international financial

---

[1] This holds only for the currencies of the major industrialized countries. A lot of countries in the world continued to peg their currencies to another key currency, i.e. maintained some form of convertibility (at fixed price). In addition, the currencies of a group of countries in Europe were pegged to each other. We discussed some of these regimes in Ch. 3.

transactions. On the contrary, the newly emerging system was characterized by a relaxation of controls in many countries. What emerged, therefore, was a system without commitments and with a lot of freedom. In other words, in many countries residents became freer to convert domestic currency into foreign currency (and gold), without, however, enjoying a price guarantee.[2]

In this chapter we analyse in a general way the major problems of this new system without commitments and without coercion. In the following chapters, some of these problems will be analysed in greater detail.

1. Problems with a world without commitments

The movement towards flexible exchange rates solved the credibility problem of the Bretton Woods system. However, by rejecting all price commitments it introduced new problems. We first analyse the problem of exchange rate variability.

1.1. Excessive exchange rate variability?

It is clear even to the most casual observer that exchange rates have become much more variable since the major currencies started to float. This is illustrated in Figs 5.1 and 5.2, which show the yearly changes of the dollar/DM and the yen/dollar exchange rates since 1960. It is immediately clear that since the early 1970s something fundamental has happened in the way exchange rates behave.

In order to learn more about the nature of this increased variability of exchange rates, we have to compare these movements to a benchmark. One very useful benchmark is the variability of *expected* exchange rate changes. Why is this so?

Many economic decisions to export and to invest are based on expectations about future exchange rates. If economic agents are able to correctly anticipate changes in future exchange rates, the observed variability of exchange rates may not matter much. However, if exchange rates are difficult to predict, an increase in exchange rate fluctuations will involve an increase in risk. This will affect the behaviour of economic agents in their decisions to export and to invest. Put differently, the evidence of Figs 5.1 and 5.2 does not really tell us much about the kind of uncertainty faced by economic agents in the floating exchange rate system. We have to know whether these observed changes were expected or not.

---

[2] US residents, who were prohibited from holding gold, were granted complete freedom to hold the yellow metal at the end of the 1970s.

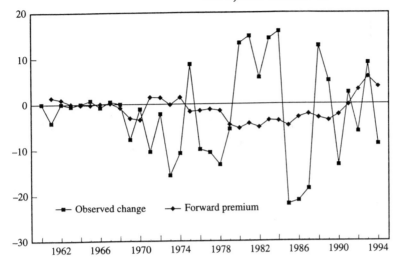

FIG. 5.1. DM/dollar exchange rate (yearly change in per cent)
Source: IMF, *International Financial Statistics*

How can we know this? The interest parity theory comes in very handy here to answer this question (see Chapter 3, Box 3.1, for a discussion of the interest parity theory). What this theory says (among other things) is that the forward premium is the best available forecast of the future change in the exchange rate. If, for example, the dollar is 5 per cent more expensive in the forward market than in the spot market, this means that speculators expect the dollar to increase in price by 5 per cent in the future. Since the forward premium is an observable variable, it provides us with an indicator of what the market expects for the future at any given moment of time, at least if the theory is right. (See Box 3.1 in Chapter 3 for a discussion of why the forward premium may not be such a good indicator of the market's expectation of future changes in the spot rate.)

In Figs 5.1 and 5.2 we present the forward premium of the dollar relative to the German mark and the yen (together with the observed changes of the dollar exchange rates). A positive/negative number means that the dollar is more expensive/cheaper in the forward market than in the spot market. This can then be interpreted to show that speculators expected an appreciation/depreciation of the dollar in the subsequent year. The series of the forward premium was shifted one year forward, so that the number we obtain in a particular year is in fact the forecast, made the previous year, of the change in the current year.

Figs 5.1 and 5.2 allow us to make some interesting observations. First, as a general rule, during the flexible exchange rate period, the *observed* changes in the exchange rate tended to be much larger than the *expected* changes (as measured

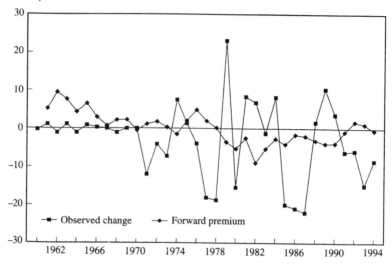

Fɪɢ. 5.2. Yen/dollar exchange rate (yearly change in per cent)
Source: IMF, International Financial Statistics

by the forward premium).[3] This means that most of the observed changes were unexpected by market participants.

This is certainly not the case during the fixed exchange rate period (1960–71). Here we see that most of the time the expected and the observed exchange rate changes were of the same (low) order of magnitude. It appears therefore that the second period was characterized by more exchange rate uncertainty than the Bretton Woods period.

A second interesting observation one can make from Figs 5.1 and 5.2 is that the forward premium (discount) quite often failed to predict the direction of the future change in exchange rates. This is particularly striking during the period 1980–4 when the dollar appreciated continuously. And yet economic agents continuously expected a depreciation of the dollar (as measured by the forward discount on the dollar). Thus, the forward exchange rate appears to have been a biased predictor of the future spot rate.[4] This is certainly a puzzling feature of the exchange markets to which we will return in a later chapter.[5] Here we only note that economic agents had great difficulties in correctly forecasting exchange rates during the flexible exchange rate period. The evidence seems to indicate that most of the actual movements of the dollar/DM and the dollar/yen exchange rates caught the speculators by surprise. Neither the magnitude, nor the direction

---

[3] This phenomenon was first noted by Mussa (1976).

[4] This conclusion is confirmed by many formal tests of the bias of the forward exchange rate. See e.g. Fama (1984), and Frankel (1986). The most common interpretation of this bias of the forward rate is the existence of risk premiums in the foreign exchange market. See Box 3.1 (Ch. 3) for more explanation.   [5] See Ch. 8.

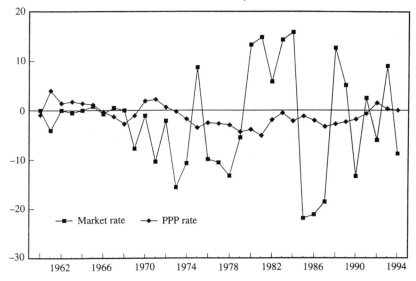

FIG. **5.3.** DM/dollar: market and PPP exchange rates (yearly change in per cent)
Source: IMF, *International Financial Statistics*

of the movements seem to have been foreseen by the people operating in the foreign exchange markets.

1.2. Exchange rate variability and price variability

A second benchmark for comparing the size of the exchange rate movements are the movements of the 'fundamental' determinants of the exchange rates. In this section we concentrate on the price level.

The purchasing power parity (PPP) theory tells us that the equilibrium exchange rate is determined by the ratio of the domestic and the foreign price level (see Box 5.1 for a more detailed description of this theory). One of the versions of this theory (the 'relative' PPP theory) then predicts that when the foreign price level increases by x per cent and the domestic price level by y per cent, the equilibrium exchange rate will increase (or decrease) by $(y - x)$ per cent. For example, if the foreign inflation rate is 10 per cent and the domestic inflation rate 5 per cent, then the domestic currency will appreciate by 5 per cent $(10 - 5)$ in equilibrium.

We can now analyse the extent to which the observed exchange rate movements reflect these fundamental price changes. Figs 5.3 and 5.4 show the observed changes in the DM/dollar and the yen/dollar rate together with the difference between German and US inflation and Japanese and US inflation, respectively.

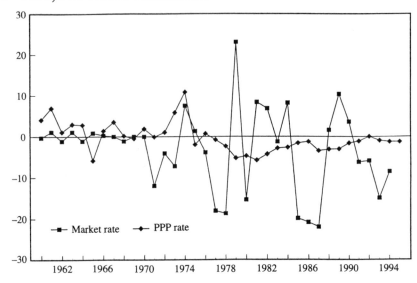

Fɪɢ. 5.4. Yen/dollar: market and PPP rates (yearly change in per cent)
Source: IMF, *International Financial Statistics*

The latter are called the PPP rates. It is immediately evident that during the period of floating exchange rates, the exchange rate movements are much larger than the inflation differentials. This does not seem to have been the case during the Bretton Woods period, where we observe changes in exchange rates and PPP rates of equal magnitude.

A second feature of these exchange rate movements is that quite often for several years in a row, the PPP rates move in the opposite direction from the exchange rates. This is particularly striking during the period 1980–4, where we find that the dollar was appreciating strongly and that the US inflation rate exceeded the German inflation rate every year. A similar problem also existed during the Bretton Woods period (see, for example, the DM/dollar rate during 1961–5). The magnitude of the discrepancies, however, was much lower than during the flexible exchange rate period.

Thus, the facts we observe concerning exchange rate movements confront us with several puzzles. Not only are they largely unexpected; in addition, these exchange rate movements are much larger than one of their fundamental determinants, price movements, and, what is even more puzzling, they often move in opposite directions.

An important implication of the fact that exchange rates move more than the national price levels is that the nominal and real exchange rates have been highly correlated during the floating exchange rate period. This is shown in Figs 5.5 and 5.6 for the DM/dollar and the yen/dollar exchange rates. (The real exchange rate is defined here as the nominal exchange rate times the ratio of the

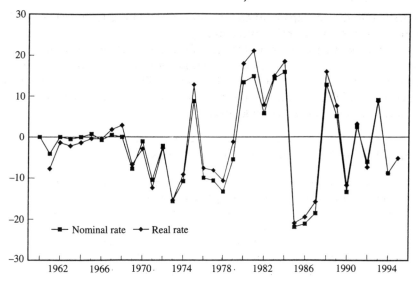

Fig. **5.5.** DM/dollar: nominal and real exchange rates (yearly change in per cent)
Source: IMF, *International Financial Statistics*

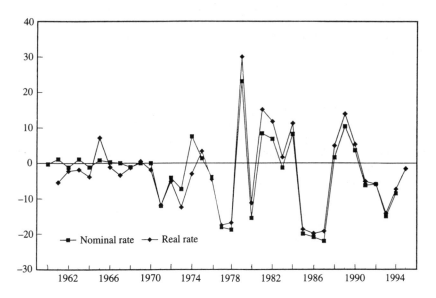

Fig. **5.6.** Yen/dollar: nominal and real exchange rates (yearly change in per cent)
Source: IMF, *International Financial Statistics*

domestic (German or Japanese) and the foreign (US) price levels (where the latter refers to the consumption price index).)[6]

It should be mentioned here that this feature of exchange rate movements does not generalize to other historical periods of floating, or to exchange rates other than those of the industrialized countries. Elsewhere it was shown that in periods of high inflation, the positive correlation between nominal and real exchange rates is reduced considerably.[7]

Box 5.1. The Purchasing Power Parity Theory

The Purchasing Power Parity theory is a very old theory. At the University of Salamanca, Spanish economists during the sixteenth century debated its virtue. In this century, Cassel (1922) can be considered to have written almost everything one wants to know about this theory.

One can start the discussion by postulating the following equilibrium relationship between the exchange rate and the price levels:

$$S = kP/P_w \qquad (5.1)$$

where S is the exchange rate (the price of the foreign currency in units of the domestic currency), P is the domestic price level, and P_w is the foreign price level; k is the factor of proportionality. In its simplest form the PPP theory says that k is a constant, so that when P doubles, the equilibrium exchange rate also doubles (for a given foreign price level). k can also be defined as the real exchange rate. We then have

$$k = SP_w/P. \qquad (5.2)$$

Equation (5.1) is represented graphically in Fig. 5.7. In Fig. 5.7 we set the domestic price level on the vertical axis, the exchange rate on the horizontal axis. Given the foreign price level, we have a proportional relationship between the domestic price level and the exchange rate, represented by the PPP line.

It is important to see that the PPP relationship is an equilibrium relationship, and not a causal relation from say the price level to the exchange rate, or vice versa. Suppose the economy is initially at point A. Assume that an exogenous disturbance shifts the economy away from the PPP line to point C. (Such a disturbance could have occurred, for example, as a result of an expansion of the domestic money stock, which lowered the domestic interest rate, led to a capital outflow, and a depreciation of the currency.) At C one can say that the domestic currency is too cheap (undervalued). This will tend to make domestic producers more competitive. Foreign demand for domestic products increases. This will in turn lead to an increase in the prices of domestic goods. The economy will be pushed up towards the PPP line. Over time PPP will be re-established.

The initial disturbance can also bring the economy to a point like D. In that case the domestic currency can be said to be too expensive (overvalued). Domestic pro-

---

[6] See also Box 5.1 in this ch.   [7] See De Grauwe, *et al.* (1985).

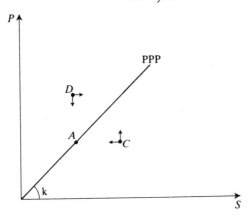

FIG. 5.7. The PPP line and the adjustment mechanism

ducers have lost competitiveness, and will be forced to make price concessions. The dynamics of the movements of the economy is downwards. In Chapter 3 it was stressed that in a fixed exchange rate environment this dynamics may be very slow, because of downward rigidity of wages and prices. In a flexible exchange rate environment, exchange rate changes may help in the adjustment process towards PPP. In this case, the exchange rate will tend to increase. This depreciation of the domestic currency is likely to be triggered at some point by the trade deficits which the country accumulates as a result of reduced competitiveness.

The preceding discussion can also be phrased in terms of movements in the real exchange rate. When the economy moves from A to C, it can be said that the real exchange rate increases (there is a real depreciation of the domestic currency). The dynamics of the adjustment then forces the real exchange rate to decline again. In the end the *real* exchange rate should return to its initial value. A similar formulation in terms of real exchange rate movements can be made in the case when the economy jumps from A to D.

We learn from this analysis that there are forces that tend to restore the equilibrium PPP relationship in the economy, when the latter is disturbed.[8] This adjustment mechanism, however, may be a long one. In this sense, it must be said that the PPP theory describes a *long-run* relationship between the price level and the exchange rate.

1.3. Long-run exchange rate variability

In the previous sections we looked at the size of the yearly variations of exchange rates. Our focus was essentially short term. We found that there is very little relation between yearly movements of the exchange rates and yearly changes in

---

[8] In a later section it will be made clear that this does not hold for all disturbances.

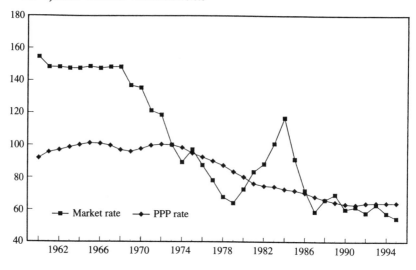

Fɪɢ. 5.8. DM/dollar: market and PPP rates (1973 = 100)
Source: IMF, International Financial Statistics

the price level. From this evidence one would be tempted to reject the purchasing power parity theory as an explanation of exchange rate movements. This would be unfair to the theory, however. The purchasing power parity theory describes a *long-run* equilibrium relationship between price levels and exchange rates. The short-term deviations from PPP we observed in the previous section are not incompatible with a situation in which exchange rates tend to return to their PPP value over the long run. A long-run analysis, therefore, can tell us whether, and how, in the flexible exchange rate system exchange rates tend to return to their (purchasing power) equilibrium level.

In Fig. 5.8, we show the evolution of the DM/dollar rate (called the market rate) and compare it with the ratio of the price levels in the US and Germany (called the PPP rate). When this ratio increases/declines the price level increases faster/slower in Germany than in the US. Thus the equilibrium price (PPP) of the dollar increases/declines. Fig. 5.9 does the same for the yen/dollar rate. In Fig. 5.10 real exchange rates are represented. These real exchange rates are obtained by multiplying the market rate by the PPP rate (see also the formula (5.2) in Box 5.1).

In Figs 5.8 to 5.10 we have used 1973 as the base year to calculate the indices. This means that we implicitly believe that in 1973 the exchange rate was close to its equilibrium (PPP) value. This choice of the base year is of great importance. It colours our view of whether the exchange rate was in equilibrium or in disequilibrium during the whole period. There is now some consensus that the period around the years 1973–5 was close to an equilibrium situation for these two exchange rates (see Williamson (1983), who studies the role of variables other than price levels in determining the equilibrium exchange rates).[9]

---

[9] In the next chapter we analyse the role of variables other than the price level.

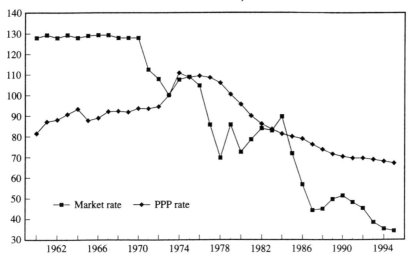

FIG. 5.9. Yen/dollar: market and PPP rates (1973 = 100)
Source: IMF, *International Financial Statistics*

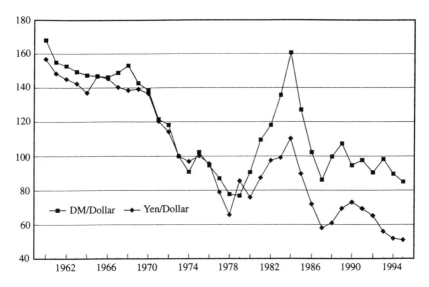

FIG. 5.10. Real exchange rates (1973 = 100)
Source: IMF, *International Financial Statistics*

The choice of the base period, however, is of no relevance for establishing the empirical phenomenon stressed here. This is the fact that exchange rates have diverged from their PPP values for long periods. Or, put differently, real exchange rates have exhibited very long cycles. For example, if we take the early 1970s as the starting-point we find that the dollar goes through a first cycle declining

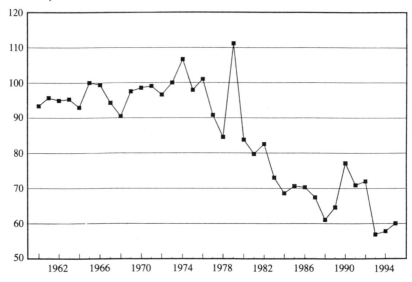

FIG. 5.11. Real exchange rate of the yen/DM (1973 = 100)
Source: IMF, International Financial Statistics

(in real terms) from 1970 to 1979 to go back to its initial level in the first half of the 1980s.

Another feature present in the data is a long-term drift of real exchange rates. This is especially evident in the case of the yen/dollar. From 1960 to 1995 the real yen/dollar rate declines by more than 100 per cent (i.e. the yen appreciates in real terms by more than 100 per cent). The same phenomenon of long-term drift is present in other exchange rates. In Fig. 5.11 we show the real DM/yen rate. We can see that from the middle of the 1970s the real DM/yen rate exhibits substantial downward drift. It could be, of course, that this is only the first leg in a cyclical movement. If this is the case, the cycle is an extremely long one and exceeds by far the typical length of a business cycle.[10]

The simple PPP theory leaves us with a problem. How can we explain the sizeable and prolonged deviations of exchange rates from their purchasing power parity values? The long run seems to be very long indeed. In addition, we have observed that in a number of cases there does not seem to be a clear tendency for the exchange rates to return to their PPP values over periods as long as twenty years. It must, therefore, be admitted that the simple PPP theory, as formulated up to now, is incomplete.

---

[10] The more technically oriented reader will recognize that the real exchange rate may exhibit a unit root. This means that when we regress the real exchange rate on its lagged value, the coefficient we obtain is not significantly different from unity. When the real exchange rate exhibits a unit root this also implies that a shock produced today has a permanent effect on the future real exchange rate. For more evidence see Engel and Hamilton (1990), and Frankel and Rose (1994).

2. The purchasing power parity theory and real disturbances

The incompleteness of the PPP theory to fully account for exchange rate movements was first recognized by Gustav Cassel (1922). One of the major insights of Cassel was that the PPP theory only holds if the sources of the price disturbances are monetary.[11] Put differently, the PPP theory predicts that when a monetary shock occurs, for example, an increase in the money stock, both the domestic price level and the exchange rate will increase in the same proportion. When all adjustments have taken place, an increase in the money stock will reduce the purchasing power of money, both in terms of a domestic basket of goods, and in terms of a foreign basket of goods. In this sense, the PPP theory is in fact an extension of the quantity theory of money to an open economy.[12]

The PPP theory, however, does not predict that when a *real* shock occurs, the proportionality between the price level and the exchange rate will be maintained. To take an example: if the terms of trade of a country improve (because of, say, an increase in the demand for its main export product), the country will experience an improvement of its current account. It may then need a real appreciation of its currency to re-equilibrate the current account. We will then observe that the exchange rate and the domestic price level do not change in the same proportions. They may even have to move in opposite directions. In Box 5.2 we pursue these ideas further.

The question now becomes whether the strong deviations from PPP we have observed, can be due to the occurrence of real shocks. In the next section we concentrate on one of these real disturbances. In the following chapter we concentrate on a number of other real disturbances.

Box 5.2. The PPP theory, the quantity theory and real disturbances

In this box we analyse the effects of two kinds of shocks, one monetary, one real. Let us use the same graphical device as in Box 5.1. In Fig. 5.12, we represent the PPP relationship by the PPP$_1$ line. (Note that this line is defined for a given foreign price level.)

The economy is initially at point A. Suppose now that the monetary authorities double the money stock. The quantity theory of money tells us that in the long run (if nothing else happens) the domestic price level will also double. By the same token the exchange rate will also double in the long run. In Fig. 5.12, the new long-run equilibrium point is B. As a result, all the relative prices (in particular, the real exchange rate) will be restored to their initial value. In the long run, money is a veil. In this sense, the PPP theory is a necessary addendum to the quantity theory applied to the open economy.

The dynamics of the adjustment to the long-run equilibrium can be quite complicated. In other words, the path taken by the economy to move from A

---

[11] See also Frenkel (1976) on this doctrinal issue.
[12] See also Niehans (1985) on this issue. The reader will notice that in Ch. 4 we used this idea when we developed the Krugman model.

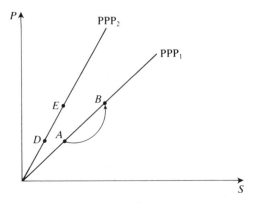

Fig. **5.12.** The PPP line and real disturbances

to *B* is difficult to predict. One possibility is presented in Fig. 5.12 by the arrow from *A* to *B*. This is, however, only one of the many possibilities. We will return to this issue of the dynamics of the exchange rate and price path in the next chapter when we discuss popular exchange rate models.

When the economy is hit by a real disturbance the proportionality between exchange rate and price level will not hold. This basic insight is illustrated in Fig. 5.12. Suppose that world demand shifts its preferences in favour of the domestic output. Given the price level and the exchange rate, there will be excess demand for the domestic output. As a result, the new equilibrium price must increase. Put differently, the terms of trade improve. Graphically, the PPP line shifts upwards to PPP$_2$. The economy will have to move to the new PPP line, and the proportionality between the exchange rate and the price level will be lost. More precisely, the domestic price level will have to increase more than the exchange rate. In other words, the real exchange rate must decline (a real appreciation of the domestic currency).

Where exactly the new equilibrium on the PPP$_2$ line will be located is impossible to say without modelling the goods market and the money market. It could be a point like *D* or one like *E*. In all these cases the domestic currency experiences a real appreciation. In the first case, this is brought about by a nominal appreciation (*S* declines). In the second case the real appreciation is realized by an increase in the price of the domestic good.

3. Real exchange rates and productivity differentials

We know from our previous discussion that the proportionality between prices and exchange rate only holds if the changes in the price levels are due to monetary shocks. It is clear, however, that the equilibrium exchange rate can also change because of non-monetary disturbances. In particular, shocks that affect the relative price of tradables and non-tradables will also influence the equilibrium exchange rate. Prominent among these shocks are productivity changes.

In general, the growth of productivity is higher in the tradable goods sector (which includes most of the manufacturing sector) than in the non-tradable goods sector (which includes many service industries and the government sector). These differential growth rates have important implications. In order to make this clear let us take the example of the US and Japan. During the postwar period the growth of productivity has been higher in the tradable goods sectors of these two countries than in the non-tradable goods sector. In addition, the productivity growth in the Japanese tradable goods sector has been substantially higher than in the US tradable goods sector. This has allowed Japanese wages to increase faster than in the US without endangering the Japanese competitive position. Put differently, wages in Japan could increase faster than in the US because the higher growth of productivity allowed unit labour costs in Japan to remain at the US level.

The higher wage increase in Japan, however, has been transmitted to the non-tradable goods sector, so that Japanese prices in this sector have increased faster than in the US non-traded goods sector. As a result, the Japanese aggregate price level, which is an average of the price level in the two sectors had to increase faster than the US aggregate price level. Thus, external equilibrium was compatible with a higher rate of inflation in Japan than in the US without the need for the yen to depreciate relative to the dollar. Or alternatively, with the same rate of inflation in Japan and the US, the yen had to appreciate relative to the dollar. The reason is that with equal inflation (and wage increases) in the two countries, the unit labour costs in the Japanese tradable goods sector declined relative to the US. This made Japanese exports increasingly competitive leading to increasing export surpluses for Japan.[13]

The previous ideas allow us to compute equilibrium exchange rates which take into account both the price developments and the productivity changes. The results are presented in Figs 5.13 and 5.14.[14] We now find that using the simple PPP relationship we overestimated the degree of overvaluation of the dollar during 1960–70, and underestimated it significantly during 1980–5 (especially for the yen/dollar rate). This has to do with the fact that labour productivity was increasing faster in Japan and Germany than in the US, so that the equilibrium price of the dollar was pushed down.

The results of Figs 5.13 and 5.14 also show that we can explain most of the long-run decline of the dollar relative to the German mark and the Japanese yen by the PPP theory and the theory of productivity differentials. This is especially clear in the case of the dollar/yen rate. From 1960 to 1995 the dollar dropped to one-third of its initial value against the yen. This long-run decline of the dollar can be explained almost completely by higher inflation and lower productivity growth in the US compared to Japan. In the case of the dollar/DM rate we find that we can explain a large part of the long-term decline of the dollar by the fact that inflation was higher and productivity growth was lower in the US compared to Germany.

---

[13] See Balassa (1964). See also Marston (1987*a*), for a recent analysis applied to the dollar/yen rate, and Kravis and Lipsey (1987).

[14] For more detail about the computations and the statistical sources see Appendix to this chapter.

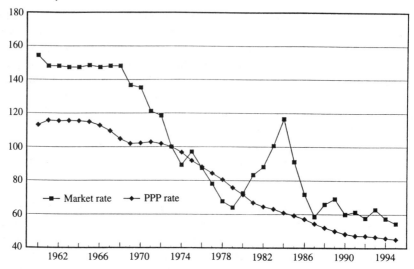

FIG. 5.13. DM/dollar: market and PPP rates (corrected for productivity differentials) (1973 = 100)

Source: IMF, *International Financial Statistics*

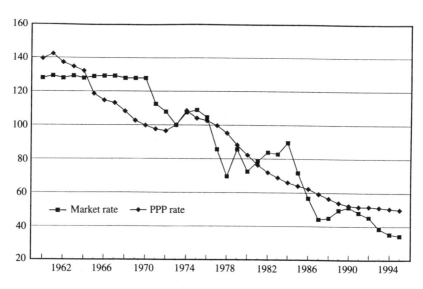

FIG. 5.14. Yen/dollar: market and PPP rates (corrected for productivity differentials) (1973 = 100)

Source: IMF, *International Financial Statistics*

TABLE 5.1. *Output per employed person (average yearly growth rate)*

	US	Japan	Germany
1961–70	1.9	8.9	4.2
1971–80	0.6	3.7	2.6
1981–90	0.8	2.9	1.7
1991–95	1.1	0.7	1.7

Note: The productivity measures relate to the whole economy and not only to the traded goods sector. It is generally accepted that the differential productivity growth rates find their origin in the tradable (industrial) sector, and that these differentials are small when comparing non-tradable (service) sectors across countries.

Source: European Commission, *European Economy*, 59, 1995

One interesting question that arises here is whether this long-run decline of the dollar against the yen and the DM is likely to continue in the future. Although the future will always be difficult, if not impossible to predict, history can be of some help. A large part of the long-run decline in the dollar has been due to the differential in the growth of labour productivity between the US on the one hand and Japan and Germany on the other. There is now increasing evidence that this differential has narrowed considerably, and has almost disappeared. In Table 5.1 we show some evidence.[15]

It is likely that productivity growth differentials between these major countries will be small in the future. Therefore one of the major sources of the long-run decline of the dollar is likely to disappear. If the US monetary authorities manage to keep inflation low and comparable with Japan and Germany, there is little reason to expect that the dollar will continue its long-run downward slide against the yen and the DM.

Although the PPP theory and the theory of productivity differentials explain the long-run trends rather well, it is also clear from Figs 5.13 and 5.14 that they cannot explain the short-term (yearly) movements of the exchange rates. The degree of short-term variation around the long-term trend is substantial. And we observe here again that the short term is longer than just a few months; it lasts several years.

We can represent the data of Figs 5.13 and 5.14 in a more synthetic way by dividing the observed exchange rates by their equilibrium values (i.e. the PPP values corrected for productivity differentials). This is done in Fig. 5.15. The indices we obtain can also be called real exchange rates, because they measure the deviations of the DM/dollar and the yen/dollar rates from the (productivity-corrected) PPP values. Fig. 5.15 confirms what was just said. PPP and productivity differentials do quite well in explaining the long-term trend. (This can be seen by the fact that the real exchange rate, corrected for productivity differentials, shows no trend.) They are not good at explaining movements over

---

[15] The OECD publishes similar data for the business sector indicating that the productivity growth differentials have been reduced considerably.

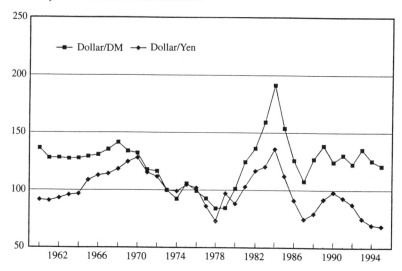

FIG. **5.15**. Real exchange rates (corrected for productivity differentials) (1973 = 100)
Source: IMF, *International Financial Statistics*. See also appendix

time spans below 10 years. For example, these two theories can in no way explain what happened during the 1980s when the dollar first increased by 50 per cent against the yen and 100 per cent against the DM, and later dropped by approximately the same amounts. Clearly other things must have happened besides inflation differentials and productivity shocks to explain such large cyclical movements in the dollar exchange rates.

The evidence of Fig. 5.15 also teaches us something about the different behaviour of exchange rates in fixed and flexible exchange rate regimes. When we compare the period of floating with the Bretton Woods period we arrive at the following conclusion. First, significant 'misalignments' (i.e. deviations from productivity-corrected PPP values) occurred in the two exchange rate regimes.[16]

A second observation which can be made from Fig. 5.15 is that the size of the misalignments was larger during the flexible exchange rate period. Especially during the 1980s the misalignments of the dollar took historically large proportions. This evidence is corroborated by many empirical studies comparing the exchange rate movements of currencies that floated freely and of currencies that were pegged after the collapse of the Bretton Woods system (see Mussa (1979), Frankel and Rose (1994)). It appears that the size of the misalignments has been much larger with freely floating exchange rates than with pegged exchange rates.

What are the explanations of these phenomena? To this question we turn in the next chapter.

[16] Some economists will object to the use of the word misalignment. This word suggests that the observed exchange rates are incorrectly valued or out of equilibrium. One should not exclude the possibility that the movements of exchange rates during the 1980s e.g. responded to shocks (other than prices and productivity) so that the observed rates were equilibrium rates. Misalignment is then a misnomer. We return to these issues in the following chapters.

APPENDIX. CALCULATING THE PPP EXCHANGE RATE CORRECTED FOR PRODUCTIVITY DIFFERENTIALS

Let us start from the definition of the general price index p_C in the home country (in logs):

$$p_C = ap_T + (1 - a)p_N \tag{A1}$$

where p_T = the price index of traded goods
$\quad\quad p_N$ = the price index of non-traded goods
$\quad\quad a$ = the share of traded goods in the consumption basket.
Analogously we have for the foreign country:

$$p_C^* = a^*p_T^* + (1 - a^*)p_N^*. \tag{A2}$$

The equilibrium prices in the tradables and the non-tradables sectors are assumed to be equal to the ratio of wages to productivity (unit labour costs). In logs this yields

$$\begin{array}{cc} p_T = w - q & p_N = w - v \\ p_N^* = w^* - q^* & p_N^* = w^* - v^* \end{array} \tag{A3}$$

where w, w^* are the (log of the) wage rate in the domestic and the foreign country, respectively. Note the assumption that wages are equalized in the traded and non-traded goods sectors;

$\quad q$, q^* are the (log of the) productivity levels in the tradables sectors in the two countries;

$\quad v$, v^* are the (log of the) productivity levels in the non-tradables sector in the two countries.

Substituting (A3) into (A1) and (A2) yields, after rearranging:

$$p_C = ap_T + (1 - a)(p_T + q - v) \tag{A4}$$

$$p_C^* = a^*p_T^* + (1 - a^*)(p_T^* + q^* - v^*). \tag{A5}$$

We now introduce the assumption that PPP holds in the tradable goods sector:

$$p_T = S^{PPP} + p_T^* \tag{A6}$$

where S^{PPP} is the exchange rate when PPP holds in the tradable goods sector.

If we furthermore assume that the shares of tradables and non-tradables in the consumption basket of the two countries are identical ($a = a^*$), and that the productivity in the non-tradables sector is the same in both countries ($v = v^*$), we can write

$$p_C - p_C^* = aS^{PPP} + (1 - a)(S^{PPP} + q - q^*). \tag{A7}$$

Solving for S^{PPP}, we obtain an expression which can be interpreted as the productivity-adjusted PPP rate:

$$S^{PPP} = (p_C - p_C^*) - (1 - a)(q - q^*). \tag{A8}$$

In the computations of this productivity-adjusted PPP rate we used the productivity measures of Table 5.1. The share of traded goods in the consumption basket (a) was set equal to 0.3.

6

MODELLING NOMINAL AND REAL EXCHANGE RATE VARIABILITY

In the previous chapter we diagnosed several problems with the present floating exchange rate system. One is the high degree of exchange rate variability, the size and the direction of which was typically not reflected in the forward premiums or discounts. Second, we observed a strong correlation of nominal and real exchange rates, which follows from the fact that nominal exchange rates fluctuate much more than national price levels. Third, we found that real exchange rates exhibit long cyclical movements (one of which was more than ten years in duration). Put differently, exchange rates show a tendency to wander away from their equilibrium levels as measured by their PPP values. These long swings in the real exchange rates were not eliminated by taking into account the differential growth rates of productivity.

How can we explain these three stylized facts concerning the nature of the variability of the exchange rates? Do we have theories which allow for a consistent explanation? To these questions we now turn.

1. Why are exchange rates so volatile?

The starting-point for analysing this question is again the interest parity theory. We have derived the basic equation in a previous chapter.[1] For the sake of convenience it is reproduced here:

$$\frac{1+r_t}{1+r_{ft}} = \frac{E_t(S_{t+1})}{S_t}. \tag{6.1}$$

Equation (6.1) tells us that the rate at which the exchange rate is expected to change must be equal to the interest differential. As will be remembered, equation (6.1) which is the open interest parity condition, holds if there are no risk

[1] See Box 3.1, Ch. 3.

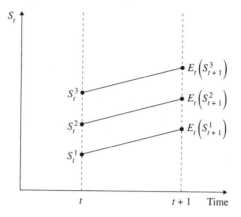

FIG. **6.1.** Flexible exchange rates: many exchange rate paths

premiums. This is certainly a serious limitation. Nevertheless, as a starting-point it is a useful device to highlight some of the fundamentals of exchange rate determination.

The basic insight we can gain from equation (6.1) is that there is an infinite number of exchange rates that satisfy this condition. For example, if the future exchange rate is expected to be 10 per cent higher than the present spot rate, equation (6.1) can be satisfied with a spot rate equal to 1 and an expected future rate equal to 1.1. Other combinations, however, are equally possible, e.g. 2.0 and 2.2, or 3.0 and 3.3, etc. Thus, equilibrium of the financial markets is compatible with an infinite number of different exchange rates.

The same problem can also be formulated as follows. For every expected future exchange rate there is an exchange rate today that will ensure that the interest parity condition holds. Thus, expectations about the future exchange rate are self-fulfilling.[2] If, for example, a financial guru convinces people that the future exchange rate will not be, say, 2.0 but 2.5 then this will be reflected immediately in the present exchange rate. We conclude that there is a basic indeterminacy in equation (6.1).

This problem of indeterminacy of the equilibrium paths for the exchange rates is illustrated in Fig. 6.1. Given the interest rate differential, we have an infinity of paths linking the present spot rate with the expected future one. This is shown in Fig. 6.1 by a collection of parallel lines which connect the spot rate with the expected future spot rate.

Which path will be selected? In a flexible exchange rate system this will essentially be determined by the expectations agents have about the future. Once they have made up their mind about the future exchange rate, a unique

---

[2] Note that we encountered this problem also in the context of fixed exchange rates when we discussed the Obstfeld model.

exchange rate path will result.[3] We will, therefore, have to analyse how these expectations are formed. We will see that these expectations are influenced not only by the fundamental variables (such as the price levels, the productivity changes, or other economic variables), but also by seemingly irrelevant variables.

2. The fixed exchange rate solution: providing an anchor

Before analysing this process of expectations formation, it is useful to remember how this problem of indeterminacy is taken care of in a fixed exchange rate system. In such a system the authorities fix the present exchange rate (S_t). In terms of Fig. 6.1, the authorities fix the initial value of the exchange rate path. Given the interest rates, this determines a unique path for the exchange rate. In this sense the authorities provide an anchor for the expectations of economic agents.

The fixed exchange rate system in fact went further than that. To the extent that the commitment of the authorities towards fixed exchange rates was credible, i.e. if economic agents were confident that the same fixed exchange rate would be maintained in the future, then $S_t = E_t(S_{t+1})$. From equation (6.1) we can see that this restricts the interest rates in both countries to be the same.[4] Thus, a credible system of fixed exchange rates imposed strong conditions on interest rate differentials. This, in a sense was the price for the public provision of an anchor for exchange rate expectations.

What happened when the credibility of the commitment towards fixed exchange rates was undermined? For example, suppose that economic agents expected a future devaluation of the national currency (i.e. the future exchange rate was expected to be higher than the present fixed one). Equation (6.1) tells us that in that case the domestic interest rate had to increase relative to the foreign interest rate. Such an interest rate increase quite often did not prevent a speculative crisis when speculators expected that the authorities would not be willing to keep a high domestic interest rate. We have discussed models that describe the collapse in Chapter 4. The fixed exchange rate system then ceases to provide an anchor.

3. Floating exchange rates: no fixed point

In a floating exchange rate environment, there are no commitments by the authorities to fix a particular exchange rate. This leads to the basic problem

---

[3] Mathematically oriented readers will recognize that the problem is the same as the problem of finding a solution to a differential or a difference equation. Without restrictions on the initial (or on the final) conditions there are infinitely many equilibrium paths the variable can take.

[4] Note that because in practice exchange rates were not rigidly fixed but could move between an upper and lower limit, there was also some leeway for interest rates to differ. Also, the previous analysis disregards the possibility that monetary authorities introduce capital controls. These lead to deviations from interest parities. We will return to this problem later.

of indeterminacy. Economic agents' forecasts of the future exchange rate will be the driving force determining today's exchange rate. If they change their expectations about the future exchange rate, this will immediately be reflected in the exchange rate today. What then determines these expectations?

There are several competing theories that explain how economic agents set their expectations. One class of theories assumes rational behaviour, another assumes that rationality in the formation of expectations is limited.

4. Exchange rates and rational behaviour

The central idea of the theory of rational expectations is that it is in the interest of economic agents, who have to forecast the future, to use the available and relevant information. Throwing away readily available and important information is not good policy for profit maximizing individuals. Those who do this will be confronted by smarter individuals who are not as stupid, and who therefore will make better forecasts. As a result, these smarter individuals will make less mistakes, and also more profits. In the long run they will drive out from the market-place the stupid ones who fail to use the available information, and who therefore make less profits. Thus, the theory of rational expectations is no different from the theory which says that profit maximizing firms will look for ways to minimize costs. Those firms who fail to do this make less profit and tend to disappear, at least in a competitive environment.

What do these general ideas imply for exchange rates?

Economic agents who need to know the future value of the foreign currency have an interest in making reliable forecasts. What is the relevant information for them to use? First, there is the past history of the exchange rates. If something systematic occurs in the series of exchange rates (e.g. an increase at the end of each year), then this information will be used by rational economic agents. A failure to use this systematic (and thus predictable) movement in the series will lead to a systematic forecast error. Those who exploit this systematic component will make better forecasts, and thus more profits.

Second, and more importantly, economic agents will use not only past observations of the exchange rates, but also other information that can be useful in forecasting the future exchange rates. For example, when the monetary authorities announce a new policy aimed at reducing the growth rate of the domestic money stock, economic agents will work out whether and to what extent this new policy will affect the exchange rate. In doing this, they will necessarily use a model of the economy which describes the link between the money stock and the exchange rate.

More generally, it will be in the interest of the economic agents to obtain a representation of the economy (a model), which describes how the exchange rate is determined and how changes in exogenous variables affect the exchange rate. If they trust the model, they will use it to calculate how the changes they observe in important variables are likely to affect the exchange rate.[5] Similarly, they will use the model to evaluate how *expected* changes in these variables are likely to influence the exchange rate. In more technical jargon we say that the subjective distribution of the future expected exchange rate is equal to the objective distribution, i.e. the one produced by the model.

A basic characteristic of this theory is that it stresses the forward-looking nature of the exchange rate. Let us return to Fig. 6.1 to make this point clear. Based on a view about the future path of important exogenous variables and on a model of the economy, economic agents fix the future exchange rate (for example $E_t(S_{t+1}^2)$). This then determines uniquely the exchange rate (S_t^2) needed today to bring the economy to this end-point, along a path determined by the interest parity condition. This process is the opposite of the one we described when we discussed the fixed exchange rate regime. In the latter, the present exchange rate is anchored, so that the interest parity condition (the slope of the exchange rate path) determines how the exchange rate will move to the end-point.

The forward-looking nature of the exchange rate in a floating exchange rate regime has an important implication. The future expected exchange rate is unlikely to be fixed for very long. The economy is continuously disturbed by new shocks which were previously unanticipated. Therefore, economic agents will in this rational expectations view of the world, continuously re-evaluate the effects of these new shocks for the future value of the currency. Thus, the end-point in Fig. 6.1 is a continuously moving target. As a result, the exchange rate today will have to jump around continuously to allow the economy to find the right track.

The previous very general discussion of the forward-looking rational expectations theory of exchange rates allows us to explain the first of the three stylized facts discussed in the previous chapter, i.e. the short-term variability of exchange rates. It is insufficient, however, to explain the other two empirical phenomena. In order to do this, we have to add more economic structure into the very general discussion of this section.

Broadly speaking, two approaches have been followed in modelling exchange rates.[6] One can be called the disequilibrium approach, the other the equilibrium approach. The former assumes some sluggishness in the adjustment of economic variables (for example prices) towards their equilibrium values; the latter assumes that all variables adjust instantaneously. The disequilibrium models (sometimes also labelled the fixed-price models) have clearly become the more popular ones for analysing exchange rate behaviour. We, therefore, discuss them first, and we ask the question whether these models are able to explain the positive correlation between nominal and real exchange rates, and the long swings in real exchange rates.

---

[5] We will come back to this. As we will argue, occasions may arise when economic agents lose their trust in economic models as instruments for predicting the future. In that case, the only information they may be willing to use is the present and past exchange rates.

[6] For a recent survey of exchange rate theories, see Taylor (1994), Isard (1995), and Rosenberg (1996).

5. Disequilibrium models

Two versions of the disequilibrium models have become popular. One is the Dornbusch model, the other is the portfolio balance model. The former assumes that goods prices are sluggish, the latter that the current account takes time to move to its equilibrium value.

5.1. The Dornbusch ('overshooting') model

In this section we give an intuitive account of the main features of the Dornbusch model. In Box 6.1 we present the model in a more formal way.

Let us assume the following about the structure of the economy. First, in the long run both the quantity theory and purchasing power parity hold. This means that if the money stock doubles this must lead in the long run to a doubling of the domestic price level and to a doubling of the exchange rate (assuming nothing happens in the rest of the world).

Second, in the short run prices are sticky, i.e. prices react with a lag to disturbances, such as an increase in the money stock.

Third, (open) interest parity holds at each moment of time. This means that the exchange rate and the interest rate must adjust instantaneously so that the expected rates of return on domestic and foreign assets remain the same at every moment in time. In other words, there are no risk premiums.

A fourth assumption is that expectations are formed rationally. In fact in the Dornbusch model *perfect foresight* is assumed. Economic agents know the structure of the economy as spelled out in the previous three points, and also know the future values of the exogenous variables driving the model.

With this structure in mind we can analyse the effects of disturbances. Suppose that the monetary authorities announce and immediately implement a policy increasing the domestic money stock. In the rest of the world nothing happens. What are the effects of such a policy announcement in the exchange market?

We present the effects in Fig. 6.2. The initial expected future exchange rate is $E_t(S_{t+1}^1)$. The new expected future exchange rate increases to $E_t(S_{t+1}^2)$ because economic agents know that such a permanent increase in the money stock must in the long run increase the price level and because they know the PPP theory underlying the model. In addition, the domestic interest rate must decline. This is so because the higher supply of money creates an excess supply of money. Since neither the price level nor the output level can increase instantaneously, the interest rate must decline. This so-called liquidity effect is needed to induce economic agents to hold the higher domestic money stock.[7]

The effect of the decline in the domestic interest rate is to reduce the ratio

---

[7] Over time when the price level starts increasing, the transactions demand for money will go up. At that moment the domestic interest rate will start increasing.

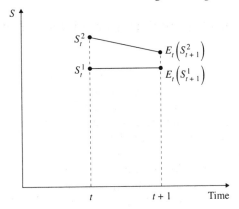

FIG. 6.2. Perfect foresight model

$(1 + r_t)/(1 + r_{ft})$ in equation (6.1). Since we assumed that initially domestic and foreign interest rates were equal, this ratio becomes less than unity. This means that the present exchange rate must be higher than the expected future exchange rate. In Fig. 6.2 we represent the initial spot exchange rate by S_t^1. Thus, when the policy shock occurs, the exchange rate will have to jump from S_t^1 to S_t^2. In the process the exchange rate will overshoot its long-run value, $E_t(S_{t+1}^2)$, given by the purchasing power parity condition.

This overshooting result is obtained here because we have assumed that goods prices are slow to react. As a result, financial variables, in particular the interest rate and the exchange rate, have to take the full burden of adjusting to the exogenous disturbance. In the example given here, this necessitates an overshooting of the exchange rate. The intuition underlying this overshooting of the exchange rate is the following. The monetary shock lowers the return on domestic assets, and thereby makes the holding of foreign assets more attract-ive. In order to keep foreign and domestic assets equally attractive, the price of the foreign currency must increase sufficiently so as to generate an expectation that from now on it can only decline in price. This expected future decline in the price of the foreign currency reduces the total expected return on foreign asset holdings and brings it in line with the return on domestic assets. (This expected depreciation of the foreign currency is represented by the negative slope of the line linking S_t^2 to $E_t(S_{t+1}^2)$ in Fig. 6.2.) Thus, the overshooting of the exchange rate is necessary to maintain equality of expected yields on domestic and foreign assets.

This overshooting model can be extended to analyse other shocks, for example, fiscal policy shocks. In Box 6.1 this matter is pursued. There it is shown that a fiscal policy shock which is not financed by issuing money leads to an appreciation of the currency in the Dornbusch model. In addition, although we still need a jump in the exchange rate, this jump is not of the overshooting variety.

5.2. The Dornbusch model as an explanation of exchange rate variability

The Dornbusch model of exchange rate determination provides a basis for explaining some of the empirical phenomena observed earlier. In particular, it explains not only why exchange rates have tended to be very volatile, but also why nominal and real exchange rate movements are strongly correlated. In a world where the authorities frequently change their monetary and fiscal policies, there will be frequent jumps in the exchange rate. Quite often, these jumps are also of the 'overshooting' type as illustrated by the example of a monetary policy shock. In these cases the overshooting phenomenon will lead to amplified effects of these policy shocks on the exchange rates. In addition, since prices are sluggish at adjusting, the high nominal exchange rate variability will also be reflected in a high variability of real exchange rates.[8]

There are a number of problems, however, which have called this model into question as a complete explanation of exchange rate movements. We will return to this in greater detail in the next chapter. Here we just list the problems. A first problem relates to the assumption that the open interest parity holds, i.e. that there are no risk premiums. This feature in fact is shared by many exchange rate models. A second has to do with the fact that although the model provides an explanation for the short-term variability of the exchange rates, it is not clear how it can explain the long-run movements of the real exchange rates which were documented in the previous chapter. Certainly the Dornbusch model predicts that exchange rates must exhibit cycles. For example, monetary shocks will push the exchange rate in one direction which must be corrected later by reverse movements. The issue, however, is whether the overshooting dynamics predicted by the Dornbusch model comes close to explaining the long cycles documented in the previous chapter. As we observed in the previous chapter, these movements have exhibited cycles of very long and unequal duration, which have been longer than a typical business cycle. It is unclear how such a long cycle can be made to fit into the overshooting cycle predicted by the Dornbusch model. We will come back to this issue in the next chapter.

Box 6.1. The Dornbusch model: a formal analysis

The Dornbusch model in its simplest form can be derived as follows.[9] We begin with the money market. The money demand can be specified in a loglinear form:

$$m = p_c + \alpha y - \beta r \qquad (6.2)$$

---

[8] It can be argued that this explanation is very *ad hoc*. After all, the Dornbusch model starts out by assuming price rigidity, without giving an economic rationale for it. As a result, it 'explains' the high correlation between the nominal and real exchange rate by assuming it.

[9] The Dornbusch model presented here is a simplified version of the original one. In particular it does not make a distinction between traded and non-traded goods. For the original article see Dornbusch (1976).

where m is the log of the money stock, p_c is the log of the consumption price index, y is the log of the output level, and r is the domestic interest rate. The consumption price index is defined as a weighted average of the price of the domestic good (p) and the price of the foreign good expressed in domestic currency $(s + p_f)$:[10]

$$p_c = \sigma p + (1 - \sigma)(s + p_f). \tag{6.3}$$

In the freely flexible exchange rate system considered here, the supply of money (m_s) can be controlled by the domestic monetary authorities. Money market equilibrium then implies that

$$m_s = p_c + \alpha y - \beta r. \tag{6.4}$$

Assuming open interest parity yields

$$r = r_f + \mu \tag{6.5}$$

where we define μ as the expected rate of depreciation of the domestic currency, and r_f as the foreign interest rate.

In the framework of a deterministic model, rational expectations imply perfect foresight. Put differently, in this model there is no uncertainty about the parameters nor about the future exogenous variables. One can, therefore, write that

$$\mu = \dot{s} \tag{6.6}$$

where $\dot{s}$ is the realized rate of change in the exchange rate,[11] i.e. the expected rate of change in the exchange rate must equal the realized rate of change.

We can now combine the previous equations (6.3) to (6.6) into one equation which describes the financial equilibrium (money market equilibrium and interest parity) in a perfect foresight world. Substitute (6.6) into (6.5), and (6.5) and (6.3) into (6.4), and rearrange:

$$\dot{s} = \frac{\sigma}{\beta}p + \frac{1-\sigma}{\beta}s + \frac{1}{\beta}z \tag{6.7}$$

where $z = (1 - \sigma)p_f + \alpha y - \beta r_f - m_s$; this variable represents all the exogenous influences in the financial markets.

We obtain a first order differential equation which describes the motion of the exchange rate in a perfect foresight environment.

In order to complete the model we have to specify an equation which describes the law of motion of the price of the domestic good, p. (In this simple Dornbusch model the output level is assumed to be exogenous.) We use the PPP theory, and postulate that when the exchange rate is above its PPP value (which means that the currency is undervalued), the price level is pushed upwards. This mechanism was explained in Box 5.1 of the previous chapter. Similarly, when the currency is overvalued, the price level is pushed downwards. More formally we have

$$\dot{p} = \delta(s - \bar{s}) \tag{6.8}$$

[10] Note that the foreign price and the exchange rate appear in additive form from now on because both variables are expressed in logs here.

[11] Technically $\dot{s}$ is the derivative of the log of the exchange rate with respect to time.

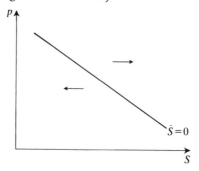

Fɪɢ. 6.3. Financial market equilibrium

where $\dot{p}$ is the rate of change of the price level and $\bar{s}$ is the PPP value of the exchange rate. Since $\delta > 0$, $\dot{p} > 0$ when $s > \bar{s}$. The PPP value of the exchange rate can also be written as follows

$$\bar{s} = \kappa + p - p_f. \tag{6.9}$$

Note that we have written the PPP relationship in loglinear form. It corresponds to the equation we used in the previous chapter and which was then specified as $S = kP/P_f$. κ can be interpreted as a variable expressing the 'real' influences on the equilibrium exchange rates.

Substituting (6.9) into (6.8) yields

$$\dot{p} = \delta s - \delta p + \delta(p_f - \kappa). \tag{6.10}$$

The model is fully described by the two first order differential equations (6.7) and (6.10). We can now derive the phase diagram of this system of two differential equations.

First set $\dot{s} = 0$ in equation (6.7). We then obtain an equation which defines under what condition the exchange rate is at rest. This yields

$$p = -((1 - \sigma)/\sigma)s - (1/\sigma)z. \tag{6.11}$$

Since equation (6.11) describes the financial submodel, it also defines under what condition the financial markets are in equilibrium. We can represent this equilibrium condition graphically in Fig. 6.3 by a negatively sloped line. The negative slope follows from the fact that the coefficient of s in equation (6.11) is negative.

In addition, we can define in Fig. 6.3 the motion of the exchange rate when the financial markets are not in equilibrium. When p is above the $\dot{s} = 0$ line the exchange rate must be increasing. This can be seen from equation (6.7). In that case $\dot{s} > 0$. Similarly when p is below the $\dot{s} = 0$ line, the exchange rate must be declining. We represent this dynamics by the arrows in Fig. 6.3.

The second differential equation (6.10) describes the dynamics in the goods market. The goods market is in equilibrium when $\dot{p} = 0$. The condition for this to be true can be derived from (6.10) to be

$$s = p - p_f + \kappa. \tag{6.12}$$

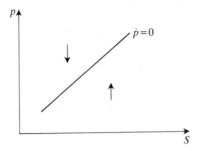

FIG. **6.4.** Goods market equilibrium

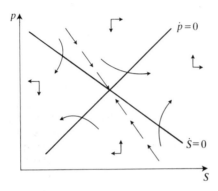

FIG. **6.5.** Phase diagram of the Dornbusch model

This is nothing but the PPP relation. We can represent this by an upward sloping line as in Fig. 6.4. When the price level is above the PPP line, the price level is pushed downwards. When the price level is below the PPP line, it increases. We represent this dynamics by the arrows in Fig. 6.4.

We are now in a position to describe the full dynamics of the model. This is done in Fig. 6.5 where the two previous graphs have been superimposed. The phase diagram in Fig. 6.5 has the following characteristics. The dynamics of the model exhibits a 'saddle point', which is typical of every perfect foresight model. That is, there is only one stable path that will bring the economy to equilibrium at the intersection of the $\dot{s} = 0$ and $\dot{p} = 0$ lines. Every other path is explosive, and will lead to an increasing divergence from the equilibrium. Thus, the model does not exclude the possibility of increasing deviations from the fundamentals, as expressed by the equilibrium conditions of the model.

The model can now be used to analyse the effects of exogenous disturbances. This is done in Fig. 6.6. Suppose, for example, that the money stock is increased unexpectedly.[12] This shifts the $\dot{s} = 0$ line upwards, as can be seen from

---

[12] Note that only unexpected shocks of exogenous variables can be analysed in this version of the model. Expected shocks must already have been incorporated into expectations. For an analysis of expected disturbances see Wilson (1979).

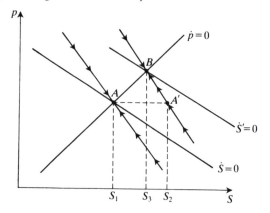

FIG. 6.6. Monetary expansion and overshooting

equation (6.11). The new price level which equilibrates the financial markets must increase. How is equilibrium achieved after this unexpected disturbance?

We know that the economy must move from the initial equilibrium point A to the final equilibrium point B. If the price and exchange rate flexibility is absolute, this adjustment can be achieved instantaneously. Suppose, however, that prices adjust sluggishly and therefore that they cannot adjust instantaneously. In that case there is only one possible adjustment path: the exchange rate must 'jump' immediately from s_1 to s_2. From then on it will move backwards again along the stable path given by the arrows from A'. This is the only adjustment path which will bring us to the final equilibrium point B. If the exchange rate did not jump instantaneously to s_2, the initial conditions would be such that the economy would be on an explosive path, which would lead to increasing deviations from the fundamentals.

We conclude that in this perfect foresight model, the exchange rate must be a 'jumping' variable, to allow for a movement towards equilibrium. In addition, the adjustment in the exchange rate is of the overshooting variety: the instantaneous jump of the exchange rate exceeds the increase needed in the final equilibrium B. Thus, over time the exchange rate will have to return part of the way.

The overshooting of the exchange rate does not necessarily accompany other disturbances. Take for example the effect of an increase in government spending. More spending by the government creates excess demand in the goods market. The real exchange rate must now change. More precisely, κ must decline, i.e. we must have a real appreciation of the domestic currency in the new long-run equilibrium. This real appreciation is needed so as to reduce the level of aggregate demand (by reducing foreign demand for the domestic good). The effects are shown in Fig. 6.7. The $\dot{p} = 0$ line shifts upwards. The new long-run equilibrium point is given by C. The dynamics of the adjustment is as follows. The exchange rate must jump downwards from s_1 to s_3. From then on the exchange rate continues to decline along the 'saddle path' described by the arrows. Thus, although the exchange rate jumps instantaneously, there is no overshooting.

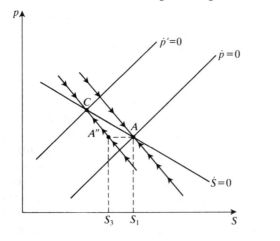

FIG. 6.7. Fiscal policy in the Dornbusch model

5.3. The portfolio balance model

Pioneering work in developing these models was done by Kouri (1976) and Branson (1977). Contrary to the Dornbusch model, the portfolio balance models do not assume that the open interest parity holds. In other words the existence of risk premiums is explicitly allowed for. In a sense it can be said that the portfolio balance models are models which explain the occurrence of risk premiums.

The portfolio balance models start from the well-known identity which says that the *changes* in the foreign asset position of a country are equal to the current account of the country. A country which is running a current account surplus during a given period of time will find itself with an increased net foreign asset position at the end of the period as compared with the beginning of the period. The opposite holds true for a country running a current account deficit.

We can write this identity as follows:

$$NF_t - NF_{t-1} = CA_t \tag{6.13}$$

where NF_t and NF_{t-1} are the net foreign asset positions of the country in period t and $t - 1$; CA_t is the current account during period t. Note that NF_t and NF_{t-1} are stocks, whereas CA_t is a flow variable.

We can now decompose NF into two components, the net foreign asset position of the monetary authorities and the net foreign asset position of the private sector. Thus

$$NF_t = NFO_t + NFP_t \tag{6.14}$$

where NFO_t is the net foreign asset position of the monetary authorities; NFP_t is the net foreign asset position of the private sector.[13]

Substituting equation (6.14) into equation (6.13) yields

$$NFO_t - NFO_{t-1} = CA_t - (NFP_t - NFP_{t-1}). \tag{6.15}$$

This equation helps to understand an essential difference between fixed and flexible exchange rate systems. In a fixed exchange rate system, the left-hand side is a residual variable, which adjusts to whatever values appear on the right-hand side of the equation. Put differently, private agents decide about how much to export and import, and this determines the current account CA_t. In addition, these private agents decide how much of their wealth to keep in domestic and in foreign assets. This then determines the capital account $(NFP_t - NFP_{t-1})$. In general, these two decisions will not be such that the current and the capital account offset each other. As a result, the central bank will have to intervene in the foreign exchange market by selling or buying foreign exchange so as to exactly match the sum of the current and capital account. A failure to do so would inevitably lead to a change in the exchange rate.

In a pure flexible exchange rate system, the monetary authorities abstain from any intervention in the foreign exchange market. As a result, the left-hand side of the equation is always equal to zero. We can then rewrite equation (6.15) as follows

$$CA_t = (NFP_t - NFP_{t-1}). \tag{6.16}$$

Equation (6.16) makes clear that the exchange rate will have to be such that the decisions which determine the current account are consistent with the decisions which determine the capital account of the balance of payments.

The next step in the analysis is to introduce the assumption that in the very short run the current account is sluggish. That is, imports and exports cannot adjust instantaneously. It usually takes time for economic agents to change their plans to spend and to produce. As a result, if we take a very short-term point of view (for example a day), we can consider the current account to be given by decisions made earlier. We can then say that the current account is predetermined during that particular day.

This has important implications. For, if economic agents in a country decide on a particular day that they would want to increase their net foreign assets holdings, they will not be able to do this instantaneously, because the current account cannot change instantaneously.[14] The net foreign asset position is essentially fixed. Therefore, the exchange rate will have to adjust instantaneously so as to make sure that agents willingly hold the existing stock of net foreign assets. Only over time, when the current account changes, can the stock of net

---

[13] We disregard the government sector here. This could easily be added.

[14] Of course, one individual agent in this country can change his net foreign asset position, provided he can convince another resident to sell him foreign assets. The net foreign asset position of the country as a whole, however, is not affected by this transaction.

foreign assets change so as to reflect economic agents' wishes to accumulate (or decumulate) foreign assets.

We can now ask the question of how monetary disturbances affect the exchange rate. Suppose an unexpected monetary expansion occurs. This lowers the domestic interest rate. Economic agents now find themselves holding domestic assets with a lower return than the foreign assets. They will therefore try to switch out of domestic into foreign assets. However, in the very short run, domestic residents as a whole cannot increase their net foreign asset position. For the latter to be possible, the current account would have to show an increase in the surplus. But we assume that in the very short run the current account does not react. As a result, the exchange rate will have to jump up, sufficiently so that the purchase of foreign assets is made unattractively expensive.

The depreciation of the currency will then start a dynamic process tending to improve the current account. Over time, therefore, domestic residents will have to accumulate foreign assets.

An interesting aspect of this model concerns the relation between the current account and the exchange rate during this dynamic adjustment process. The portfolio balance model predicts that current account surpluses are correlated with appreciations of the domestic currency. Why?

The answer has to do with the fact that the portfolio balance model does not assume the open interest parity to hold. It allows for risk premiums. The current account surpluses increase the supply of net foreign assets. In order for domestic residents to be willing to accumulate more foreign assets in their portfolio, they must receive an extra return, i.e. a risk premium. Such a risk premium comes about as a result of a lowering of the price of the foreign currency. The latter makes the holdings of foreign assets more attractive. Thus, the portfolio balance model adds an interesting feature, which has to do with the interaction of the exchange rate and the current account. One can represent this dynamics graphically as follows (see Fig. 6.8). In period t_1 the authorities increase the money stock. This leads to an immediate jump in the exchange rate. At that point the current account does not yet react. However, over time a current account surplus is building up. At the same time the exchange rate starts declining (the domestic currency appreciates). This dynamics must go on until economic agents have accumulated the desired level of foreign assets. When this is achieved, the current account surplus has gone down to zero again and the exchange rate stops declining.[15] (Note an implication of the dynamics described in Fig. 6.8: there is a first phase during which the appreciation of the currency is associated with increasing current account surpluses, and there is a second phase during which the appreciation coincides with a declining current account surplus.)

---

[15] We disregard here the dynamics of interest payments on foreign assets. As residents have accumulated foreign assets they will earn interest on these assets. These then tend to lead to current account surpluses. If the current account must go to zero this implies that the trade account must show a deficit (to offset the positive interest receipts). This also implies that the exchange rate will not return to its initial level. It will drop below the initial value (i.e. there will be a real appreciation of the domestic currency) to produce the required trade account deficit.

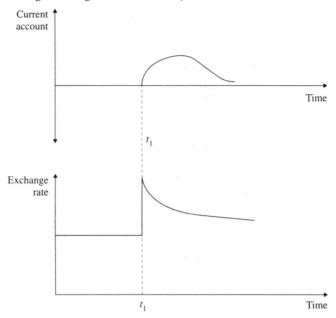

FIG. **6.8.** Exchange rate and current account after a monetary shock in the portfolio balance model

Let us now return to our question whether the portfolio balance model provides for a good explanation of the three stylized facts documented earlier.

Both the short-term variability of the exchange rates and the fact that nominal and real exchange rates are highly correlated can be explained rather well by the portfolio balance model. Shocks in exogenous variables (for example the money stock) lead to attempts by wealth owners to change the domestic and foreign composition of their portfolios. The existing stock of foreign assets held by residents cannot change quickly, because the current account changes slowly. Therefore, the exchange rate must jump immediately to maintain asset market equilibrium. This theory also implies that the nominal and the real exchange rates will be correlated in the short run, because the exchange rate reacts much faster than the price level.

The portfolio balance model also contains a dynamic feature which could explain the long swings in real exchange rates. As mentioned earlier, the model predicts a negative correlation between the current account and the exchange rate: current account surpluses go together with an appreciating currency. Do we find such cycles in the interaction between the current account and the real exchange rate? In the next chapter we discuss some empirical evidence. We will show that, although sometimes such a correlation pattern can be found in the data, in many other cases there is little correlation or worse the correlation goes in the other direction.

5.4. The portfolio balance model and risk premiums

As was pointed out earlier, the portfolio balance model can be interpreted as a model explaining the risk premiums in the foreign exchange market. This can be made clear by starting from the interest parity equation (with a risk premium):[16]

$$r - r_f = \mu + \Pi \tag{6.17}$$

where μ is the expected depreciation of the domestic currency, and Π the risk premium from holding domestic assets. As argued earlier, this risk premium can be positive or negative. The portfolio balance model now provides a theory of how the risk premium is determined. It says that the risk premium is a function of the relative supply of the domestic and foreign assets:

$$\Pi = \Pi(A/A_f) \tag{6.18}$$

where A is the supply of domestic assets and A_f is the supply of foreign assets. If the supply of domestic assets increases faster than the supply of foreign assets (for example, because the government budget deficit is larger in the home country than in the foreign country), then investors will only be willing to hold these extra domestic assets if they obtain an extra return (a risk premium) on domestic assets. This is so because after the increase in the supply of the domestic assets, investors who previously held an optimal portfolio must be induced to change the optimal composition of their portfolio and to hold more domestic assets. Assuming that the domestic and the foreign assets are not perfect substitutes, they can only be induced to do so, if the return on domestic assets increases relative to the foreign asset.[17]

Empirical testing of this model has been very disappointing. In general, it must be said that although the risk premiums tend to be important, their modelling along the lines suggested by the portfolio balance model has been unsuccessful up to now.[18] More precisely, it has appeared to be impossible to find a stable relationship between the supply of assets and the risk premiums (excess returns). Risk premiums tend to jump around and seem to elude any systematic explanation.[19] Again we will return to these empirical issues in greater detail in the next chapter.

6. The Mundell–Fleming model

If anything, the Mundell–Fleming model has been used as the workhorse to analyse macroeconomic problems in open economies, and more particularly to

---

[16] This equation was derived in Ch. 3 (Box 3.1). Note that the risk premium on domestic assets = – risk premium on foreign assets.

[17] It should be stressed here that the portfolio balance models also incorporate the variance and the covariance of the returns as explanatory variables of the risk premiums. See e.g. Dornbusch (1982), Fukao (1983), Frankel (1982), Bomhoff (1987) and Engel (1995).

[18] See Frankel (1982).

[19] In Ch. 9 we present an interpretation of the elusive behaviour of risk premiums.

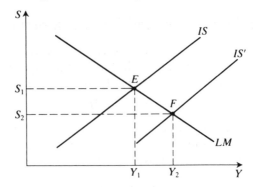

FIG. 6.9. Fiscal policies in the Mundell–Fleming model

study how monetary and fiscal policy shocks affect the exchange rate. As will be seen it is very similar in structure to the Dornbusch model. It allows us, however, to better distinguish between the effects of monetary and fiscal policies on the exchange rate, and to concentrate on the importance of different policy mixes for the exchange rate.

We will use a version of the model in which we assume that the domestic and foreign financial markets are perfectly integrated. This allows us to use the interest parity condition in the same way as in the Dornbusch model. Let us rewrite it here as follows.

$$r = r_f + \mu$$

where μ is the expected rate of depreciation of the domestic currency. As in the Dornbusch model, we disregard problems which occur when risk premiums are allowed for. We can also write the expected depreciation μ as follows:

$$\mu = \frac{(E_t S_{t+1} - S_t)}{S_t}$$

where $E_t S_{t+1}$ is the expectation prevailing in period t about period $t + 1$'s exchange rate; S_t is the exchange rate in period t. In the version of the model discussed here it is assumed that the future expected exchange rate is exogenous. In Box 6.2 we endogenize expectations by introducing the (perfect foresight) rational expectations hypothesis.

Apart from the interest parity condition, the model consists of an equilibrium condition in the goods market and an equilibrium condition in the money market. We represent these in Fig. 6.9. On the vertical axis we show the exchange rate (S), on the horizontal axis the level of output (Y). The *IS* curve represents the combinations of exchange rate and output for which the domestic goods market is in equilibrium. It is a positively sloped line for the following reason. When the exchange rate increases (the domestic currency depreciates) the demand for domestic goods is increased. This is so because in this model with sticky prices, a nominal depreciation is also a real depreciation. As a result, domestic goods become more competitive. It also follows that an increase in output is necessary in order to maintain equilibrium in the domestic goods market. Thus, the *IS* curve is positively sloped. Note that the *IS* curve in Fig. 6.9 is a translation of the traditional *IS* curve (which is drawn in the interest rate–output space) into the exchange rate–output space. The reversal in the slope has to do with the fact that according to the interest parity relation the interest rate and the exchange rate are inversely related (for a given level of expected future exchange rate).

The *LM* curve in Fig. 6.9 describes the relation between the exchange rate and the output level needed to maintain equilibrium in the money market. It is negatively sloped for the following reason. When the exchange rate increases the price of imported goods increases.[20] As a result, the consumption price index increases so that the supply of real cash balances declines. This necessitates a decline in output so as to reduce the demand for real cash balances.

A fiscal expansion can be represented by a shift of the *IS* curve to the right. This is so because the fiscal expansion generates more demand and therefore requires an expansion of output so as to maintain equilibrium in the goods market. The effect of this fiscal expansion is represented in Fig. 6.9 by the displacement of the equilibrium point from E to F. The exchange rate declines from S_1 to S_2 (i.e. the currency appreciates).[21]

Note that we have left the dynamics of the adjustment in the dark. As a result, this model is only capable of analysing comparative statics results, i.e. comparing two equilibrium positions. In Box 6.2 we add some dynamics to the model in the context of the (perfect foresight) rational expectations assumption. It is shown there that the adjustment path of the exchange rate will then involve an instantaneous jump and a 'slow' adjustment afterwards.

We now come to an important point concerning the nature of the effect of fiscal policy shocks. The fiscal expansion leads to a real appreciation of the domestic currency because we assume that the (nominal) stock of money remains unchanged. Thus, the fiscal expansion is not financed by printing money, but by issuing government bonds. If the same fiscal expansion were to be financed by issuing money, as is quite frequently the case in many countries where the central bank is just a branch of the fiscal authorities, the effect on the exchange rate would be quite different.

We can show this by first analysing how a monetary expansion affects the exchange rate. This is done in Fig. 6.10. The increase in the money stock shifts

---

[20] Note that this model assumes some asymmetry in price stickiness. The price of imported goods increases automatically, whereas the price of domestic goods is sticky. It also follows that a depreciation of the currency increases the relative price of imported goods by the same amount as the depreciation.

[21] Note that this appreciation leads to (partial) crowding out. Full crowding out occurs when the *LM* curve is vertical. This is the case when there is no real balance effect of exchange rate changes. In that case the appreciation of the currency is so strong as to completely offset the positive demand effects of the fiscal expansion.

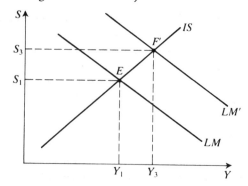

FIG. 6.10. Monetary policies in the Mundell–Fleming model

the *LM* curve to the right. That is, the increased supply of money must be absorbed by an increase in output in order to maintain equilibrium in the money market. The effect on the exchange rate is positive. A monetary expansion leads to a depreciation of the domestic currency.

Comparing Figs 6.9 and 6.10 leads to the conclusion that a fiscal expansion which is financed by issuing money has ambiguous effects on the exchange rate, and that a depreciation of the currency cannot be excluded in the Mundell–Fleming model. It also follows that we can only evaluate the effect of fiscal policies on the exchange rate by introducing monetary policies into the analysis. Thus, what matters is the fiscal–monetary policy mix.

7. Equilibrium models of exchange rate determination

In contrast to the previously discussed models, equilibrium models do not make assumptions of price stickiness (or stickiness in other variables). In equilibrium models it is assumed that markets clear instantaneously. This assumption holds not only for the asset markets, but also for the goods markets.

During the 1970s, one particular brand of equilibrium models became quite popular. This is the monetarist model. The ingredients of this model are the same as the Dornbusch model except that prices are assumed to adjust instantaneously so that the goods markets clear instantaneously. As a result, the monetarist model becomes a model where the quantity theory and purchasing power parity hold at each point in time. (Note that we used this model in our discussion of Krugman's theory about speculative attacks; see Chapter 4.) Thus, for example, when the money stock increases by x per cent, the domestic price level and the exchange rate increase by x per cent. There is clearly no overshooting in this model.

The contrast between the equilibrium and the disequilibrium models is illustrated in Fig. 6.11. We show the PPP relationship (as derived from Box 5.1 in the

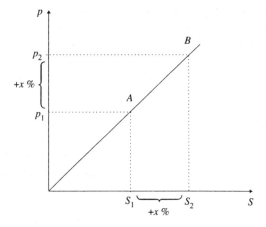

FIG. **6.11**. The monetary model of the exchange rate: nominal shocks

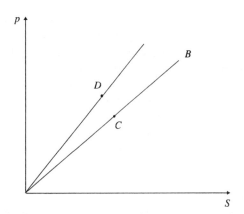

FIG. **6.12**. The monetarist model of the exchange rate: real shocks

previous chapter). Starting at point A, an increase in the money stock of x per cent leads to an increase in the domestic price level of x per cent (by the quantity theory of money) and an increase in the price level of x per cent (by the purchasing power parity theory). We end up at point B.

The monetarist (equilibrium) model does not preclude changes from occurring in the real exchange rate. These changes will happen when real shocks occur. We show an example in Fig. 6.12. Suppose an exogenous increase in the demand for the domestic good relative to the foreign good occurs. This will lead to an improvement in the terms of trade of the country. Graphically we have an upward shift in the PPP line. This means that for every level of the exchange rate, a higher price of the domestic good is necessary to equilibrate the domestic goods market. It follows that if the economy was initially, say, at point C, after the demand shock it will have to move to a point, say D, on the new PPP line. Therefore, the price level and the exchange rate will not increase in the same proportion. In other words, the real exchange rate will be affected.

How exactly the price level and the exchange rate change when the relative demand for the domestic good increases depends on the underlying structure of the model. In order to see this problem clearly a full general equilibrium model must be specified, describing the preferences of the consumers and the production technology. Such models have been developed by Alan Stockman (1987), among others.

An important implication of this equilibrium approach to the exchange rate is that real exchange rate changes can only happen because real shocks occur (such as changes in the structure of demand, or shocks in the supply like productivity shocks). Monetary shocks have no effect on the real exchange rate, they only affect the nominal exchange rate. This conclusion contrasts with disequilibrium models where we have seen that monetary disturbances produce (temporary) changes in the real exchange rate. The empirical evidence that has been accumulating over the years has made clear that this monetarist (equilibrium) model could not be used for explaining the short-term behaviour of exchange rates (see Frankel and Rose (1994)). For example, there is practically no relation between the growth rates of the money stock and the exchange rates on a monthly, quarterly, or even yearly basis. It is fair to say that the accumulated evidence against the monetarist model is such that it cannot seriously be considered as a useful short-term model, in the sense of being able to explain the short-term movements of the exchange rates.[22]

If the model has any value it can only be as a predictor of long-run tendencies. Much in the same way as the quantity theory can only be interpreted as a long-run theory, and not as a theory which explains short-term price movements. In order to explain the long swings in real exchange rates it has to rely on exogenous real disturbances that exhibit sufficient persistence. In the next chapter we analyse whether there have been enough of these real disturbances to explain the large and persistent movements in real exchange rates.

Box 6.2. The Mundell–Fleming model and perfect foresight

In Section 6 of this chapter we discussed the effect of monetary and fiscal policies in a static expectations version of the Mundell–Fleming model. In this box we extend the model by assuming perfect foresight instead.

The *LM* part of the model is essentially identical to the financial submodel of the Dornbusch model, except that the output level is now the endogenous

---

[22] It has been claimed that the monetarist model is useful in explaining short-term exchange rate movements in a situation of hyperinflation (see Frenkel (1976)). The idea is that during periods of hyperinflation, the size of the monetary disturbances is such that it overwhelms all other (real) shocks. Under those conditions the monetarists' predictions are likely to hold even in the short run. For a criticism see De Grauwe, *et al.* (1985). In the latter paper, it is stressed that during hyperinflation, the deviations from PPP tend to become very large, which is the contrary of what the monetarist model postulates.

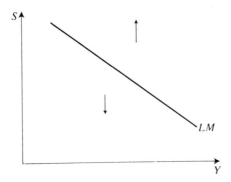

FIG. **6.13.** The *LM* curve and the exchange rate dynamics

variable, instead of the price level. (This also implies that in this *IS–LM* model the price level is rigid.) Money market equilibrium is obtained when

$$m_s = p_c + \alpha y - \beta r \qquad (6.19)$$

where

$$p_c = \sigma p + (1 - \sigma)(s + p_f). \qquad (6.20)$$

As in the Dornbusch model we also use the open interest parity condition:

$$r = r_f + \mu. \qquad (6.21)$$

Using the perfect foresight assumption, we can now postulate that

$$\mu = \dot{s}. \qquad (6.22)$$

Substituting (6.22) into (6.21), and (6.21) and (6.20) into (6.19) yields

$$\dot{s} = \frac{\alpha}{\beta}y + \frac{1-\sigma}{\beta}s + \frac{1}{\beta}z' \qquad (6.23)$$

where $z' = \sigma p + (1 - \sigma)p_f - br_f - m_s$.

This first order differential equation describes the dynamics in the money market. Equilibrium is obtained when $\dot{s} = 0$, i.e.

$$y = -((1 - \sigma)/\alpha)s - (1/\alpha)z'. \qquad (6.24)$$

This is nothing but the *LM* curve, which we used in the previous chapter. Thus, along the *LM* curve the exchange rate is at rest because the money market is in equilibrium. Note here also the similarity with the Dornbusch model, except for the fact that in the latter model the price level is endogenous.

When the exchange rate is above the *LM* line it must increase. This can be seen from the fact that in equation (6.23) the coefficient of s is positive. Similarly, when the exchange rate is below the *LM* curve, it must decline. We show this dynamics in Fig. 6.13. In order to complete the model we have to specify the dynamics in the goods market. We assume, as is commonly done in the *IS–LM* model, that when there is excess demand in the goods market, the output level increases. When there is excess supply, the output level declines:

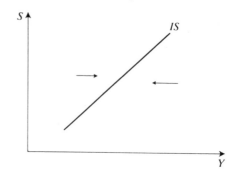

FIG. **6.14**. The *IS* curve and the dynamics of output

$$\dot{y} = \varepsilon(D - y) \tag{6.25}$$

where $\dot{y}$ is the rate of change of output and D is the aggregate demand for the domestic good. It consists of private demand, which is assumed to be a positive function of the real exchange rate ($\kappa = s - p + p_f$), and of government demand g. Thus

$$D = a(s - p + p_f) + g. \tag{6.26}$$

So that

$$\dot{y} = \varepsilon(as - ap + ap_f + g - y). \tag{6.27}$$

Setting $\dot{y} = 0$ yields the equilibrium condition in the goods market (the *IS* curve)

$$y = as - ap + ap_f + g. \tag{6.28}$$

When the output level is above the (positively sloped) *IS* curve, output must decline, and vice versa. This dynamics is shown in Fig. 6.14. The full dynamic interaction in the money and goods market is represented by the phase diagram (Fig. 6.15).

We can now contrast the effects of monetary and fiscal policies. A monetary expansion shifts the *LM* curve to the right. See Fig. 6.16. Starting from the initial equilibrium point *A* the economy has to move to point *B*. Assuming that output is a variable which cannot adjust instantaneously, the exchange rate will have to do the 'jumping'. In this case it will have to increase instantaneously from s_1 to s_3, so as to be on the saddle path which will then move it down again until point *B* is reached. Note that, as in the Dornbusch model, we obtain overshooting of the exchange rate.

The effect of fiscal policies is represented in Fig. 6.17. The fiscal expansion shifts the *IS* curve to the right. The economy will have to move to point *C*. The instantaneous effect, however, requires the exchange rate to jump downwards to s_2. From then on it will continue to decline along the saddle path described by the arrows. Thus, as in the Dornbusch model, the exchange rate jumps, but 'undershoots' its long-run equilibrium value obtained at point *C*.

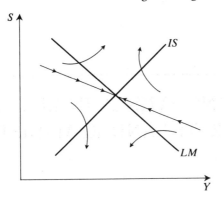

Fɪɢ. **6.15.** The phase diagram in the *IS–LM* model

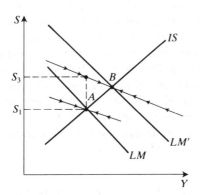

Fɪɢ. **6.16.** Monetary policy

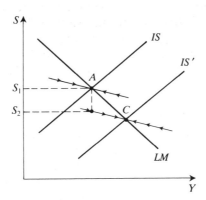

Fɪɢ. **6.17.** Fiscal policy

7

THE LONG SWINGS IN REAL EXCHANGE RATES AND REAL DISTURBANCES

In the previous chapter we presented some popular models of the exchange rate. We argued that these models are capable of explaining some features of exchange rate dynamics. In particular, all these models do rather well in explaining why exchange rates are volatile. In addition, those models that assume price stickiness explain why we observe a high correlation between nominal and real exchange rate movements. However, we hinted at the fact that these popular models may not be as successful in explaining other important features of exchange rate behaviour. In this chapter we analyse in more detail how well these models have fared in empirical application. We first discuss the econometric results and then present some case-studies. We conclude this chapter by discussing some alternative modelling attempts.

1. Formal empirical tests of exchange rate models

The first generation tests consisted of specifying econometric equations that explain the exchange rate by the fundamental variables, as identified in the theoretical models. The best-known econometric models are those of Frenkel (1976), Bilson (1978), Frankel (1979), Hooper and Morton (1982), and Frankel (1984). The formal empirical testing procedure consisted of checking whether the coefficients of the fundamental variables (e.g. money stocks, prices, current account, budget deficits, etc.) had the sign as predicted by the theory. When applied to the 1970s many of these tests tended to support the theory. A disturbing feature of these econometric tests, however, was that the inclusion of more data from the 1980s had the effect of changing the value of the coefficients significantly.

The second generation tests were pioneered by Meese and Rogoff in 1983. These tests were devastating for all the theoretical models. The method Meese and Rogoff used to show this was the following. They first estimated the models during a given sample period (1973–81). They then used this estimated econometric model to 'forecast' the exchange rate, out of sample, i.e. during the next year (1982) using the observed values of all the explanatory variables during that year (which were available since they were doing this in 1983). The result was that these forecasts were worse than a naïve forecast which consisted of setting the future exchange rate equal to today's exchange rate (this is also known as the random walk model). We show some of these results in the following table.

TABLE **7.1.** *Out-of-sample forecasting performance of different exchange rate models* (root mean squared error of forecasts 1, 6, and 12 months ahead)

	Random walk	Monetary (equilibrium)	Dornbusch	Portfolio balance
$/DM				
1 month	3.7	3.2	3.7	3.5
6 months	8.7	9.6	12.0	10.0
12 months	13.0	16.1	18.9	15.7
$/Yen				
1 month	3.7	4.1	4.4	4.2
6 months	11.6	13.4	13.9	11.9
12 months	18.3	18.6	20.4	19.0
$/£				
1 month	2.6	2.8	2.9	2.7
6 months	6.5	8.9	8.9	7.2
12 months	9.9	14.6	13.7	14.6

Source: Meese and Rogoff (1983)

We observe that the naïve random walk model is a better predictor of the future exchange rate for almost all currencies and all forecasting periods. This is quite devastating. It implies that even if in 1981 we had had perfect information about the fundamental variables driving the exchange rate in 1982, the use of the econometric model to make a forecast of the exchange rate would have made the forecast worse than not using the model at all. Note also that the naïve model (random walk) does not use any information about the fundamentals driving the exchange rate. In other words, although the random walk model uses no theory and no information on the underlying fundamental variables, it performs better as an instrument for forecasting exchange rates than the models that use all this information.

The Meese and Rogoff results had quite an impact. They were confirmed by other studies later (see Frankel and Rose (1994) for a survey). They completely discredited the econometric models of the exchange rates. They should also have discredited the theoretical models that were used to specify the econometric equations. A stronger rejection of these models was difficult to envisage. And yet, surprisingly, this did not happen. The same theoretical models continued to be taught in the classrooms, up to this day.

More damaging econometric evidence for the popular exchange rate models discussed in the previous chapter was recently provided by Flood and Rose (1993). These authors compared fixed and flexible exchange rate regimes. They found that whereas the variability of the exchange rates was on average two to three times higher in countries with flexible exchange rates than in countries with a fixed exchange rate, the variability of the underlying fundamental variables (money stocks, output changes, fiscal policies) was of the same order of magnitude in these two exchange rate regimes. This suggests that the exchange rate movements in flexible exchange rate systems tend to be dissociated from the fundamental variables that the theory tells us matter. We will come back to this feature of flexible exchange rate systems in a later chapter.

2. Case-studies

In this section we present some case-studies illustrating the problems of the existing theoretical models. This will also allow us better to understand the practical nature of the Meese and Rogoff empirical tests.

Let us start from the empirical regularity of the flexible exchange rate regime that we identified in the previous chapter. This is that the exchange rates of the major currencies have tended to wander away from their purchasing power parities during long periods of time. Even after introducing a correction for differential productivity growth rates, we found that the real exchange rates of major currencies have been going through long cycles of 'misalignment'. These cycles in real exchange rates have been longer than a typical business cycle.

This empirical regularity can be explained in two ways. One consists in invoking the dynamics of existing exchange rate models. We will present a case-study in which we try to explain a long cycle in the exchange rate by invoking the Dornbusch overshooting dynamics. In another case-study we will look at the dynamic interaction between the current account and the exchange rate.

A second explanation invokes the occurrence of a series of exogenous disturbances which tended to move exchange rates in the same direction for relatively long periods.[1] We will analyse periods during which large disturbances in monetary and fiscal policies occurred to see whether the transmission from these disturbances to the exchange rate are in the direction predicted by the theoretical models.

Case-study 1: the exchange rate cycle of the 1980s and the Dornbusch model

The Dornbusch and the Mundell–Fleming model predict dynamics of the exchange rate following monetary and fiscal shocks that will often lead to over-

---

[1] In technical jargon we say that the exogenous disturbances must be serially correlated to explain serially correlated real exchange rates.

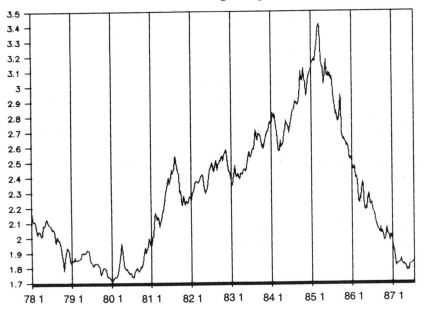

FIG. 7.1. DM/dollar rate
Source: Chase Econometrics

shooting of the exchange rate (see previous chapter for an exposition). Do we detect such dynamics in reality? We selected the 1980s to check this. We reproduce here the time path of the DM/dollar exchange rate during 1979–87 (see Fig. 7.1). What is striking is the 'creeping' appreciation of the dollar from the start of 1980 until February of 1985, i.e. an appreciation stretched over a period of more than four years. After 1985 there is a decline lasting two years. We find very little of the dynamics predicted by the perfect foresight Dornbusch (or Mundell–Fleming) model, which is one of instantaneous jumps in the exchange rate followed by slow movements after the jump. On the contrary, we tend to find inertia in the exchange rate. The surprising fact is not that the observed exchange rate moves quickly, but that it moves too slowly to be consistent with the perfect foresight dynamics.[2] In 1981 for example when the change in fiscal policies in the US was announced, one would have expected a large instantaneous appreciation of the dollar. Instead the dollar's appreciation (against the DM) stretched over many years. Of course, there may have been additional fiscal policy surprises during the years. In particular, the size of the ensuing budget deficit may have come as a surprise, and may therefore have acted as a new unanticipated shock. Nevertheless, the time pattern of the exchange rate is such that one would have needed an unreasonably large number of policy

[2] Bui and Pippinger (1987) show that the exchange rates of the major currencies moved much slower than the prices of major commodities.

surprises to produce a time profile of the exchange rate like the one presented in Fig. 7.1.

Another feature of the observed exchange rate cycle of the 1980s is the extremely long duration of that cycle. As will be remembered, the overshooting cycle predicted by the Dornbusch model is produced by price stickiness. It is very implausible, however, that price stickiness is such that exchange rates sometimes need up to ten years to go back to their PPP values.

One can conclude that the Dornbusch model does not do well in explaining the time profile of the observed exchange rate movements during 1979–82. The same can be said about other models which incorporate the rational expectations (perfect foresight) assumption, such as the Mundell–Fleming model.

Case-study 2: the exchange rate, the current account, and the risk premium during 1970–86

The portfolio balance model predicts that there will be a positive correlation between the exchange rate and the current account. Do we find this in the actual behaviour of these two variables?

Figs 7.2 and 7.3 present the current accounts of Germany and Japan (as a

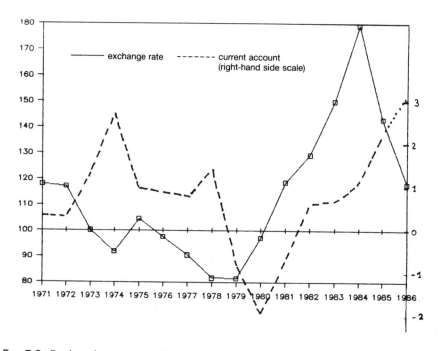

FIG. 7.2. Real exchange rate DM/dollar, and German current account (per cent of GDP)

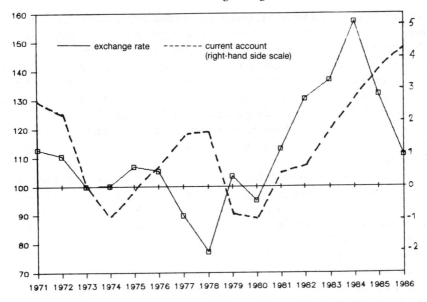

Fig. 7.3. Real exchange rate yen/dollar, and Japanese current account (per cent of GDP)

percentage of GDP) and their real exchange rates. It can clearly be seen that during the 1970s a negative correlation between the two variables existed. However, after the early 1980s, this negative correlation tends to disappear. In the early 1980s, the Japanese and the German current accounts start to improve significantly. It takes, however, close to four years for the portfolio effect to influence the exchange rate. We observe that from 1981–2 until 1984–5 these two countries accumulate current account surpluses to an unprecedented extent, and yet the yen and the DM continue to depreciate in real terms. In the end (i.e. in 1985) the portfolio effect predicted by the theory occurs, and both currencies begin a process of real appreciation. The startling thing is that during the 1980s the effect of current account surpluses on the real exchange rates took so long to operate, whereas during the 1970s this seemed to come about relatively quickly. Thus, the dynamics implied by the portfolio balance model is certainly too simple as a guide for explaining the long swings in real exchange rates.

One of the puzzles we observed in Chapter 4 is the behaviour of the forward premium (or discount) as a predictor of future exchange rate changes. We found that quite often, and for long periods of time, the forward premium (discount) systematically errs in predicting the direction of future exchange rate changes. As an illustration consider the dollar during the 1980s. During the period 1980–5 the dollar appreciated substantially. This period coincided with the existence of a forward discount on the dollar (in relation to the mark and the yen, for example). As was pointed out earlier, this is very difficult to explain in the context of the simple open interest parity theory. For this would have meant that during five years when the dollar appreciated substantially, investors continually expected the dollar to decline: an extremely implausible situation. This phenomenon has been analysed in great detail (see, for example, Fama (1984) who first identified the problem; for a recent survey see Engel (1995)). It has been found that the forward premium (discount) is a biased predictor of future exchange rate changes, i.e. it forecasts movements in the exchange rate in the wrong direction. This finding is very general and holds for many exchange rates and many periods. A lot of econometric research has been performed to try to explain this puzzle. In an appendix we give an overview of the empirical research.

In principle, the portfolio balance model could be used to explain this puzzle. For it could be that risk premiums interfere, i.e. the forward premium (discount) contains not only an expectations term but also a risk premium. In the context of the portfolio balance model this is explained by changes in the relative supply of assets. Thus, during 1980–5, the supply of US assets was increasing faster than the German and Japanese supplies (mainly as a result of more expansionary fiscal policies in the US). As a result, the risk premium on US assets increased continuously. Thus the positive interest differential in favour of the US (a forward discount on the dollar) arose not necessarily because investors expected a depreciation of the dollar (they may even have expected future appreciations), but rather because of increasing risk premiums on dollar holdings.

This interpretation becomes more difficult to maintain after 1985. The government budget deficits continued to be larger in the US than in Germany and Japan. Thus, the risk premium must have continued to increase. In addition, from 1985, when the dollar dropped significantly, the expectations of future declines of the dollar must have been stronger than ever. All this suggests that from 1985 the forward discounts of the dollar should have increased. This, however, did not happen as is made clear in Figs 7.4 and 7.5, which show the interest differentials between US bonds and German and Japanese bonds, respectively. There is no tendency for this differential to increase. On the contrary during 1985–6, this differential declines. Thus, the portfolio balance model, which seems to be doing well in explaining a particular historical episode, fails to do so when applied to other periods. This feature of the portfolio balance model is not unique. It is applicable to most of the existing exchange rate models.

Case-study 3: exchange rates and changing fiscal and monetary policy mixes

In order to understand the persistence of the real exchange rate movements we should concentrate our attention on those exogenous disturbances which exhibited sufficient persistence. Fiscal policies come to mind as possible explanatory variables. To what extent then can the movements of fiscal policies be held responsible for the long swings in the real exchange rates?

Major swings in fiscal policies of the large industrial countries have occurred

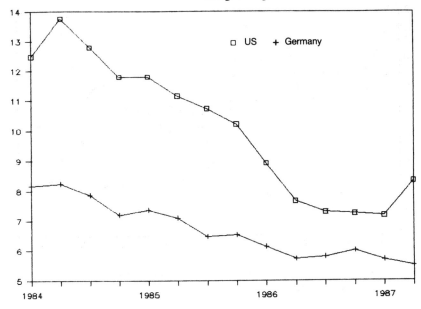

FIG. 7.4. Government bond yields, the US and Germany
Source: IMF, *International Financial Statistics*

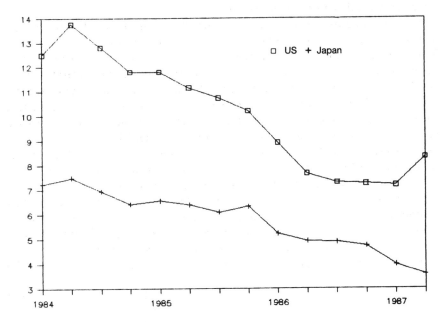

FIG. 7.5. Government bond yields, the US and Japan
Source: IMF, *International Financial Statistics*

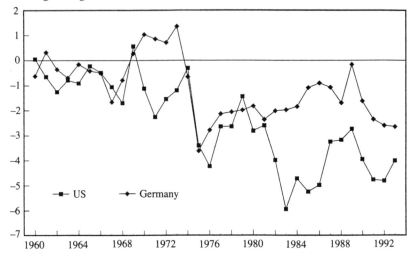

Fɪɢ. 7.6. US and German budget surplus/deficit (per cent of GDP)
Source: IMF, *International Financial Statistics*

during the flexible exchange rate period. These cycles in fiscal policies are illustrated in Figs 7.6 and 7.7. In Fig. 7.6 we show the government budget deficit (as a percentage of GDP) in the US and in Germany. In Fig. 7.7 we compare the same US fiscal deficits with the Japanese.

Two observations can be made. First, after the middle of the 1970s the budget deficits in these three countries increased significantly. Second, the divergencies in fiscal policies between these countries become more pronounced, compared to the fixed exchange rate period.[3] The period of the 1980s is particularly important. We see a substantial increase in the US budget deficit after 1981, whereas Germany and, to a lesser degree Japan, begin a process of budgetary contraction. (Note, however, that during the second half of the 1970s the roles were reversed: Japan allowed its budgetary deficit to increase substantially, while the US did the opposite.) Thus, there appear to have been a lot of fiscal policy disturbances which could help to explain the movements in the real exchange rates.

The question we have to analyse now is what the theory tells us about the effects of fiscal policies on the real exchange rate. We have discussed models that describe the transmission mechanism of fiscal policy shocks to the real exchange rates. The consensus is that a policy of fiscal expansion, coupled with monetary tightness, will lead to a real appreciation of the domestic currency in a world of high capital mobility. This result is found both in the Dornbusch and the Mundell–Fleming models.[4]

At the most intuitive level the transmission of fiscal policy shocks to the real

---

[3] In a later section we address the issue of why this divergence in policies occurred.
[4] This result is also found in most portfolio balance models. See also Frenkel and Razin (1986a) for a more recent intertemporal model.

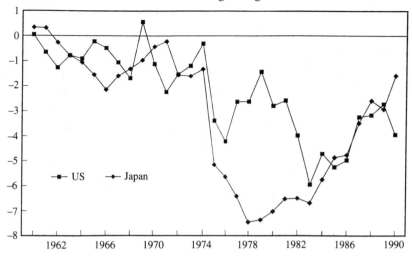

Fɪɢ. 7.7. US and Japanese budget surplus/deficit (per cent of GDP)
Source: IMF, International Financial Statistics

exchange rate can be explained as follows in the Mundell–Fleming model. A fiscal expansion (either through an increased level of government spending or a reduction of taxes) raises domestic output and the domestic interest rate. The output effect leads to more imports, and therefore to a deterioration of the current account. The interest rate effect leads to a capital inflow. In a world of free capital movements, the second effect will dominate the first one. As a result, a fiscal expansion leads to an appreciation of the domestic currency. (Note, however, that if capital is not very mobile, the current account transmission effect will dominate, and the currency depreciates.)[5] A fiscal expansion, however, financed by issuing money is more likely to lead to a depreciation of the currency. In the sticky price models such as the Mundell–Fleming and Dornbusch models, this will also be a real depreciation.

This very simple theory forms the core of the now generally accepted explanation of the strong appreciation of the dollar during 1980–5. The US budget deficits which increased substantially after 1980, together with a policy of monetary restriction initiated by the Fed in 1979, raised US interest rates and induced massive capital movements to the US. These capital movements then explain the dollar appreciation. Put differently, according to this explanation, the strong and increasing misalignment of the dollar during the 1980–5 period was due to the 'misalignment' of the fiscal policies of the major industrial countries during the same period, whereby the US engaged in a multi-year programme of expansionary fiscal policies and the other industrialized countries contracted theirs. (For a well-known statement see M. Feldstein (1986*b*).)

Thus, at first sight a case could be made for arguing that the Mundell–Fleming

---

[5] For a lucid explanation see Williamson (1983), ch. 10.

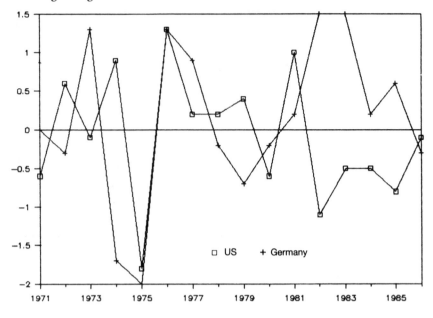

FIG. 7.8. OECD fiscal impulse, the US and Germany (+ = contraction)

and the Dornbusch models did relatively well at explaining the large upward movements of the dollar during 1980–5. However as we shall see immediately this case is weak. In addition, these models fail even more markedly to explain subsequent real exchange rate movements.

Let us analyse more systematically the movements of monetary and fiscal policy variables to see whether they explain the movements of the real exchange rates. One obvious problem in analysing such a question is the choice of the indicators of fiscal and monetary policies. The problem is especially acute for fiscal policies. Government budget deficits, as presented in Figs 7.6 and 7.7, are sensitive to the business cycle, in that during a recession the deficit tends to increase as a result of 'automatic stabilizers'. Thus, the observed data of the budget deficits do not always reflect the stance of fiscal policies accurately.

Here we will use the OECD measure of fiscal impulse. This measure is obtained by correcting the raw data of the budget deficits for the business-cycle-induced changes in the budget.[6] As our measure of monetary policies we select the yearly growth rate of M2. (Due to financial innovations, the narrower concept of M1 has become notoriously unreliable, especially in the US.) The data are presented in Figs 7.8 to 7.9. We concentrate on the first fifteen years of the floating exchange

[6] See OECD, Economic Outlook, *Occasional Studies*, Paris, June 1983. Other but similar measures are produced by the IMF. For a comparison of some of these measures, see Heller, *et al.* (1986). These measures of the fiscal stance have been criticized by Buiter (1985), who argues that one needs a model of the economy in order to gauge the expansionary or contractionary stance of the government budget.

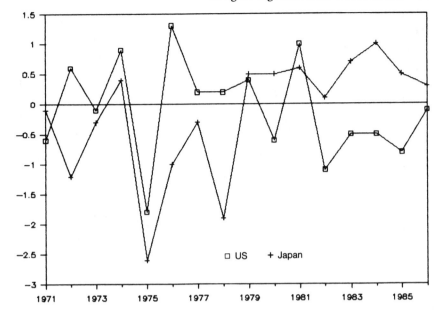

Fig. 7.9. OECD fiscal impulse, the US and Japan (+ = contraction)

Source: OECD, 'Economic Outlook', *Occasional Studies,* June 1983

TABLE 7.2. *Growth rates of M2 and OECD fiscal impulse in the US, Germany, and Japan*

	US	Germany	Japan
Growth of M2			
1976–78	11.4	9.7	12.8
1979–82	6.4	5.7	9.2
OECD fiscal impulse			
1976–78	0.6	0.7	−1.1
1979–82	−0.1	0.2	0.4

Source: IMF, *International Financial Statistics;* and OECD, 'Economic Outlook', *Occasional Studies,* June 1983

rate period. As we want to explain movements of the dollar/yen and the dollar/ DM respectively, we contrast in each figure the US policy indicator with the Japanese and German indicators, respectively. In Table 7.2 we summarize the evidence for the period 1979–82, and compare it with the period immediately preceding it, when the dollar was very weak.

As can be seen from the evidence presented in Table 7.2 the US monetary policies become contractionary in 1979–82. This is also a period of monetary contraction in Japan and Germany, however. The main difference, therefore, in the policy stance of the US versus Japan and Germany is in the conduct of

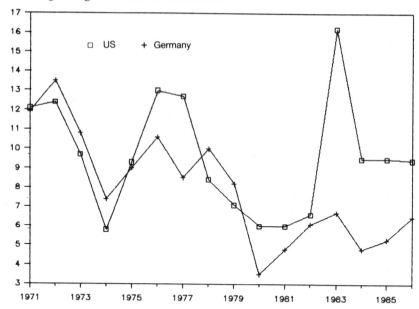

Fɪɢ. 7.10. Growth of M2 in the US and Germany (in per cent per year)
Source: IMF, International Financial Statistics

fiscal policies. From 1981 on (see Figs 7.8 and 7.9), the US shifts towards fiscal expansion, whereas Germany and Japan start a process of fiscal contraction. Thus, during 1981–82 one can invoke Mundell–Fleming (and Dornbusch) to explain the real appreciation of the dollar.

Problems with this explanation of the real appreciation of the dollar based on shocks in the fiscal–monetary mix appear during the period after 1982. From the middle of 1982, the Federal Reserve shifted towards an expansionary monetary policy, which was comparable to the high money growth episodes of the Carter administration. This can clearly be seen in Figs 7.10 and 7.11, where we observe a spectacular increase in the growth rate of M2 after 1982. In contrast to the US, the monetary policies of Germany and Japan remain relatively restrictive. We summarize this turnaround in US policies in Table 7.3.

One observes a doubling of the US growth rate of M2 after 1982, whereas no change, or even a decline, is observed in the other countries.

The consensus model (whether Mundell–Fleming or Dornbusch) which we used to explain the real appreciation of the dollar during 1981–82, would have predicted that after 1982 the dollar might have become a candidate for a depreciation, certainly not an appreciation. And yet, that is what happened. During 1983–84 the US dollar experienced a spectacular further appreciation in real terms.

Problems arise also for the *post-1985 period*. After 1985 the dollar started to decline spectacularly. Can this real depreciation of the dollar be associated with

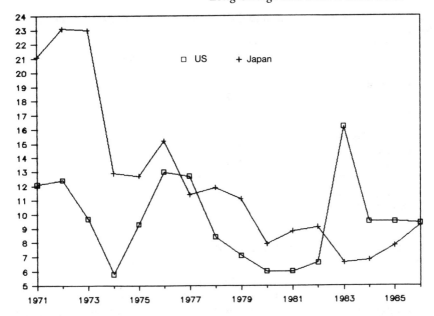

FIG. 7.11. Growth of M2 in the US and Japan (in per cent per year)
Source: IMF, *International Financial Statistics*

TABLE 7.3. *Growth rates of M2 in the US, Germany, and Japan*

	US	Germany	Japan
1979–82	6.4	5.7	9.2
1983–84	12.9	5.8	6.7

Source: IMF, *International Financial Statistics*

policy disturbances? Table 7.4 reveals the following. Fiscal policies remained relatively expansionary in the US compared to the other countries. The gap in fiscal policy between the US, on the one hand, and Germany and Japan, on the other hand, tends to narrow. Thus, the Mundell–Fleming model correctly predicts that the mark and the yen should have strengthened relative to the dollar, as they did. The problem with this explanation of the post-1985 real exchange rate movements has to do with monetary policies, especially in Japan. As can be seen from Table 7.4 (and Fig. 7.11), monetary policies became more expansionary in Japan in 1986. Little change is observed in German monetary policies. Thus, the fiscal–monetary policy mix in Japan turned towards more fiscal relaxation and monetary expansion. In Germany the mix changed towards fiscal relaxation with no change in monetary policy. In the US the fiscal impulse remained unchanged but monetary policy become more restrictive. This is a

TABLE 7.4. *Growth rates of M2 and OECD fiscal impulse in the US, Germany, and Japan*

	US	Germany	Japan
Growth of M2			
1983–84	12.9	5.8	6.7
1985–86	9.5	5.9	8.5
OECD fiscal impulse			
1983–84	−0.5	0.9	0.9
1985–86	−0.5	0.2	0.4

Source: IMF, *International Financial Statistics*; and OECD, 'Economic Outlook', *Occasional Studies*, June 1983

change in policy mixes which can hardly explain the appreciation of the mark and the yen which during 1985–86 approached 50 per cent.

It is clear that we have problems with the explanation of the movements of the real exchange rate of the dollar based on disturbances in the fiscal and monetary policy mixes. Certainly the model does well in explaining the 1981–82 surge of the dollar, but performs badly as a guide for the post-1982 period. Thus, either there is something wrong with the underlying model, or other exogenous real disturbances have occurred during the post-1982 period which more than offset the effects of disturbances in the fiscal–monetary policy mixes. We return to this problem in case-study 5 to search for other possible real shocks.

Case-study 4: the dollar exchange rates during the 1970s

Before making a final judgement on the importance of fiscal–monetary policy mixes, let us look at two other historical episodes of clear misalignment of the dollar. These are in the period 1976–9, when the dollar depreciated by 20 per cent in real terms against the DM, and during 1976–8 when the dollar also depreciated by 20 per cent in real terms against the yen. We first discuss the dollar/yen rate and subsequently the dollar/DM exchange rate.

There is some prima-facie evidence that the real appreciation of the yen during 1976–8 could be related to shocks in the monetary–fiscal policy mix. As noted in the previous section, Japan followed a programme of strong fiscal expansion during 1976–8. At the same time the US was engaged in a policy of fiscal restriction. This appears both in Fig. 7.7 which shows the actual budget deficits in the two countries, and in Fig. 7.9 which presents the OECD fiscal impulse variables.[7] At the same time monetary policies were broadly similar in

[7] It can also be seen from these figures that the fiscal expansion in Japan started in 1975, when the US was also following a policy of fiscal expansion to counter the ongoing recession. It is from 1976 on that the two countries sharply diverged in their fiscal policies.

TABLE 7.5. *Growth of M2 and OECD fiscal impulse (as percentage of GDP) in US and Japan during 1976–1978* (yearly averages)

	US	Japan
Growth of M2	11.4	12.8
OECD fiscal impulse	0.6	−1.1

Source: IMF, *International Financial Statistics*; and OECD, 'Economic Outlook', *Occasional Studies*, June 1983

TABLE 7.6. *Growth of M2 and OECD fiscal impulse (as percentage of GDP) in US and Germany during 1976–1979* (yearly averages)

	US	Germany
Growth of M2	10.3	9.3
OECD fiscal impulse	0.5	0.3

Source: IMF, *International Financial Statistics*; and OECD, 'Economic Outlook', *Occasional Studies*, June 1983

both countries. Table 7.5 summarizes the evidence on the US and Japanese fiscal–monetary policy mix during 1976–8. It is interesting to note that the divergence in fiscal policies between the US and Japan was of a similar order of magnitude during 1976–8 as during the early 1980s (1983–4) (see Table 7.4). The difference is that the roles were reversed, with Japan expanding in the first period, and the US expanding in the second period.

It is important to stress here that the perfect capital mobility version of the Mundell–Fleming model cannot be applied to the Japanese situation during the 1970s. During this period considerable controls on capital movements existed in Japan, which were eliminated in the early 1980s only. Thus, the version of the model with imperfect capital mobility is more appropriate. If capital is imperfectly mobile, the effect of a fiscal expansion on the real exchange rate is ambiguous, depending on the degree of imperfection of capital mobility. If this imperfection is strong enough, the negative current account effects of a fiscal expansion will tend to dominate and will produce a real depreciation of the domestic currency. We conclude that it is unclear whether the fiscal expansion followed in Japan during 1976–8 can be held responsible for the real appreciation of the yen during the same period.

What about the real appreciation of the DM relative to the dollar during 1976–9? Can it be associated with shocks in policy mixes in the US and Germany? We summarize the evidence in Table 7.6.

The evidence indicates that the US and Germany were following broadly similar monetary and fiscal policies during 1976–9. The US followed a slightly more restrictive fiscal policy than Germany, and as a result was able to reduce its budget deficit somewhat faster than Germany. Similarly, monetary policies were on a parallel path, with the US pursuing a more expansionary monetary policy than Germany during 1976–7, and a more contractionary one during 1978–9. This broad similarity of the fiscal and monetary policy mixes pursued by the US and Germany, however, did not prevent the dollar from depreciating by more than 20 per cent in real terms against the DM during the same period.

We can summarize the evidence on the importance of shocks in the fiscal–monetary policy mixes as follows. The real exchange rate movements of the major currencies which have been large and persistent can only in a very small number of cases be explained by shifting policy mixes of the countries involved. In fact we found only one episode of major real exchange rate movements which could be explained by fiscal and monetary policies. This is the episode of strong real appreciation of the dollar during 1979–82, which can be explained by the mix of fiscal expansion and monetary contraction in the US. Most other large real changes in the exchange rates seem to be unrelated with shocks in fiscal and monetary policies. Sometimes these real exchange rate movements appear to go counter to what the standard theory teaches us about the effects of monetary and fiscal policies. This is particularly the case for the period 1983–4 when the dollar continued its steep upward climb at a time of considerable monetary laxity in the US. Similar puzzling episodes were detected during the 1970s.

As we mentioned several times before, other shocks might have occurred which tended to offset the effects of fiscal and monetary policies on the exchange rates. Let us now turn to these other real shocks.

Case-study 5: the real exchange rate and oil shocks

Let us concentrate on variables other than fiscal policies in our quest to understand the large swings in real exchange rates. One important candidate is the oil price shocks which occurred first in 1973–4 and later in 1979–80. These shocks were quite important. They implied a substantial transfer of purchasing power from the oil consuming nations to the oil producers. One can obtain an idea of the quantitative importance of these shocks from Table 7.7. It presents estimates

TABLE 7.7. *Effect of the increase of 1980 and the decline of 1986 of the oil price on national income (in per cent of GDP)*

	1980	1986
US	−1.0	0.3
Germany	−2.1	2.4
Japan	−4.5	2.5

Source: IMF, *World Economic Outlook*, Apr. 1986, p. 27

of the effects of the oil price increase of 1980 on the national income of the US, Germany, and Japan. The effects of the oil price increase of 1973–4 are generally considered to be of similar magnitude. Table 7.11 also presents the effects on the national income of the same countries of the reverse shock which occurred in 1986, when oil prices declined sharply. The reader can see that these oil shocks were relatively large, especially in Germany and Japan, where they involved a transfer of purchasing power of 2 to 4 per cent of GDP.

The question we now have to analyse is how the oil price increases (and later the decline) may have affected the real exchange rates of the major currencies.

There is a very strong theoretical presumption that countries which make a transfer (the oil consuming countries) will experience a real depreciation of their currency. This presumption dates back to the old literature on the 'transfer problem'. In a nutshell the mechanism is as follows. The oil consuming country, which experiences a deficit in its current account, will have to build up a surplus on its non-oil trade to pay for the higher oil bill. It can realize this surplus by a real depreciation. The latter can come about either by a nominal depreciation (for a given domestic price level), or by a reduction of domestic spending which will improve the non-oil trade balance. By the same token, this expenditure reducing policy tends to reduce the domestic price level relative to the price level in the oil producing country.[8] In other words the domestic currency experiences a real depreciation.

A similar conclusion can be reached using the standard Mundell–Fleming model. In that model, the oil transfer can be considered as a tax imposed by the oil producers on the residents of the oil consuming countries. Its effects are, therefore, qualitatively the same as the effects of a contractionary fiscal policy. If monetary policies do not change, this model predicts a real depreciation of the domestic currency.

When applying this model to the dollar/DM and the dollar/yen exchange rates we face the problem that the three countries involved are net importers of oil. These countries, however, are not dependent on imported oil in the same degree. The US, for example, is also a large producer of oil. As a result, one can expect that the deflationary macroeconomic effect of the oil price increase was significantly lower in the US than in Germany and Japan. (This is also confirmed by the figures in Table 7.7.) As a result, one can expect that the deflationary macroeconomic effect of the oil price increase was significantly lower in the US than in Germany and Japan. This reasoning implies that the real depreciation of the dollar relative to the currencies of the oil countries is lower than the real depreciation of the other two currencies. Put differently, this analysis leads to the conclusion that the oil price increases of 1973–4 and 1979–80 induced a real appreciation of the dollar relative to the DM and the yen.

It should be clear that the effects of an oil price decline go in the opposite

---

[8] The dynamics of the adjustment to oil shocks is considerably more complicated, and has led to a burgeoning literature, in which almost anything can happen. We will come back to this literature when we discuss the need for intertemporal optimization models for a correct understanding of the effects of fiscal policies and oil shocks.

TABLE 7.8. *Change in the 'real' DM/dollar and yen/dollar rates* (in per cent) (– = depreciation of the dollar; + = appreciation)

	DM/dollar	Yen/dollar
1973–4	–28	+1
1979–80	+10	+7
1986–7	–30	–30

Source: IMF, *International Financial Statistics*

TABLE 7.9. *Growth of M2 and OECD fiscal impulse (as percentage of GDP) in US and Germany during 1973–1974* (yearly averages)

	US	Germany
Growth of M2	7.8	9.0
OECD fiscal impulse	0.4	–0.2

Source: IMF, *International Financial Statistics*; and OECD, 'Economic Outlook', *Occasional Studies*, June 1983

direction. Therefore, one can also conclude that, according to the theory, the DM and the yen had to appreciate in real terms relative to the dollar after 1986 when the oil price started to decline abruptly.

Does this theoretical analysis lead to the correct prediction of real exchange rate movements? We will analyse the three oil shocks consecutively.

A. The first oil shock (1973–4)

Table 7.8 summarizes the exchange rate movements observed during that period. We observe that the dollar depreciated substantially against the DM, but remained practically unchanged relative to the yen during the first oil shock. The depreciation of the dollar relative to the DM is particularly troublesome, since the theory would have predicted an appreciation of the dollar. Clearly, yet other factors could have been responsible for this puzzling behaviour of the dollar/DM rate.

Monetary and fiscal policies followed by the US and Germany during this episode of oil price increases do not help to explain the puzzle. In particular, monetary *and* fiscal policies (the former measured by M2, the latter by the OECD fiscal impulse variable) were more expansionary in Germany than in the US. This is shown in Table 7.9 (see also Figs 7.8 and 7.10 for the yearly developments). Thus the monetary–fiscal policy mix followed by these two countries cannot explain the real depreciation of the dollar against the mark.

B. The second oil shock (1979–80)

The contrast between the second and the first oils shocks is large. As can be seen from Table 7.8, contrary to the first oil shock, during the second one the dollar appreciated both against the mark and the yen. This appreciation was certainly helped by the strong contractionary monetary policies in the US during that period. Thus, during the second period of oil price increases, the dollar moved in the direction predicted by the theoretical model. The puzzling thing, therefore, is the difference one observes during the two periods of oil price rises.

C. The third oil shock (1986–7)

In 1986 crude oil prices declined sharply. At the end of 1986 they had dropped to almost half the level attained in 1985. As Table 7.8 indicates, this period also coincided with a significant weakening of the dollar. However, it is less evident that this sharp depreciation of the dollar had much to do with the oil price decline. For the drop in the dollar started almost a full year prior to the drop in crude oil prices. The latter may have accelerated the depreciation of the dollar during 1986–7. It can, however, not be considered as the cause of the dollar slide observed since the beginning of 1985.

The oil shocks of 1973–4 and 1979–80 were major (and largely unexpected) real disturbances. Our historical analysis of the 1970s and the 1980s, however, reveals that the effects of these real disturbances on the real exchange rates were quite unpredictable. Sometimes the oil shock affected real exchange rates in a way predicted by standard economic models. At other times, real exchange rates were driven in the opposite direction or were barely affected by these real disturbances.[9]

D. A different model for each different period?

A general feature of the existing econometric models of the exchange rates is that once we use the models outside the period which is the focus of the analysis, they usually fail to predict which direction the exchange rate will take when a particular shock occurs in one of explanatory variables. This is a troublesome feature of present exchange rate models. If we need a different theory for each historical episode, theorizing is not very useful. Also it leads to a situation where

[9] Although the shifts in fiscal and monetary policies and the oil shocks have been the major real disturbances since the early 1970s, other real shocks have occurred, which could also have affected the movement of real exchange rates. For example, tax changes have occurred in the US which may have boosted the dollar. These real disturbances, however, did not have the same kind of persistence as the monetary–fiscal policy mix, and therefore cannot easily account for the persistence in the movement of the exchange rates. Only rich enough endogenous dynamics can transform stochastic disturbances into long cyclical movements of the exchange rates.

ex post we can explain everything by special factors, but where ex ante the theory has no predictive power.

This weakness of current exchange rate theorizing can also be illustrated by reading what economists thought about the effects of, for example, fiscal policies on the exchange rate in the 1970s when the dollar was weak, in the early 1980s when the dollar was strong, and after 1985 when the dollar weakened again.

In his classic study, *The International Monetary System*, Robert Solomon writes that on 9 May 1973, 'the German Government had announced a stringent program of budgetary restraint designed to combat inflation. It was widely believed that, on top of a tight monetary policy, one result of this program would be to increase Germany's trade surplus and *strengthen the mark*. Sales of dollars in Europe were reported to be of "panic" proportions' (p. 277, italics added).[10] The same belief can be found in the OECD reports ('Economic Outlook') during the 1970s. These reports can be considered as reflecting widespread views about the working of the international economic system and are representative of what mainstream economists believed at that time.

During the 1980s this belief that a policy of fiscal restriction would strengthen the currency was turned upside down, and Germany was often urged to relax its fiscal stance so as to strengthen the mark relative to the dollar. Now it was said that an expansionary fiscal policy would draw foreign savings to the domestic economy and lead to an appreciation of the currency. This view was popularized by, among others, Martin Feldstein (1986b) and Stephen Marris (1985). The latter argued in his influential book, *Deficits and the Dollar: The World Economy at Risk*, that the US deficits 'sucked foreign savings into the US economy's financial markets faster than the US economy's need to finance its growing current account deficit' (p. 31). These capital flows then led to the strong appreciation of the dollar.[11]

The beliefs of economists concerning the effects of fiscal policies changed again during the 1990s. The view that prevailed during the 1970s was resuscitated. Now, as in the 1970s, most economists argued that large budget deficits were the source of weakness of a currency, and that a reduction in government budget deficits was necessary to strengthen a currency.

This view again became the conventional wisdom and can be found in the *World Economic Outlook* of the IMF and the 'Economic Outlook' of the OECD. This view was also enshrined in the Maastricht Treaty which forced European countries to reduce their government budget deficits so as to strengthen their currencies.

Thus, it appears that the models we use today to understand exchange rate

---

[10] This belief could of course have been based on the simple Mundell–Fleming model with low capital mobility. We have seen that in the low capital mobility version of the Mundell–Fleming model a policy mix of fiscal and monetary contraction produces a real appreciation of the currency. It should be pointed out, however, that Germany (in contrast to Japan) had no capital controls, so that the high capital mobility version of the Mundell–Fleming model is the relevant one. And as we know, this version produces the opposite result.   [11] Marris (1985).

movements are not only unsuitable for predicting the future, they are not always useful in understanding the past.

3. Exchange rates and speculative bubbles

The failure of attempts at explaining the long-run movements of real exchange rates has led to the popularity of dynamic models, called 'bubble' models. One of the issues which has been discussed here is whether the dynamics inherent in the bubbles model is consistent with rational behaviour. In that case we have a consistent alternative explanation for the movements of the real exchange rates.

A bubble is an explosive path of the exchange rate which brings it progressively farther away from the economic fundamentals. Put differently, it is a movement of the exchange rate which leads to an increasing divergence of the exchange rate from its equilibrium value as determined by an economic model. Such a bubble can be recognized as such by economic agents, who nevertheless continue to 'ride it out'. They do this because they expect such a ride to be profitable.

Can such explosive behaviour of the exchange rates be consistent with a (perfect foresight) rational expectations view of the world?

Although the perfect foresight rational expectations models of the exchange rates cannot exclude the exchange rate from following an explosive path which brings it further and further from its fundamentals,[12] it is inconsistent with the occurrence of a 'bubble' which invariably bursts. The reason is easy to understand. Suppose the exchange rate moves along an explosive upward path. Economic agents are aware of this. However, in the logic of the (perfect foresight) rational expectations model, in which economic agents know the true structure of the model, these agents are able to predict a crash. This will induce rational speculators to sell the foreign currency the instant before the crash, so as to reap infinite profits. Since everybody will do this, the event of the crash will be brought forward in time. This will then induce agents to sell an instant before the new time of the crash. We can go on with this reasoning. It leads to the conclusion that the speculative bubble can never materialize. Thus, a speculative bubble (with a crash) can never occur in a rational expectations model, in which economic agents can predict the timing of the crash.

Although speculative bubbles are not consistent with the simple (perfect foresight) rational expectations model in which economic agents can predict the timing of the collapse, they could arise in a situation in which the timing of the crash cannot be predicted with certainty. Such models have been made popular by Blanchard (1979) and Dornbusch (1982).[13] In Box 7.1 a simple model is presented which leads to such a speculative bubble with a crash. These speculative bubbles typically arise in situations where speculators attach a low probability to the occurrence of the crash (a large change in the exchange rate) in the

---

[12] See the discussion of the perfect foresight Dornbusch model in Ch. 6.
[13] Blanchard (1979), and Dornbusch (1982).

next period, and a large probability of a continuation of the bubble movement (a small change in the exchange rate) in the next period. As a result, they will 'ride out' the bubble, expecting a continuing increase in the price of the foreign currency. In addition, they typically expect to be able to 'jump out' before the crash materializes.

Have speculative bubbles of this type been important as an explanation of exchange rate movements? Much empirical research has been devoted to answering this question. The question is still unsettled, with most authors concluding that speculative bubbles have been relatively rare (see Obstfeld (1987) and Frankel (1985)).

Some authors, however, give evidence that the upward movement of the dollar against the yen during 1981–2 exhibited characteristics of a speculative bubble (Okina, (1985)). Similarly Borensztein (1987) concludes that the 1980–5 run up of the dollar against the mark may be due to a speculative bubble. The evidence however is far from conclusive. Frankel (1985), for example, has argued that the observed real exchange rate movements lasted too long to be consistent with the rational bubble model.

The lack of conclusive evidence for the speculative bubble model can be explained as follows. First, one of the fundamental problems in testing whether a speculative bubble has occurred is that each test is a test of two hypotheses. Since a bubble is defined as a persistent deviation of the exchange rate from the equilibrium value as predicted by an economic model, one has to specify a model which produces these equilibrium values. As a result, if we find that the observed exchange rate deviates from these equilibrium values this finding can be interpreted in two ways. It can mean that indeed we have a speculative bubble. Alternatively it can also be the case that we have used the wrong model to compute the equilibrium value. The persistent deviation from the 'equilibrium' exchange rate is then the result of computing a wrong equilibrium rate. It will remain difficult to avoid this problem.[14]

A second reason why it is difficult to detect speculative bubbles is that the movement we observe in the exchange rate may be due to an expectation held in the market that the monetary–fiscal policy mix is going to change in the near future. This leads to a particular movement of the exchange rate in one or the other direction. However, as long as the policies are not changed, it gives the impression that the exchange rate is moving away from the fundamentals. This impression can last for some time if the authorities fail to change their policies (although they are continually expected to have the intention of doing so).

This problem has been called the Peso problem, in reference to the Mexican situation during the second half of the 1970s. The Mexican government was

---

[14] This problem also arises with so-called variance bound tests. Here we compare the variability of the observed exchange rates with the variability of the 'fundamentals', i.e. with the variability of the equilibrium values of the exchange rate as produced by a model. This procedure has been applied to the stock markets (see Shiller (1981)) and to the exchange markets (Meese and Rogoff (1983)). The finding that exchange rates are more volatile than their underlying fundamentals is not a convincing test of a speculative bubble.

expected to devalue the currency. As a result, speculation was set in motion and the black market price of the dollar (in terms of pesos) shot up, together with domestic interest rates. However, as the devaluation did not materialize until 1982, these movements of exchange rate and interest rate seemed to be dissociated from observable policies. In addition, during this whole period, one had the impression that economic agents were making systematically wrong forecasts. Only afterwards, when the devaluation took place, did it turn out that the expectations were correct.

To conclude, the main problem of the bubbles explanation of the large movements in real exchange rates is that while it may explain a few episodes of large exchange rate movements, there is very little evidence that bubbles are a *general* phenomenon allowing us to explain the persistence and the long duration of the departures of exchange rates from their PPP values.

Box 7.1. Rational speculative bubbles

O. Blanchard (1979) was the first to show formally that in an uncertain environment speculative bubbles can arise. The analysis is relatively simple, and starts (again) from the interest parity condition:

$$r_t - r_{ft} = \mu_t \qquad (7.1)$$

where μ_t is the expected rate of depreciation of the domestic currency during the next period (say one month). Put differently, μ_t is the expected rate of increase in the price of the foreign currency.

Let us now assume that speculators expect with a probability $(1 - p)$ that the current 'bubble' in the exchange rate will continue during the next month. However, they attach a probability p that the bubble will burst during the next month so that the exchange rate S returns to its 'fundamental' value $\bar{S}$. We have

$$\mu_t = p(\bar{S} - S_t) + (1 - p)a_t \qquad (7.2)$$

where a_t is the rate of appreciation of the foreign currency, if the exchange rate stays on its speculative bubble path.

Combining (7.1) and (7.2) yields

$$r_t - r_{ft} = p(\bar{S} - S_t) + (1 - p)a_t. \qquad (7.3)$$

Equation (7.3) allows us to understand why a currency may continue to appreciate in the market while it shows a forward discount. (Note that $r_t - r_{ft}$ = forward premium of the foreign currency.) Let us take the example of the dollar during the first part of the 1970s, and let us consider the dollar as the foreign currency. As will be remembered the dollar then exhibited a forward discount relative to the mark (i.e the dollar interest rate exceeded the German interest rate). At the same time the dollar was appreciating substantially. Equation (7.3) allows us to make sense of this puzzling phenomenon. It shows that a negative interest differential could have been the result of the following forecast by speculators: they expected the dollar to continue to appreciate during the next month ($a_t > 0$) with a probability $1 - p$; however, at the same time they attached a probability p to a large enough crash of the dollar ($\bar{S} - S_t < 0$) so that the right-hand side of (7.3) became negative.

Equation (7.3) can also be manipulated to obtain:

$$a_t = \frac{1}{1-p}(r_t - r_{ft}) + \frac{p}{1-p}(S_t - \bar{S}).\qquad(7.4)$$

It can be interpreted as follows. If the exchange rate is on a speculative bubble path with a rate of increase a_t, this rate of increase will accelerate as the exchange rate gets further away from the fundamental rate. Thus, when during the bubble development the deviation between S_t and $\bar{S}$ increases, the rate of appreciation of the foreign currency increases. This accelerating movement of the exchange rate has rarely been found in the foreign exchange market.

Although this theory about the dynamics of speculative bubbles adds interesting insights into the behaviour of exchange rates, the evidence that it has been an important phenomenon is limited. It may explain a few (relatively short) episodes of exchange rate behaviour. It fails, however, to explain the long cycles in exchange rates observed since 1973.

4. Conclusion

The main lesson of this chapter is very simple. The exchange rate models that have become popular since the 1970s cannot be used to understand the large movements of the exchange rates during the last twenty years, let alone for predictive purposes. We established this point first by reviewing the econometric evidence. The studies of Meese and Rogoff stand out here, indicating that the information content of the existing exchange rate models is close to zero. Second, we presented a number of case-studies illustrating the empirical failure of the popular exchange rate models.

These failures manifest themselves at different levels. First, the models fail to explain the bias of the forward premiums as forecasts of future exchange rates. The portfolio balance model which is an attempt at explaining this bias by modelling the risk premiums, has as yet not been able to come up with a satisfactory explanation of the variability of these premiums. Other models have been equally unsuccessful.

Second, these popular exchange rate models fail to explain the long swings in real exchange rates which we observe since the early 1970s. The case-studies in this chapter illustrate this. We searched for real shocks which could explain the large movements of the real exchange rates observed since the early 1970s. It has to be concluded that this search was not very successful. We found that sometimes particular disturbances were important in affecting real exchange rate movements. At other times similar disturbances had quite different effects. Thus, on the whole the large real shocks, such as fiscal policies and oil price changes, had quite unpredictable effects on the real exchange rates.

The problem with the real shock explanation of the large 'misalignments' of the dollar exchange rates is that one simply cannot find a series of disturbances which first drove the dollar down (in real terms) during the 1970s, then pushed it up during six years from 1979 to 1985, to bring it back at its level of the 1970s at the end of the 1980s.

We have to conclude that the real exchange rate movements of the last twenty years cannot easily be explained by models which rely on real shocks. There have simply not been sufficiently persistent disturbances which, in the context of our popular exchange rate models, could explain the persistence of real exchange rate movements in a predictable way.

We also analysed whether the dynamics predicted by the models could be detected in the data. Our conclusion here was equally negative. The overshooting models do not help us in explaining the large and protracted movements in the real exchange rates observed since the early 1970s, neither can the bubbles model.

Why has it been difficult to develop models of the exchange rates which will outlast the exchange rate cycle during which they were constructed?

The answer has something to do with intertemporal budget constraints. The importance of intertemporal budget constraints has been stressed by a new theoretical approach on how the current account, the government budget, and the exchange rate interact. This new theory[15] starts from the proposition that the current account surplus/deficit is the outcome of a decision to spend less/ more today and more/less tomorrow. In order to understand this process, we need models which take the intertemporal nature of the problem explicitly into account. As we will see in the next chapter this new view helps to understand why it is difficult to predict how fiscal policies affect the real exchange rate, and how the exchange rate and the current account are related to each other.

To conclude, it should be stressed that although we understand very little about the short-term movements of the exchange rates, we know a little more about the fundamental variables that drive the exchange rates in the very long run. As was illustrated in Chapter 5, inflation and productivity growth have been fundamental forces explaining why the yen, for example, has more than doubled *vis-à-vis* the dollar during the last twenty-five years. What we fail to understand is why the movements around these long-term trends have been so large and often so protracted.

---

[15] See e.g. Stockman (1980), Lucas (1982), Obstfeld and Stockman (1985), and Svensson (1985).

APPENDIX. THE BIAS IN THE FORWARD PREMIUM AND RISK PREMIUMS

In this appendix we discuss the literature that has analysed the bias in the forward premium. As was indicated in this and in previous chapters, a very systematic finding is that the forward premium systematically errs in predicting the direction of future exchange rate changes. The best-known study establishing this is the article by Fama (1984). Fama went about it as follows.

The forward rate can be written as

$$f_t = E(s_{t+1}) + \pi_t \tag{7.5}$$

where f_t is the log of the forward exchange rate, s_{t+1} is the log of the spot exchange rate in period $t + 1$; $E(s_{t+1})$ is the rationally expected exchange rate; π_t is the risk premium.

Subtracting s_t from both sides yields

$$f_t - s_t = E(s_{t+1} - s_t) + \pi_t. \tag{7.6}$$

One can obtain information on the risk premium in the following way. Consider two regression equations using the forward premium, $(f_t - s_t)$, as an explanatory variable and each of the two components of the forward premium, i.e. the forecast error $(f_t - s_{t+1})$, and the actual change in the spot rate $(s_{t+1} - s_t)$, as the dependent variable:

$$f_t - s_{t+1} = a_1 + b_1(f_t - s_t) + \varepsilon_{1t} \tag{7.7}$$

$$s_{t+1} - s_t = a_2 + b_2(f_t - s_t) + \varepsilon_{2t}. \tag{7.8}$$

The efficient market hypothesis implies (in the absence of risk premiums) that $a_2 = 0$, $b_2 = 1$ and ε_{2t} is white noise. (This is also a necessary condition for rational expectations to hold.) Failure to find this can then be interpreted as evidence of market inefficiency (non-rational expectations) or of the existence of risk premiums.

Assuming that the expected future spot rate in (7.6) is rational, it can be shown that

$$b_1 = \frac{\operatorname{cov}(f_t - s_{t+1}, f_t - s_t)}{\operatorname{var}(f_t - s_t)}$$

can also be written as

$$b_1 = \frac{\operatorname{var}(\pi_t) + \operatorname{cov}(\pi_t, E(s_{t+1} - s_t))}{\operatorname{var}(f_t - s_t)} \tag{7.9}$$

and

$$b_2 = \frac{\operatorname{cov}(s_{t+1} - s_t, f_t - s_t)}{\operatorname{var}(f_t - s_t)}$$

can be written as

$$b_2 = \frac{\text{var}(E(s_{t+1} - s_t)) + \text{cov}(\pi_t, E(s_{t+1} - s_t))}{\text{var}(f_t - s_t)}. \tag{7.10}$$

Thus it appears from (7.9) and (7.10) that the estimated coefficients of the regression equations (7.7) and (7.8) allow us to infer certain characteristics of the risk premium and its correlation pattern with the expected changes in the exchange rate. In addition, if we subtract (7.10) from (7.9) we obtain

$$b_1 - b_2 = \frac{\text{var}(\pi_t) - \text{var}(E(s_{t+1} - s_t))}{\text{var}(f_t - s_t)}.$$

Thus, a comparison of the coefficients b_1 and b_2 teaches us something about the relative importance of the variability of the risk premium relative to the variability of the expected exchange rate changes.

We show the results of estimating equations (7.7) and (7.8) in Table 7.10 for different exchange rates. We have made a distinction between floating exchange rates and exchange rates within the EMS. The results can be summarized as follows.

First, for the floating exchange rates we invariably find that b_2 is negative and most often significantly so. (This empirical result has been found many times in the literature (see Engel (1995).) This is not the case with the EMS exchange rates, where we find positive b_2s (although smaller than unity). Thus the bias of the forward premium is most pronounced in the case of floating exchange rates. What is more, in a floating exchange rate environment the forward premium systematically errs in forecasting future exchange rate changes, while this is not the case in the EMS. We will come back to this remarkable result in order to explain it.[16]

Second, from the negative sign of the coefficient b_2 it can be concluded that the risk premium and the expected future changes in the dollar exchange rates of the three major currencies are negatively correlated. This conclusion follows from equation (7.10) defining b_2: since $\text{var}(E(s_{t+1} - s_t))$ is always positive, a negative sign on b_2 implies that $\text{cov}(\pi_t, E(s_{t+1} - s_t))$ is negative. Since the estimated b_2s in the EMS are generally positive no such conclusion can be drawn for the EMS exchange rates.

Third, the variance of the risk premium is larger than the variance of the expected exchange rate changes. This can be seen from the expression $b_1 - b_2$ which is positive for all the dollar exchange rates. It is also significantly positive in four out of seven cases. Again we find something quite different in the case of the EMS currencies. In this case $b_1 - b_2$ turns out to be negative, indicating that the variance of the expected exchange rate changes within the EMS is higher than the variance of the risk premiums.

---

[16] This distinction between floating exchange rates and EMS exchange rates was also found by Flood and Rose (1994*b*).

TABLE 7.10. *Estimation of equations (7.7) and (7.8) for non-EMS and EMS exchange rates, (Sample period: 1979.01–1988.04) (OLS estimation)*

	a_1	b_1	a_2	b_2	s(a)	s(b)	R^2	$\bar{R}^2$	DW
Non-EMS									
DM/$	-0.01	4.03	0.01	-3.03	0.01	1.72	0.04	0.02	1.97
Yen/$	-0.01	2.90	0.01	-1.90	0.01	1.02	0.06	0.03	1.86
Pound/$	0.01	6.31	-0.01	-5.31	0.00	1.08	0.22	0.17	2.07
FF/$	0.00	1.29	0.00	-0.29	0.00	0.78	0.02	0.01	1.96
Lira/$	0.00	1.15	0.00	-0.15	0.00	0.42	0.06	0.01	1.83
BF/$	0.00	1.76	0.00	-0.76	0.00	0.98	0.03	0.01	1.84
Guilder/$	-0.01	4.22	0.01	-3.22	0.00	1.30	0.08	0.05	2.01
EMS									
FF/DM	-0.01	0.04	0.01	0.96	0.00	0.32	0.00	0.07	2.12
Lira/DM	0.00	0.35	0.00	0.65	0.00	0.19	0.03	0.09	2.29
BF/DM	0.00	0.39	0.00	0.61	0.00	0.28	0.02	0.04	1.69
Guild/DM	0.00	1.49	0.00	-0.49	0.00	0.26	0.22	0.03	2.26

Note: s(a) and s(b) are the standard errors of a and b respectively
Source: P. De Grauwe (1989)

TABLE 7.11. *Test of large risk premium and negative covariance*

	$t(b_1 - b_2)$	$t(b_2)$	SER (in %)
Non-EMS			
DM/$	2.06	-1.76	3.2
Yen/$	2.35	-1.86	3.5
Pound/$	5.38	-4.92	2.8
FF/$	1.03	-0.37	3.3
Lira/$	1.55	-0.36	2.9
BF/$	1.29	-0.78	3.4
Guilder/$	2.86	-2.48	3.1
EMS			
FF/DM	-1.44	3.00	1.3
Lira/DM	-0.79	3.42	1.3
BF/DM	-0.39	2.18	0.9
Guild/DM	3.81	-1.88	0.5

Note: SER = standard error of the regression
Source: P. De Grauwe (1989)

8

THE EXCHANGE RATE AND RICARDO'S EQUIVALENCE THEOREM

1. Introduction

In the previous chapter we argued that we lack models which are able to predict the direction and the time path followed by the exchange rate when the economy is disturbed by shocks such as fiscal policies or oil shocks. As a result, we have been unable to explain these exchange rate movements, except in an *ad hoc* way.

The question arises why it has proved so difficult to develop such models. In this chapter it will be argued that our failure to develop useful exchange rate models has something to do with the fact that changes in the exchange rates and in the current account are the outcome of an intertemporal maximization problem, and that most of the empirical models in use have, as yet, not incorporated this fundamental idea.

2. The intertemporal budget constraint of a country

Like an individual, a country faces an intertemporal budget constraint. If a country issues debt today, it will have to service this debt in the future. How is a country led to issue debt and how can it service its debt?

Take the situation of a country which initially has no foreign debt and no international reserves. In the first period, it increases total spending (absorption) on goods and services relative to output. As a result, the country will have a deficit on its current account of the balance of payments. The only way this current account deficit can be financed is by issuing debt, say bonds, which will be held by the rest of the world. One can write that:

$$B_1 = \text{current account deficit}$$

where B_1 is the foreign debt issued by the country in the first period.

The existence of a foreign debt, B_1, will necessitate the payment of interest in future periods, and a repayment of the principal when the foreign debt comes to maturity. This repayment may of course be postponed indefinitely, by issuing new debt when the old debt expires. In that case the country is faced with the need to pay interest on its foreign debt for the indefinite future. Let us assume that this is the case. How can a country pay interest on its outstanding debt in the future? The answer is that it will have to run current account surpluses in the future. These surpluses will then allow the country to acquire the foreign exchange needed to make the interest payments.[1] Without these current account surpluses in the future, the country will be unable to pay interest on its foreign debt. It also follows that if the country increases its foreign debt today, it will have to generate larger current account surpluses in the future. Since a current account surplus is the difference between output and spending, the former will have to increase faster than the latter in the future.

One can formulate these ideas in a somewhat different way. The ability to generate future current account surpluses determines the amount a country can borrow today. A country which is believed to be able to generate large current account surpluses in the future (for example because of a high expected growth rate of output) can issue more foreign debt today than a country which is not expected to generate large surpluses.

How much debt can a country issue today? The answer is given by the intertemporal budget constraint (which is sometimes also called a solvency constraint). This can be formulated as follows: the foreign debt which a country can issue today cannot be larger than the present value of all expected future current account surpluses and deficits.[2] If it is larger, foreign creditors realize that the country will be unable to earn foreign exchange in sufficient amounts to service the debt in the future. They will then be unwilling to hold the debt issued by this country.

Thus if the government is increasing its deficit so that total spending in the country increases relative to output, the whole future time path of government budget deficits and surpluses will have to change. In general, more deficits today imply that less deficits will be possible in the future.

Box 8.1. The current account and the intertemporal debt constraint

Let us use a very simple two-period model. The model is deliberately kept as simple as possible. We will discuss possible complications at a later stage.

The country we consider here has a choice between consumption today or tomorrow. Let us first assume a closed economy. In Fig. 8.1 we present the main elements of the model. On the horizontal axis we have consumption in period 1 (today), on the vertical axis consumption in period 2 (tomorrow). The intertemporal transformation curve is represented by the concave line. Total output today is

---

[1] The country can of course issue new debt in the future in order to repay the interest on its existing debt. This strategy, however, cannot be continued indefinitely, because it will lead to a ballooning of the foreign debt, and ever increasing interest payments. Sooner or later the country will have to earn the interest payments by running current account surpluses.

[2] For a more formal treatment see Box 8.1.

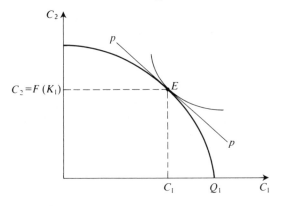

FIG. 8.1. Two-period consumption model (closed economy)

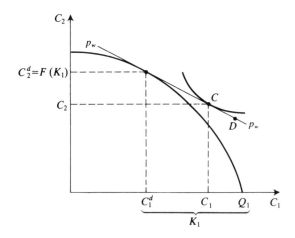

FIG. 8.2. Two-period consumption model (open economy)

given by Q_1. This can be used for producing consumption goods, say C_1, or capital goods, $K_1 = Q_1 - C_1$. The latter produce consumption goods in the second period ($C_2 = F(K_1)$). That is, capital goods today are transformed into consumption goods tomorrow.

In the closed economy we represent in Fig. 8.1 the equilibrium is achieved at point E. This is the point where the indifference curve of the representative individual is tangential to the transformation curve. The interest rate which sustains the equilibrium is given by the slope of the straight line pp. Note that in this closed economy there can be no net borrowing for the country as a whole. At point E the production of capital goods $Q_1 - C_1$ is made possible by the willingness of residents not to consume the whole output Q_1.

When we open up the economy, it becomes possible for the country to be a net borrower. We now look at Fig. 8.2. The domestic transformation curve is the same as in Fig. 8.1. We now, however, assume that the country is able to borrow freely at the international interest rate given by the slope of the line $p_w p_w$. Note that we assume that the $p_w p_w$ line is flatter than the pp line in Fig. 8.1. This means that the world interest rate is lower than the domestic interest rate in the closed economy.

The country can now increase its consumption opportunities today, because the latter do not have to coincide with the transformation curve. It can choose a point on the $p_w p_w$ line, say point F. Total consumption is then C_1. Since it is producing Q_1, of which K_1 are capital goods, the domestic production of consumption goods is $C_1^d = Q_1 - K_1$. Thus, there is a 'deficit', which is nothing but the current account deficit, equal to:

$$B_1 = C_1 - C_1^d = C_1 - (Q_1 - K_1) \tag{8.1}$$

where B_1 is defined as the current account deficit.

This current account deficit is also the amount the country will have to borrow in the international capital market (a capital inflow) to sustain the high level of consumption in the present period.

What happens next period? Because the country is consuming so much today, and in order to do so is borrowing today, it will have to do the reverse tomorrow. In period 2, the consumption level will be C_2, which is below the amount of consumption goods produced in period 2 ($C_2^d = F(K_1)$). Put differently, in period 2 the country will have to run a current account surplus equal to $F(K_1) - C_2$.

We can find the present value of this future current account surplus by the formula

$$\frac{-B_2}{(1 + r)} = \frac{F(K_1) - C_2}{(1 + r)} \tag{8.2}$$

where B_2 is the current account deficit in period 2; we have added a negative sign because the country has a surplus in period 2.

The model now makes clear that this expression is equal to the current account deficit today. Thus, we can write that

$$\frac{-B_2}{(1 + r)} = B_1. \tag{8.3}$$

This can also be seen graphically as follows. Rewrite equation (8.3) as follows:

$$\frac{-B_2}{B_1} = (1 + r). \tag{8.4}$$

The right-hand side is the slope of the $P_w P_w$ line. It also defines the intertemporal budget constraint of the country. Given the foreign interest rate, an increase in today's borrowing (B_1) will have to lead to increased repayments in the next period, or, put differently, the intertemporal budget constraint tells us that an increase in today's current account deficit must lead to an increased current account surplus in the next period.

This result is of basic significance. Suppose the country increases its preference for consumption today. This could take the form of more spending by the government. We then move to the right on the budget line $P_w P_w$, say to point D. As a result, there will be a higher current account deficit today. This, however, will be matched by a higher current account surplus tomorrow. Put differently, the increase in today's borrowing to finance the current account deficit will be compensated by increased repayments of the external debt in the next period.

We can easily generalize the intertemporal foreign debt constraint specified in equation (8.3) to many periods. We then obtain

$$B_1 = \frac{-B_2}{(1 + r)} + \frac{-B_3}{(1 + r)^2} + \frac{-B_4}{(1 + r)^3} \cdots \tag{8.5}$$

or

$$B_1 = \sum_{i=1}^{\infty} \frac{-B_{i+1}}{(1 + r)^i} \cdots \tag{8.6}$$

This equation says that the foreign debt created today (B_1) must be equal to the future repayments of the debt. Another way to interpret this equation is as follows. The right-hand side defines the present value of the future current account surpluses and deficits. This value then also determines how large the current account deficit can be today.

It is important to note here that B_1 is the total net issue of debt instruments (let us call them bonds) by the domestic private and government sector and held by non-residents. These are usually called outside assets (bonds).

We can go one step further in our interpretation of the intertemporal debt constraint (sometimes also called a solvency constraint) by using the definition of B_i. We have

$$B_i = A_i - Q_i \tag{8.7}$$

where Q_i is the domestic output in period i, and $A_i = C_i + K_i$, i.e. total spending for consumption and capital goods, by the private and the government sector. Substituting in equation (8.6) we obtain

$$A_1 - Q_1 = \sum_{i=1}^{\infty} \frac{Q_{i+1} - A_{i+1}}{(1 + r)^i} \cdots \tag{8.8}$$

This equation says that if spending increases today relative to output, the whole future time path of spending relative to output will have to change to maintain the solvency constraint. Thus if the government is increasing its deficit so that spending increases relative to output, the whole future time path of government budget deficits and surpluses will have to change. In general, more deficits today imply that less deficits will be possible in the future.

3. Intertemporal debt constraint and the exchange rate

The existence of an intertemporal debt constraint is of great importance for the theory of exchange rate determination. In this section we present an intuitive analysis of the link between this debt constraint and the exchange rate. In Box 8.2 a more formal analysis is presented.

In a perfect foresight world, economic agents set the exchange rate based on their expectation of the present and the future supplies of assets (money, bonds).

In addition, they are aware that the intertemporal debt constraint links tomorrow's bond issue by a country to today's. Thus if a country issues more foreign debt today because of an increased budget deficit of the government which is produced by a reduction in taxes, economic agents forecast lower deficits and/ or higher surpluses in the future. The present value of these higher surpluses must be equal to the deficit today.

This has important implications for the exchange rate. If today's budget deficit, induced by a reduction of taxes, leads to a real appreciation of the domestic currency, as the traditional models predict, then the future budget surpluses must have the opposite effects on the future exchange rate. In a perfect foresight world, economic agents are aware of this. As a result, the expected future depreciation will immediately be reflected in today's exchange rate. This then prevents the currency from appreciating in the first place. It follows that the effect of today's deficit on the exchange rate is exactly offset by the expected higher surpluses in the future.[3]

This result is akin to the so-called Ricardian equivalence theorem, which says that a higher budget deficit today, produced by a reduction in taxes, has no effect on the interest rate, because economic agents know that the intertemporal budget constraint will force the government to increase taxes in the future, i.e. to service the debt incurred today. The present value of these expected future budget surpluses exactly offsets the deficit created today.[4]

We have made a number of implicit assumptions to arrive at this result. Relaxing these assumptions generally leads to exceptions to the Ricardian equivalence theorem. Nevertheless, it is a useful benchmark to compare other models with. In addition, it creates a presumption that the effect of a fiscal expansion on the real exchange rate is ambiguous once we take the intertemporal nature of the problem into account. Let us discuss some of the complications that can be added to the analysis. We will consider three complications which have some relevance for our analysis.

3.1. Budget deficits and government spending

The previous analysis only holds if the increased government budget deficit is due to a reduction of taxes. These taxes should not produce distortions.[5] In that case agents consider today's bond issue as a substitute for taxes. If, however, the budget deficit arises from an increase in government spending, the effects will be different. For in that case the claim made by the government on domestic resources increases. This will in general have real effects, i.e. it will change relative prices, and therefore also the real exchange rate.

---

[3] Note that we assume throughout that the government is expected to remain solvent.
[4] See Ricardo (1951). Robert Barro has popularized this idea. See Barro (1974).
[5] This condition has been stressed in the literature on Ricardian equivalence. It restricts the kind of taxation that can be used to lump-sum taxes.

The direction of this effect on the real exchange rate, however, will generally be difficult to predict.[6] It depends on the type of goods and services the government spends on. For example, the government may increase its spending mainly on non-traded goods. This will tend to raise the price of non-traded goods relative to traded goods. As a result, resources move out of the traded goods sector into the non-traded goods sector. At the same time domestic residents increase their demand for the cheaper traded goods. The net effect is that the trade account deteriorates, requiring a real depreciation of the currency.[7]

The government may also decide to spend more on investment goods, instead of on consumption goods. This decision will also affect the real exchange rate. If, for example, the higher budget deficit is used to finance investment in infrastructure or other public goods which raise the future growth rate of the economy, it may make it easy to generate future current account surpluses. Or alternatively, the government may use the proceeds of the issue of bonds to finance consumption. In that case, the future current account surpluses will be more difficult to generate, and may require deep spending cuts, and real depreciations.

3.2. The role of money

In the previous formulation of the Ricardian equivalence theorem, we assumed that the money stock is kept constant. We know that governments can also finance budget deficits by issuing money, instead of issuing bonds. And in contrast to the issue of bonds, there is no limit to the issue of money because the government has a monopoly in printing money. This also means that even if the government does not print money today, it may be expected to do so in the future in order to finance the budget deficit. If expectations exist that the government will finance the budget deficit by monetary expansion in the future, this will generally lead to expectations of future price increases. To the extent that agents believe in the long-run operation of purchasing power parity, they will expect a depreciation of the domestic currency. These expectations are then telescoped back into today's exchange rate. As a result, the currency will experience an immediate depreciation.

3.3. The perfect foresight assumption

The Ricardian equivalence theorem holds for the effect of the budget deficit on the exchange rate if we assume perfect foresight. This is a very strong assumption. However, when we relax it, it is unclear in what direction this changes our conclusion.

---

[6] See Frenkel and Razin (1986*b*) on this issue.

[7] For models of traded and non-traded goods, see Dixit and Norman (1980), Bruno (1976), Corden and Neary (1982).

In an uncertain environment there are many sources of risk which will affect the transmission of fiscal policy shocks. A first one can be called the inflation risk. In the previous section we considered the case of an expected future monetary expansion. In practice, there usually will be much uncertainty about this. This uncertainty will add an inflation premium for holding domestic assets. Put differently, when the government increases its budget deficit, this raises the risk of future monetary expansion and future inflation. In order to be compensated for this risk, economic agents will want a higher return on domestic assets. This higher return can be brought about by an immediate depreciation of the domestic currency.[8]

A second source of risk leads to a similar effect on the exchange rate. It is the default (or solvency) risk. There is uncertainty about the ability or the willingness of future governments to repay their debt. New governments may be elected which do not feel bound by the terms of the loans obtained by the previous government. Or the political pressure not to repay the debt may lead governments in the future to repudiate the debt. They may do this explicitly, or more likely, implicitly, by renegotiating the terms of the loans.

This default risk will generally be a function of the size of the outstanding debt. As with the inflation risk, it will add a risk premium for holders of domestic assets. As a result, the domestic currency will have to depreciate sufficiently, so as to generate an expected capital gain in the future, which will compensate them for the higher risk.

The previous discussion of the difficulties of predicting the effects of fiscal policies on today's exchange rate can be formalized in an extended version of the Mundell–Fleming model which allows risk premiums to play a role. This is done in the appendix to this chapter.

We can summarize the preceding analysis as follows. Every change in fiscal policies today changes the whole path of future fiscal policies. In addition, since in each period there is also a budget constraint requiring that a given deficit must be financed by issuing bonds or by printing money, we also know that a fiscal policy today is likely to change the whole future path of monetary policies.

This constraint on government actions is strong, and yet it leaves a lot of degrees of freedom. Future governments will still have many options and choices in the way they conduct their fiscal and monetary policies. It is the uncertainty about these future policy choices which explains why it is near impossible to know how a fiscal policy conducted today, or a disturbance like an oil price change, affects today's exchange rate, let alone the dynamic path the exchange rate will follow in the future. This indeterminacy also explains a major puzzle observed during the floating exchange rate period. This is that similar disturbances which occurred during that period had quite different effects on the real exchange rate.

We can now go one step further in the analysis and ask the question to what

---

[8] This is also the mechanism which we encountered when discussing the portfolio balance model.

extent this problem of the indeterminacy of the future path of monetary and fiscal policies is influenced by the prevailing exchange rate system.

Box 8.2. Intertemporal debt constraint and the exchange rate in a perfect foresight model

A useful starting-point of the analysis recognizes that the exchange rate in period t is determined by all the relevant exogenous variables and by the expected future change in the exchange rate:[9]

$$S_t = Z_t + bE_t \Delta S_{t+1} \qquad (8.9)$$

where Z_t is a vector of exogenous variables influencing the exchange rate; $E_t \Delta S_{t+1}$ is the expected change of the exchange rate in period $t + 1$. We can also rewrite equation (8.9) as follows

$$S_t = \frac{1}{1+b} Z_t + \frac{b}{1+b} E_t S_{t+1}. \qquad (8.10)$$

Shifting equation (8.10) one period forward and taking expectations yields

$$E_t S_{t+1} = \frac{1}{1+b} E_t Z_{t+1} + \frac{b}{1+b} E_t S_{t+2}. \qquad (8.11)$$

Substituting (8.11) into (8.10) yields

$$S_t = \frac{1}{1+b} Z_t + \left(\frac{1}{1+b}\right)\frac{b}{1+b} E_t Z_{t+1} + \left(\frac{b}{1+b}\right)^2 E_t S_{t+2}. \qquad (8.12)$$

We can repeat this procedure *ad infinitum* to obtain the following solution:

$$S_t = \frac{1}{1+b} Z_t + \frac{1}{1+b}\sum_{i=1}^{\infty}\left(\frac{b}{1+b}\right)^i E_t Z_{t+i}. \qquad (8.13)$$

The exchange rate today is determined by the current and the expected future values of the exogenous variables.[10]

The exogenous variables in equation (8.13) will typically include the money stock and other (outside) assets. In order to simplify matters, let us suppose that these assets are domestic government bonds (H_t). We then have

$$Z_t = fM_t + gH_t$$

where f and g are parameters expressing the influence of the money stock and government bonds on the exchange rate. The (static) Mundell–Fleming theory predicts that an increase in domestic bonds will lead to an increase in the domestic interest rate and therefore to an appreciation of the domestic currency (a decline in the exchange rate). Thus, g is negative.

We can now analyse the effects of an increase in the supply of outside bonds

---

[9] This formulation can be found in Mussa (1976).

[10] It should be stressed that this solution implies perfect foresight. In addition, we have selected only one solution, i.e. the one corresponding to the stable path. There are an infinite number of solutions, all unstable however. This is a typical feature of perfect foresight models.

due to a government budget deficit in period t. Let us first assume that government bonds are the only assets. (We will return to this assumption, as it is rather crucial.) We then have

$$S_t = \frac{g}{1+b}H_t + \frac{g}{1+b}\sum_{i=1}^{\infty}\left(\frac{b}{1+b}\right)^i E_t H_{t+i}. \tag{8.14}$$

We can also express this equation in first differences:

$$\Delta S_t = \frac{g}{1+b}\Delta H_t + \frac{g}{1+b}\sum_{i=1}^{\infty}\left(\frac{b}{1+b}\right)^i E_t \Delta H_{t+i}. \tag{8.15}$$

Introducing the intertemporal budget constraint, we know that the issue of bonds today means that less bonds can be issued in the future. This intertemporal budget constraint was specified as follows (see Box 8.1):

$$B_t = \sum_{i=1}^{\infty}\frac{-B_{t+i}}{(1+r)^i}\ldots \tag{8.16}$$

where B_t is the issue of new bonds in period t. It can therefore also be written as

$$B_t = H_t - H_{t-1} = \Delta H_t. \tag{8.17}$$

Substituting (8.17) into (8.15) yields

$$\Delta S_t = \frac{g}{1+b}B_t + \frac{g}{1+b}\sum_{i=1}^{\infty}\left(\frac{b}{1+b}\right)^i E_t B_{t+i}. \tag{8.18}$$

We can now immediately derive the following result. If the discount factors in equations (8.16) and (8.18) are equal, i.e. if

$$\frac{1}{(1+r)^i} = \left(\frac{b}{1+b}\right)^i \tag{8.19}$$

the effect of an increased bond issue today on the exchange rate is zero. This can be seen by substituting (8.16) into (8.18) using (8.19).

This rather powerful result has the following interpretation. In a perfect foresight world, economic agents set the exchange rate based on their expectations of the present and the future supplies of outside assets. In addition, they are aware that the intertemporal debt constraint links tomorrow's bond issue to today's. Thus, if more bonds are issued today because of an increased budget deficit, economic agents forecast lower deficits and or higher surpluses in the future. The present value of these higher budget surpluses must be equal to the deficit today. As a result, the effect of today's deficit on the exchange rate is exactly offset by the expected higher surpluses in the future.

This result is akin to the so-called Ricardian equivalence theorem, which says that a higher budget deficit today has no effect on the interest rate, because economic agents know that the intertemporal budget constraint will force the government to increase taxes in the future, i.e. to repay the debt incurred today. The present value of these expected future budget surpluses exactly offsets the deficit created today.

In the previous analysis the stock of money was disregarded. We know, however, that the authorities can also finance budget deficits by issuing money. Suppose that the government is always expected to finance a budget deficit by an issue of money. We then have

$$B_t = M_t - M_{t-1} = \Delta M_t \qquad (8.20)$$

and the exchange rate equation (in first differences becomes):

$$\Delta S_t = \frac{f}{1+b}\Delta M_t + \frac{f}{1+b}\sum_{i=1}^{\infty}\left(\frac{b}{1+b}\right)^i E_t\Delta M_{t+i}. \qquad (8.21)$$

Contrary to the case of a bond-financed fiscal policy there is no constraint on the issue of money today. Thus, if the government issues money today in order to finance a budget deficit, this does not reduce its ability to issue more money in the future. Thus, the issue of money today will unambiguously lead to an increase in the exchange rate.

4. Intertemporal budget constraints and pre-commitments

In a world where the authorities are bound by few commitments the number of future paths of debt and money will be larger than in a situation where authorities are tied by a set of (credible) pre-commitments. In the latter case the number of options the authorities have in setting the future path of monetary and fiscal policies is restricted by the commitments they have taken. As a result, we can say that the uncertainty of the effects of policy actions on the exchange rate and on a number of other macroeconomic variables is very much influenced by the nature of the commitments the authorities have taken.

There are two reasons to believe that these commitments have been loosened since the early 1970s. As a result, we now face a much more uncertain policy environment. This has to do with two institutional changes which have taken place since the early 1970s. First, there was the move to floating, which removed the fixed exchange rate commitment, and therefore, left more future options open for the authorities. Second, the development of a true international capital market allowed a significantly greater prospect of financing budget deficits for a large number of countries. This also vastly increased the number of choices the national authorities faced when setting their monetary and fiscal policies.

It is important to analyse in somewhat more detail how these two institutional changes have enlarged the policy options of the authorities. Take the move from fixed to flexible exchange rates first. In a fixed exchange rate system, in which the authorities stick to their commitment to a fixed exchange rate, and in which in addition the possibilities of financing current account deficits by capital movements are limited, the number of policy options are severely limited. Suppose, for example, that the domestic authorities engage in a policy of fiscal expansion. This is likely to lead to a current account deficit which draws down the stock of international reserves. As the stock of international reserves held by the authorities is known to economic agents, the latter can quickly calculate when the stock of international reserves will be depleted if the expansionary fiscal policy stance is maintained. A speculative run will be set in motion, forcing the authorities to return quickly to more 'orthodox' policies or to face the collapse of the fixed exchange rate regime.[11] If the authorities were to finance the budget deficit by printing money, this would only make the deficit in the current account larger, and would therefore increase the speed with which the stock of international reserves is depleted. Thus, in this rigidly fixed exchange rate system where authorities have no access to the world financial markets, there is really no other choice for the authorities but to stay in line. As a result also there is very little uncertainty about what the changes in fiscal policies will do to the economy.

Things are radically different once the fixed exchange rate commitment is relaxed. This is what happened in the early 1970s. In a world without fixed exchange rate commitments, the tightness of the restrictions on future fiscal and monetary policies is relaxed considerably. Take a fiscal expansion once more. The authorities now have a large menu of policy choices in the future. They can let the currency depreciate freely in response to the deficit in the current account. Or alternatively they can peg the exchange rate. In fact they can choose any combination of these two extremes between free floating and fixed exchange rates. Each choice also implies a different path for monetary policies. In the free float choice, there will be no drain on international reserves, so that monetary policies will not have to be restricted.

Thus, the relaxation of the fixed exchange rate commitment also multiplied the number of different time paths future monetary and fiscal policies could follow after an initial shock in the fiscal stance. Whether the explosion of policy choices for the authorities improved welfare is another matter which is not pursued here. The important point is that with floating exchange rates it became increasingly more difficult to predict the effects of policy shocks, because the flexible exchange rate system increased the size of the set of policy responses of the authorities.

There is a second institutional change which has significantly increased the number of policy options for national authorities. This is the increase in size and sophistication of international capital markets. This in turn has allowed for much easier access to foreign finance by domestic authorities, and has considerably relaxed the international reserve constraint, which during the 1950s and the 1960s reduced the policy options of the authorities. Following a domestic fiscal expansion, countries can now borrow considerably in international capital markets, thereby enlarging the menu of possible policy responses to exogenous disturbances. (In Box 8.3 we analyse this proposition more formally. We also discuss the so-called Feldstein–Horioka puzzle which casts doubt on whether capital mobility has really increased.)

---

[11] See our discussion of speculative attacks in fixed exchange rate systems in Ch. 4.

TABLE 8.1. *Standard deviation (and mean) of the growth rate of the money stock (M2) and of the government budget deficit (as percentage of GDP)*

	US	Germany	Japan
Money Stock			
Fixed rate period	1.6	1.4	3.6
(1960–70)	(6.8)	(11.9)	(19.1)
Flex rate period	3.0	2.3	4.2
(1971–93)	(9.2)	(7.4)	(11.2)
Government Budget Deficit			
Fixed rate period	0.6	0.7	0.8
(1960–70)	(−0.7)	(−0.3)	(−0.9)
Flex rate period	1.4	1.2	2.3
(1971–93)	(−3.3)	(−1.5)	(−4.5)

Note: mean in brackets

Source: IMF, *International Financial Statistics*

We conclude that the combination of relaxation of the fixed exchange rate commitment and the greatly enlarged access to international capital markets which has occurred since the early 1970s has vastly increased the freedom of action and the possible policy responses of national governments to exogenous disturbances and to fiscal policy shocks.

5. More freedom means more variability of policies

There is evidence that this increased number of options has also given incentives to authorities to experiment with more and more volatile mixes of fiscal and monetary policies.

Table 8.1 provides some evidence for this. We show the variability of fiscal and monetary policies during the fixed (1960–70) and the floating (1973–93) exchange rate periods. The variability is measured by the standard deviation of yearly observations. We also show (between brackets) the mean of these measures of monetary and fiscal policies. The results of the table suggest that the variability of these two measures of economic policies became substantially higher during the flexible exchange rate period. This evidence is consistent with the hypothesis formulated here, i.e. that the enlarged set of policy choices inherent in the floating exchange rate system (together with the increased access to foreign finance since the early 1970s) has also encouraged policy-makers to exhibit less restraint in using their policy instruments.

One can conclude from all this that the larger set of policy choices at the disposal of national authorities which has evolved since the early 1970s may have invited governments to behave in a less disciplined way. This then led to greater uncertainty about the course of future policies, and may have made it more difficult for economic agents to forecast exchange rates.

6. Interest parity and risk premiums

There is additional empirical evidence which tends to confirm the hypothesis formulated here, i.e. that the loosening of commitments during the flexible exchange rate period has reduced our ability to predict the effects of exogenous disturbances, and has led to a progressive decline in our ability to forecast the future. The evidence comes from the forward exchange markets.

We noted in Chapter 4 that during the floating exchange rate period the forward premium was not a very good predictor of the future developments of the exchange rate. In particular, we found that the forward premium tended to be much smaller than the subsequent observed changes in the exchange rates. Thus, the forward premium systematically underestimates the size of the movements that take place later. We also found that there were periods during which the forward premium was systematically wrong in predicting the direction of the future exchange rate movements. This seems to indicate that the forward premium is a biased predictor of the future exchange rate. This was also confirmed by many econometric studies (see the appendix of Chapter 7 where these studies were discussed).

One way to test the hypothesis that the flexible exchange rate environment has reduced our ability to forecast the future is to compare the quality of the forward premium as a predictor of future exchange rate changes over different exchange rate regimes. If our hypothesis is correct, the forward premium should exhibit a stronger bias in a regime of free floating than in a regime of pegged exchange rates. Such a test was performed by De Grauwe (1989) and more recently by Flood and Rose (1994b). It consists of regressing the exchange rate change in period $t + 1$ on the forward premium in period t (see Fama (1984) and the appendix to Chapter 7 where this methodology is discussed), and to do this for exchange rates that are floating (e.g. dollar/DM, dollar/yen) and for exchange rates that are pegged (the EMS exchange rates). The equation that was estimated is:

$$s_{t+1} - s_t = a + b(f_t - s_t) + u_t \tag{8.22}$$

where f_t is the log of the forward rate, s_t is the log of the spot rate (then $f_t - s_t$ is the forward premium) and u_t is the error term. In order for the forward premium to be an unbiased predictor of the future change in the exchange rate b must be equal to 1.

The results of this exercise are shown in Table 8.2. They confirm our hypothesis. The coefficient b is systematically negative in the case of the dollar exchange rates, whereas it is positive in the case of the EMS exchange rates (although it remains below its theoretical value of 1). This suggests that the bias

TABLE **8.2**. *Estimation of equation (8.22) for non-EMS and EMS exchange rates (sample period: 1979.01–1988.04)*

	a	b	s(a)	s(b)	R^2	DW
Non-EMS						
DM/\$	0.01	−3.03	0.01	1.72	1.04	1.97
Yen/\$	0.01	−1.90	0.01	1.02	0.06	1.86
£/\$	−0.01	−5.31	0.00	1.08	0.22	2.07
EMS						
FF/DM	0.01	0.96	0.00	0.32	0.07	2.12
Lira/DM	0.00	0.65	0.00	0.19	0.03	2.29
BF/DM	0.00	0.61	0.00	0.28	0.02	1.69
guilder/DM	0.00	−0.49	0.00	0.26	0.22	2.26

Note: The forward premiums are one-month premiums; s() is the standard error of the co-efficient between the brackets

Source: P. De Grauwe (1989)

in the forward premium is much larger for the dollar exchange rates than for the EMS exchange rates. In the case of the EMS, the forward premium seems on average to predict the sign of the subsequent exchange rate change correctly.

The evidence confirms that, as the international monetary system allowed more policy choices, expectations of economic agents lost an anchor which in previous systems was provided by the authorities' commitment to a particular exchange rate. As a result, the future became inherently more uncertain, and less predictable.

7. The perfect foresight model

The previous analysis also makes clear that the perfect foresight model, which has dominated academic thinking about the exchange rate, and which can now be found in most textbooks of international economics, is particularly inappropriate for use as a predictive model. This holds for both the sticky price and for the flexible price version of these models.[12] In the logic of these models, economic agents forecast the future time path of the exchange rate, based on their knowledge of the model and the future path of the exogenous variables. This future exchange rate is then used as an 'anchor' which is telescoped back into the present. Put differently, the exchange rate today must jump to the right initial value so as to bring it on a path leading to the terminal equilibrium value, which agents have computed from their knowledge of the underlying model and their forecast of the future exogenous variables.

---

[12] It also holds true for those rational expectations models which add *ad hoc* stochastic terms in the equations, but are otherwise to be considered as perfect foresight models.

We have argued that in the world as it has evolved since the early 1970s in which the national authorities of the major industrialized countries have dropped practically all commitments in their policy-making, it is impossible to forecast the future course of economic policies. There are just too many courses of action the authorities can take in a commitment-free environment.

The impossibility of forecasting the future also makes it impossible to predict how a current shock, such as a fiscal policy shock, will affect today's exchange rate. The effect of a current shock can only be known if we know how this shock will affect the future path of monetary and fiscal policies. This leads to the situation which we discussed earlier in which similar policy shocks lead to profoundly different effects on the real exchange rates. Each shock seems to be unique in that it has different implications for the exchange rate.

This is a serious problem because it makes it difficult for economic agents to detect the underlying economic model which determines the exchange rate. Each disturbance seems to be unique because it leads to different expectations about how it will affect the future course of economic policies. As a result, economic agents are never able to collect enough data to make a statistical inference.

We can call the uncertainty facing economic agents a two-stage uncertainty. In the first stage, there is uncertainty about how a shock which occurs today will affect future policies. This prevents economic agents from correctly predicting the effects of this current shock, even if they know the underlying economic model determining the exchange rate. In the second stage we have uncertainty because the inability to predict the effects of current shocks in turn prevents economic agents from correctly estimating the underlying economic model.

In such an uncertain environment one is entitled to question the usefulness of perfect foresight models of the exchange rates (including models which assume that the objective probability distribution of disturbances are known to individuals). The poor predictability of the models which use these assumptions indicates that this may not be the right approach in modelling agents' behaviour in an uncertain environment. Fortunately, there exist alternative theories of individual behaviour towards risk which are more satisfactory and which allow us to preserve the basic insights of rational expectations models.

Box 8.3. Capital mobility and policy choices

In this box we show how the free movement of capital makes it possible to increase the policy options of the authorities thereby reducing the predictability of these policies. We use the same two-country model as the one used in this chapter.

Let us assume that the world interest rate is given by the line $p_w p_w$. The domestic interest rate is given by the line $p_d p_d$. The latter is steeper implying that the domestic interest rate exceeds the world interest rate. Capital controls prevent the domestic interest rate from equalizing with the foreign interest rate. The domestic equilibrium is then given by points A and B. A is the production point: given the domestic interest rate, agents will invest an amount of capital goods

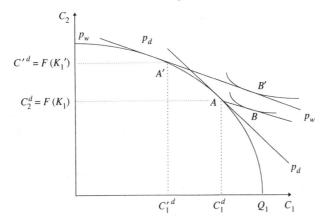

FIG. 8.3. Capital mobility and policy choices

$K_1 = Q_1 - C_1^d$, so that in period 2 they can reach the production level $F(K_1)$. Borrowing in the international capital market can be done at the international interest rate and allows residents to dissociate the consumption path from the production path. This yields the consumption point B. The current account is now given by the horizontal distance between the consumption and the production points.

We should now compare the equilibrium points obtained when capital controls exist with the equilibrium points obtained when capital is freely mobile. In the latter case the foreign and domestic interest rates will coincide. As a result, the production and consumption points become A' and B'. The result is remarkable. The country will now invest more (so as to achieve a higher future output). At the same time consumption increases and so does the current account deficit. Since future output increases (thanks to the higher investment), servicing of the higher foreign debt should be possible. We also observe that domestic welfare improves unambiguously.

Fig. 8.3 also illustrates the point made in this chapter. The free mobility of capital unambiguously increases the consumption possibilities of the country. This can be seen from the fact that the consumption possibilities are given by the line $p_w p_w$. In the case of capital controls, the consumption possibilities are given by the line which is below $p_w p_w$. As a result, the domestic government can move the economy along an expanded consumption possibilities frontier when capital is freely mobile. This creates an enhanced choice of policies.

The Feldstein–Horioka puzzle   There is a widespread consensus that capital is now moving more freely than, say, twenty years ago, and that this increased mobility of capital has contributed to creating a truly integrated world capital market. The paper of Feldstein and Horioka, published in 1980, arguing that the world is still far removed from a truly integrated capital market, and that in fact most national capital markets are still pretty much closed, came as a surprise to many observers. In order to show their point, Feldstein and Horioka regressed cross-section equations explaining the domestic rate of savings by the domestic rate of investment as follows

$$SQ_k = a + bIQ_k + u_k \qquad (8.23)$$

where S_k is the savings rate (savings/GDP) in country k, IQ_k is the investment rate (investment/GDP) in country k, and u_k is an error term.

The hypothesis of perfect capital mobility implies that when a shock occurs in the investment activity in country k (say an increase in IQ_k), the financing of this increased domestic investment will be realized by a capital inflow. The reason is that a slight increase in domestic investment leads to a slight increase in the domestic interest rate. This is sufficient to draw all the foreign capital needed to finance the increased domestic investment. Put differently, when capital is perfectly mobile, domestic savings and investment are uncorrelated. This also implies that b in equation (8.23) is zero. Feldstein and Horioka tested this hypothesis by estimating equation (8.23) for the industrialized countries during the post-war period, and rejected it. They found that b is typically close to 0.8. This means that 80 per cent of domestic investment in the industrialized countries is financed by domestic savings. Only a small fraction of domestic investment, therefore, is financed by foreign capital. Feldstein and Horioka concluded that the integration of the world capital market is still far from being realized. In a recent paper, however, Feldstein (1994) notes that the coefficient b has tended to decline since the 1960s suggesting that capital mobility has increased.

These results of Feldstein and Horioka led to a burgeoning literature (for a survey, see Frankel (1992)). Much of the initial response was to criticize the econometrics of equation (8.23). For example, it was pointed out that savings and investment are interdependent, so that a simultaneous equation bias occurs when estimating (8.23) by ordinary least squares. Estimating equation (8.23) by simultaneous equations methods, however, did not significantly change the conclusion: the coefficient b remained large. On the whole one can say that the many additional econometric studies have left the main result of Feldstein and Horioka untouched.

There is a more serious criticism that can be levied against the Feldstein and Horioka study, however. This is that estimating equation (8.23) is not a good test of capital mobility. For it can be shown that in a world of perfect capital mobility b will be close to one if savings and investment are influenced by the same exogenous shocks. Take a productivity shock for example. We use the two-country model of this chapter, and assume perfect capital market integration which implies that domestic and foreign interest rates coincide (see Fig. 8.4). We represent the productivity shock by the outward movement of the production possibility frontier. We now observe the following. Before the productivity shock, domestic investment was $Q_1 - C_1^d$ and domestic saving $Q_1 - C_1$. After the productivity shock, both domestic investment and savings increase. Thus, one can conclude that if savings and investment are influenced by the same disturbances (e.g. productivity shocks), they will be positively correlated, even if capital is perfectly mobile. Regressing an equation like (8.3) on the observed savings and investment rates will produce a high b. This cannot be considered as evidence of the lack of capital market integration.

The study of Feldstein and Horioka has certainly been helpful in the empirical analysis of the degree of capital mobility. It has also led to a more balanced view concerning the degree of capital market integration in the world.

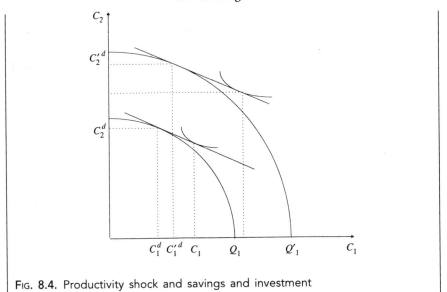

FIG. 8.4. Productivity shock and savings and investment

APPENDIX. RISK PREMIUMS IN THE MUNDELL–FLEMING MODEL

Instead of assuming interest parity as we have done up to now, we start from the following more general interest rate equation:

$$r = r_f + \mu + \pi$$

where μ was defined as the expected rate of depreciation of the domestic currency. We have now added a term π, the risk premium on domestic assets. In the previous analysis we assumed this risk premium always to be equal to zero. We can also rewrite this equation as follows:

$$\pi = r - (r_f + \mu).$$

It follows that π can be interpreted as the excess return on the domestic assets (if π is positive). If π is negative there is excess return on the foreign asset.

What are the determinants of this risk premium? Many factors may influence the risk premium. Here we concentrate on government debt.

An increase in the government budget deficit increases the amount of domestic government debt to be held by private economic agents. This leads to an increase in risk. We can distinguish three kinds of risk.

First, there is a diversification risk. This arises because economic agents now have to hold a higher proportion of their wealth in the form of domestic government bonds. As a result, they will have a less diversified portfolio. In general, they will want to obtain an additional return (risk premium) to be compensated. Note that this is the same risk premium as the one we analysed in the portfolio balance model.

A second source of risk is the one we stressed in the discussion of this chapter. The fiscal policy shock today affects the whole future path of government debt. Economic agents, however, are uncertain what this path will look like. One scenario could be a protracted increase of the debt in the future, until at a certain point hard measures will have to be taken, including possibly default. Other scenarios could be less apocalyptic. In fact, it is possible that the fiscal impetus is associated with higher government revenues in the future because it stimulates investment and future productive capacity. This risk premium may therefore be positive or negative.

The third source of risk is the inflation risk. It arises because the future debt accumulation may put pressure on the authorities to monetize the debt. This would tend to increase inflation in the future and will reduce the real value of the debt. Economic agents will only want to hold additional government bonds if they are compensated for this risk by an additional premium.

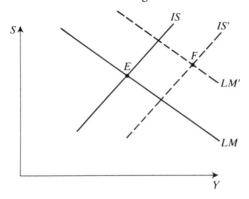

FIG. **A8.1.** Effect of fiscal policy

We can now introduce this theory of the risk premium into our analysis. This is done in Fig. A8.1. We show the same *IS–LM* framework as in Chapter 6. (Note that the exchange rate, and not the interest rate, is on the vertical axis.) A fiscal expansion shifts the *IS* curve to the right, to the new position *IS′*. At the same time it affects the risk premium. Let us assume that the risk premium is positively affected. This affects the *IS–LM* model as follows.

By increasing the domestic interest rate, it leads to an excess supply of money. In order for this excess supply of money to be absorbed, either output must increase or the exchange rate must increase (thereby increasing the domestic price level). Therefore, the *LM* curve shifts to the right, to *LM′*.

The outcome of these shifts is shown in Fig. A8.1. Initially, the economy is at point *E*. After the fiscal expansion, and taking into account the positive risk premium effect, the economy moves to point *F*. The effect on the exchange rate is ambiguous, and will depend on the strength of the risk premium effect.

This analysis can also be used to analyse the effects of an oil price increase (see Fig. A8.2). As we have seen earlier, the macroeconomic effect of an oil price increase is to shift the *IS* curve to the left. Such an oil price increase will generally also lead to a current account deficit. Therefore, foreign residents will be asked to hold more domestic debt. The same theory of the risk premium can be applied here. Foreign residents face a diversification risk, a risk related to the future time path of domestic debt, and an inflation risk. The strength of this risk premium effect will determine any further shifts in the *LM* curve. The *LM* curve shifts to the right because the higher interest rate leads to an excess supply of money. Thus, the risk premium effect tends to accentuate the depreciation of the currency.

When we want to compare two oil consuming countries, however (for example, the US and Japan), the previous analysis makes clear that there is little we will be able to say about the dollar/yen rate. Even if the initial deflationary effect on the US is lower than in Japan, which may lead to the conclusion that the dollar will appreciate relative to the yen, this conclusion may no longer hold when one takes into account the risk premiums in both countries. For example, economic agents may expect a quicker turnaround of the initial current account deficit in Japan than in the US, thereby generating a lower risk premium in Japan than in the US. As a result, the need for the yen to depreciate

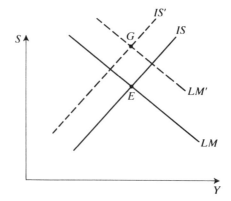

<small>FIG. A8.2. Effect of oil shock</small>

relative to the currency of the oil producer may be less pronounced than in the case of the dollar. As the future policy reactions of the US and the Japanese authorities are impossible to predict, it is almost impossible to predict how an increase (or a decline) in oil prices is going to affect the dollar/yen exchange rate.

This theoretical analysis also helps to understand why so little systematic relationship was found between oil price changes and the price of the dollar relative to other currencies.

9

RATIONAL BEHAVIOUR IN AN UNCERTAIN WORLD

1. Introduction

In the previous chapter we argued that the nature of the uncertainty is such that the equilibrium values of exchange rates cannot be known with much precision. And contrary to what one could have expected, there has been no learning curve in exchange rate forecasting. As a result, forward prices are now less of a guide for economic agents than at the outset of the floating exchange rate system.

An important implication of all this is that the simple perfect foresight rational expectations model we relied on to explain the volatility of exchange rates, is not very useful. The idea that economic agents compute a future exchange rate based on a model they believe in, and then telescope it back into the present, is of little use in a world where economic agents have great difficulty in working out what the true model of the world is, and where this uncertainty about the true model is itself the result of flexible exchange rates.

It is time to reformulate a theory of how speculators behave in such an environment. This will allow us to develop a different modelling approach, which we hope will be more successful in explaining some basic empirical phenomena. The model will be based on the concept of 'near-rationality' (limited rationality).

Box 9.1. The micro-foundations of near-rational behaviour

In this section we present a model based on individual utility maximization. This model provides the foundation for the behaviour of individuals which will be assumed in the next section.

Assume a risk-averse speculator who takes a forward position in a foreign currency. His expected profit is

$$E(\tilde{S} - F_0)W - C \tag{9.1}$$

where $\tilde{S}$ is the uncertain future exchange rate; F_0 is the current (forward) exchange rate; W is the forward purchase (sale) of the foreign currency. W can be positive or negative depending on whether the speculator buys or sells forward. It will

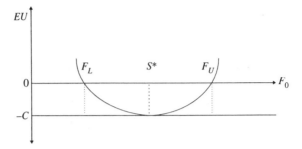

FIG. 9.1. Expected utility

be assumed that $\tilde{S}$ is normally distributed with a mean $S*$, and a variance σ^2. C is the cost of making the forecast. It will be assumed that this information cost is constant (i.e. independent of the size of the speculative position W). It will also be assumed that each time the speculator changes his speculative position, W, he makes a new forecast at the same fixed cost C. This cost may be thought of as the fee paid to consultants engaged in the forecasting business.

Assuming a utility function with a constant absolute risk aversion we obtain the following expression for the expected utility of the speculator:

$$U = E(\tilde{S} - F_0)W - C - (R/2)\,\mathrm{var}(\,(\tilde{S} - F_0)W\,) \qquad (9.2)$$

where R is the degree of absolute risk aversion, which is assumed to be constant. The first order conditions for an optimum are given by

$$(S* - F_0) - R\sigma^2 W = 0 \qquad (9.3)$$

This yields the following expression for the optimal forward position of the speculator

$$W = \frac{S* - F_0}{R\sigma^2}. \qquad (9.4)$$

This is the standard, and well-known, expression of the optimal portfolio in a mean variance framework. The optimal speculative position depends positively on the difference between the expected future exchange rate and the current forward rate, and negatively on the variance of the expected return.

We can now substitute W from (9.4) into the utility function to obtain the expected utility of the optimal portfolio:

$$EU = \frac{(S* - F_0)^2}{2R\sigma^2} - C. \qquad (9.5)$$

Equation (9.5) is represented graphically in Fig. 9.1. On the vertical axis we set out the expected utility EU; on the horizontal axis the current forward rate F_0. EU is a quadratic function. When $S* = F_0$ it is equal to $-C$. As the current rate deviates from the expected rate the expected utility gain from taking a short or long position increases in a non-linear way.

A first characteristic of the expected utility is its non-linearity. As a result, around the point where the current rate equals the expected rate ($S* = F_0$) the function is almost flat. One can say that the gains are then of second order.

A second characteristics of the expected utility has to do with the variance (σ^2) of the estimated exchange rate. When this variance increases, the expected gain declines and the function becomes flatter around the point $S* = F_0$. Thus, when the precision of the estimation of the future exchange rate declines (for example, because of increasing uncertainty), the utility gains from taking a speculative position decline.

The horizontal line $-C$ represents the fixed information cost C of changing the speculative position W. We now obtain the following result. When the expected gain from the speculative position (the first term in (9.5)) is lower than the information cost C, speculators will not change their position as long as the change in the expected future exchange rate is small enough. To see this, suppose that the current and the expected exchange rates initially coincide. An exogenous disturbance changes the current rate. If this change is small, i.e. if it remains within the bounds given by $F_L F_U$, it will not be worthwhile for economic agents to engage in a new fore-casting exercise that could lead to a change in their portfolio. We will call the range $F_L F_U$, a range of 'agnosticism'. Not in the sense that economic agents have no view of what the future exchange rate will be, but in the sense that they do not make new forecasts each time they observe a change of the current rate, as long as these changes are small enough.

It should be stressed that although the cost of obtaining information may be relatively small, these small costs may still result in a relatively large band of 'agnosticism'. This has to do with the non-linearity of the expected utility. The near flatness of this function around the equilibrium point $S* = F_0$ makes a relatively large band of agnosticism possible even if the information costs are of a second order magnitude. In a sense one can say that when the exchange rate moves within this band of agnosticism, the economic agent rationally decides not to use all available, but costly, information in order to find out whether the equilibrium exchange rate has changed. Such a behaviour has also been called 'near-rational'.[1]

An important implication of the previous analysis is the following. When the precision of the estimation of the future exchange rate declines (σ^2 increases), the range of 'agnosticism' increases. We show this in Fig. 9.2. The increase in σ^2 makes the expected utility curve flatter. With a given information cost, the range between which it will not be worthwhile to change a forward position increases from $F_L F_U$ to $F_L' F_U'$.

It may be useful to obtain an idea of the possible order of magnitude of the band of agnosticism. Equation (9.5) can help us to derive some numerical estimates of this band. We find that if

$$(S* - F_0)^2 \leq 2R\sigma^2 C$$

---

[1] The concept of near-rationality has been used by (among others) George Akerlof and Janet Yellen (1987) to argue that economic agents quite often deviate from full rational optimizing behaviour, because such behaviour does not lead to significant losses. See also Mankiw (1985) for an application in the context of imperfect competition. The existence of small 'menu' costs, even if they are of a second order of magnitude, will prevent firms from changing their price when shocks in demand occur.

or

$$S^* - F_0 \leq \pm \sigma \sqrt{(2RC)} \qquad (9.6)$$

speculators will not find it attractive to re-evaluate their estimate of the equilibrium exchange rate S^*. Thus, (9.6) is an expression of the band of agnosticism (the algebraic counterpart of $F_L F_U$ in Fig. 9.1). We can now use (9.6) to obtain a numerical estimate of the width of the band. We need information about the conditional standard deviation σ, the information cost C, and the degree of risk aversion R.

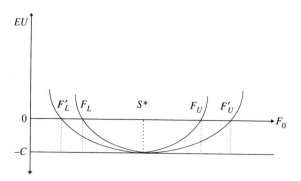

FIG. 9.2. Increasing uncertainty

Estimates of the conditional standard deviations[2] can be obtained from the results of Meese and Rogoff discussed in Chapter 7 (see Table 7.1). These results give us the size of the forecast errors when speculators use an economic model to estimate the fundamental exchange rate. Assume that the forecasting horizon is one year, then we find from that table that the conditional standard deviation is on average 18 per cent. As a measure of risk aversion we take a value $R = 2$ which is an estimate often found (see Goodhart (1988)). We have no direct estimate of the information cost C. However, what we can do is to assume different values of C and compute the implied band of agnosticism. The results are given in Table 9.1.

TABLE 9.1. *Estimates of the band of agnosticism*

Information cost (per cent)	Band of agnosticism (per cent)
0.05	16
0.1	22
0.2	32
0.3	39

[2] The conditional standard deviation measures the unexpected component of the changes in the exchange rate. Such a measure is obtained by first forecasting the exchange rate using all available information. The standard deviation of the forecast error is then a measure of the conditional standard deviation.

We observe that with relatively small information costs we still obtain sizeable bands of agnosticism. To give an example. Suppose the information cost amounts to only 0.1 per cent of the size of the speculative positions then (given the assumed values of R and σ) the implied band of agnosticism is 22 per cent. That is, the exchange rates can fluctuate within a band of 22 per cent around the rationally expected exchange rate $S*$ and yet not lead speculators to re-estimate that equilibrium exchange rate. In this sense it can be said that information costs that appear to be trivially small can still produce sizeable bands of agnosticism when the uncertainty about the true underlying exchange rate is large enough.

2. Exchange rates and limited rationality

Let us assume that there is a range within which economic agents are 'agnostic' about the precise value of the future exchange rate. (See Box 9.1 for the microeconomic foundations of this assumption.) By agnostic we mean here not that speculators have no view about what the underlying fundamental exchange rate is. They may or may not have one. The important point is that they do not find it worthwhile to re-estimate continuously the fundamental exchange rate when the observed exchange rate is changing. In a very uncertain environment such a continuous recomputing does not lead to appreciable utility gains given that the cost of information is not zero. As a result, it is as if speculators are agnostic (within a certain range) about the underlying equilibrium exchange rate.

The foregoing assumptions have important implications for the theory of exchange rate determination. We illustrate this in Figs 9.3 and 9.4 where we plot today's exchange rate and the expected exchange rate for the next period, together with the path linking these two values.

In Fig. 9.3 we represent the perfect foresight model. Economic agents forecast a future exchange rate $(E_t S_{t+1})$ based on a model and their forecast of the future exogenous variable. The interest parity condition then allows us to telescope this future rate to the present (S_t). We have

$$S_t = \frac{1+r}{1+r_f} E_t (S_{t+1})$$

where r is the domestic interest rate and r_f is the foreign interest rate. The spot rate will have to jump to the value S_t to be consistent with the forecast and the implied model.

In Fig. 9.4 the model of 'near-rationality' is represented. The range of agnosticism is represented by the line segment $E(S_L)E(S_U)$. The line segment $E(S_L)E(S_U)$ corresponds to the range of forward exchange rates between $F_L F_U$ in Fig. 9.1.

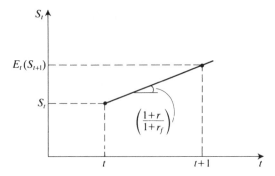

FIG. **9.3.** The perfect foresight model

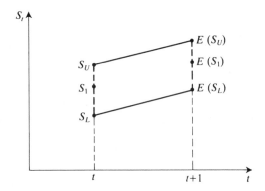

FIG. **9.4.** The near-rational model

Since $E(S_L)$ and $E(S_U)$ are the extreme values of the expected range of future exchange rates, we can telescope these back to the present, using the same interest parity condition. This yields the range $S_L S_U$.

In a full rational expectations model, economic agents would have computed the mathematical expectation of the future exchange rate, which lies somewhere between $E(S_U)$ and $E(S_L)$, say at $E(S_1)$. This then would have pinned down the present exchange rate at S_1. This fully rational behaviour ensures that expected profits will be maximized.

In the uncertain environment considered here, choosing an exchange rate other than S_1 will do almost equally well in terms of the expected utility of speculative gains, as long as the exchange rate which is selected is in the neighbourhood of the mathematically expected exchange rate (represented by the range between S_U and S_L). Selecting another such exchange rate can be called *near-rational*.

The question now is what decision criterion agents will follow to select one of the many possible exchange rates. Some decision rule will have to be followed.

The literature on near-rationality suggests several rules. One is that when the environment is extremely uncertain, economic agents allow themselves to be guided by the initial values of the price when deciding on the best price (exchange rate). These function as 'anchors' in individuals' judgement of the optimal price (exchange rate) (see Ackerlof and Yellen (1987)).

A second decision rule, which will be analysed here in greater detail, is based on 'herding' behaviour. This consists in following the behaviour of others. When the economic model underlying the exchange rate is extremely uncertain agents may decide to follow the lead of other agents. The latter are assumed to have some information not possessed by the former. The best way to know how the other agents behave is to observe the movements of the exchange rate itself. In addition, the information embodied in these exchange rate movements is public and freely available.

We now come to the following view about how speculators behave in a near-rational world. Speculators use two kinds of information. One is costly and is based on a 'fundamental' analysis, i.e. on using a model of the exchange market and on a forecast of the underlying fundamental variables. Speculators, however, choose not to re-estimate the fundamental exchange rate continuously. In an extremely uncertain environment the gains from such continuous optimizing behaviour are small compared to the costs of collecting the information. Only when the current exchange rate departs sufficiently from the (previously) estimated fundamental exchange rate will the speculator find it worthwhile to re-estimate the fundamental exchange rate. When these departures are small, speculators will use observed movements in the exchange rate as their information set to forecast the future exchange rate. These observed movements are interpreted by speculators as the result of information other market participants possess. Since this information is in the public domain it can be used freely. Recently, theoretical models have been developed in which such herding behaviour is formalized (see Hirschleifer and Welch (1995); Devenow and Welch (1996)). We will come back to such a model and show that the dynamics it generates is surprisingly complex.

In this context, it can be argued that *technical analysis* is a similar (near-rational) decision rule whereby agents observe the movements in the market as a way to extract information about what other operators do. Technical analysis (sometimes also called chartism) has become a widely used practice in forecasting exchange rates. It implies the use of techniques which aim at extrapolating some systematic tendency observed in past and present exchange rates. These rules can be relatively simple such as moving averages, or can be based on more complex models (ARIMA or other time series models). Despite the fact that it is much frowned upon by economists, technical analysis can be considered as a set of near-rational rules of behaviour. These rules of behaviour are 'near-rational' responses by economic agents to the fact that economic models do not provide reliable information to forecast the future.[3]

---

[3] See Rosenberg (1996) for an explanation of widely used methods of technical analysis.

3. How is the spot exchange rate determined in a near-rational world?

The assumptions embodied in the previous sections about how economic agents set their expectations in an uncertain environment allows us to sketch a model of how the spot exchange rate is determined.

We consider the spot exchange rate as the outcome of current events in the foreign exchange market and of expectations about the future exchange rate. More formally, we have an equation

$$S_t = aZ_t + bE_t\Delta S_{t+1} \tag{9.7}$$

where S_t is the current exchange rate; Z_t is a vector of exogenous variables which affect the demand and the supply of foreign currency today; $E_t\Delta S_{t+1}$ is the expected rate of depreciation. Note that this equation was also used as the starting-point of a perfect foresight rational expectations model (see Chapter 8). The expected rate of depreciation then had to be determined in a forward looking manner based on a forecast of the future exogenous variables Z_t.[4]

Here we assume, on the contrary, that in order to set their expectations about the future, economic agents use a combination of a backward-looking and a forward-looking rule. That is, when the exchange rate is within the margin of agnosticism (the range between S_L and S_U in Fig. 9.4), the past and present movements of the exchange rates will drive expectations in the market. In other words technical analysis or chartism (a backward-looking rule) is the only information speculators find worthwhile to use. When, however, the exchange rate is driven outside this range, i.e. when it becomes clear that the exchange rate is deviating sufficiently strongly from the previously estimated equilibrium exchange rate, it is worthwhile again to re-estimate this 'fundamental' exchange rate. As a result, the forward-looking rational expectations behaviour then tends to dominate the market's expectation. We can specify such a rule in very general terms as follows:[5]

$$E_t\Delta S_{t+1} = m\left(\sum_{i=0}^{n} c_i \Delta S_{t-i}\right) + (1 - m)(S^* - S_t) \tag{9.8}$$

The first term on the right-hand side of equation (9.8) is the backward-looking rule. It says that the expected depreciation of the exchange rate $(E_t\Delta S_{t+1})$ is some average of past and present rates of depreciation. The exact nature of that rule is determined by the coefficients c_i. These can be positive, negative, or zero. If they are positive, we have extrapolation of past and present rates of depreciation. If negative, economic agents expect a regression, i.e. a depreciation is

---

[4] See Mussa (1976), and Frenkel (1976).
[5] For previous formulations of such rules see P. De Grauwe (1983), and Frenkel and Froot (1986a). It will be shown, however, that the rule proposed by the latter is different in a fundamental sense from the one proposed here.

followed by appreciation and vice versa. Finally, if these coefficients are zero, the exchange rate is expected to follow a random walk. This backward-looking term in equation (9.8) is given a weight m. (We shall come back to the problem of how this weight is determined.)

The second term in equation (9.8) is the forward-looking component (multiplied by the weight $1 - m$). It says that economic agents will adjust the expected rate of depreciation when the current exchange rate is perceived to deviate from the equilibrium exchange rate S^*, as determined by an underlying model. More precisely, when the current exchange rate is perceived to be above/below this equilibrium rate economic agents expect the future exchange rate to go down/increase.

The weights given to these two expectation rules are determined by the parameter m. This parameter is itself a function of the degree to which the exchange rate deviates from the equilibrium. If the exchange rate is within the 'band of agnosticism', m will be close to 1. That is, economic agents give no (or almost no) weight to fundamentals and underlying economic models. The backward-looking rule dominates expectations formation. We have called this 'near-rational' behaviour.

When, however, the exchange rate deviates sufficiently from the equilibrium level, the parameter m declines, thereby increasing the weight given to the second term in equation (9.8).

In the next section we use the expectational assumption of equation (9.8) in a very simple exchange rate model. It will be shown that such a model is capable of producing a very complex dynamics of the exchange rate movements that comes surprisingly close to mimicking real life exchange rate changes.

4. Chaos in the foreign exchange markets

The basic ingredients of the model are very similar to the Dornbusch model which was discussed in Chapter 5. As will be remembered, a first building block is the money market equilibrium condition (money demand equals money supply). Second, open interest parity ensures that expected returns on domestic and foreign assets are equalized. The interest rate and the exchange rate adjust instantaneously so as to clear the money market and to maintain interest parity. Third, in the goods market prices are sticky. In the long run, however, they adjust so as to make purchasing power parity possible.

The point where we deviate from the Dornbusch model is in the formulation of expectations. Instead of assuming perfect foresight, we incorporate the expectational assumption as given in equation (9.8). We implement this as follows. In the simple Dornbusch model used here, the equilibrium (fundamental) exchange rate is the PPP value of the exchange rate. Thus, according to equation (9.8), when speculators observe a market rate above/below the PPP rate they expect it to decline/increase in the future. We also assume the rate at

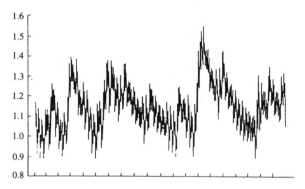

<small>Fɪɢ. **9.5.** Simulated exchange rate</small>

which they expect the exchange rate to return to its fundamental PPP value is related to the speed at which prices in the goods market adjust. When the exchange rate is close to the PPP value, the weight given to this 'fundamental' analysis is low. In the neighbourhood of the equilibrium rate, near-rational behaviour will dominate the market. We will also call this 'chartist' behaviour. This behaviour is characterized by extrapolations of past exchange rate movements (backward looking rules). We use simple moving average models. (The detail of this fundamentalist and the chartist behaviour is presented in an appendix, when we also discuss the full model.)

The essential difference between the 'fundamentalist' and the 'chartist' behaviour is that the former is forward looking in forecasting the exchange rate, while the latter is backward looking. It is this difference that drives most of the results of this model.

The central result of this model is that it is capable of generating complex (chaotic) behaviour by the exchange rate (in Box 9.2 we present some notions of chaos theory).[6] Two aspects of chaotic behaviour should be stressed here. First, the behaviour is 'aperiodic', i.e. the model generates cycles in the exchange rate, each of which, however, is unique. It is as if each cycle is driven by a unique set of variables. Second, the behaviour is characterized by extreme sensitivity to initial conditions (the 'butterfly' effect). Small disturbances in the initial conditions lead to a completely different future path for the exchange rate. All this implies that the exchange rate will exhibit a very complex pattern, which cannot easily be predicted, despite the simple nature of the underlying model. Put differently, knowledge of the underlying model and its exogenous variables will not help much in making good forecasts of the exchange rate.

We illustrate these features in Figs 9.5 and 9.6. These exhibit simulations of the exchange rate using the model described earlier, and assigning numerical values to the parameters (see De Grauwe, *et al.* (1993)). In addition, we assume

---

[6] In De Grauwe, *et al.* (1993) a more detailed analysis is provided.

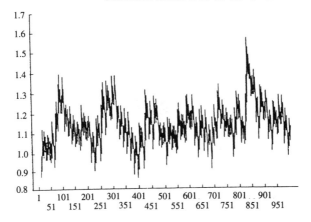

FIG. **9.6.** Simulated exchange rate (small difference in initial conditions)
Source: P. De Grauwe, *et al.* (1993), 145

that the exogenous variables (for example, the money stock) are constant through-out the simulations. Thus, the exchange rate movements are not produced by exogenous disturbances. Also, the only difference between the two simulations is a small change (1 per cent) in the initial value of the exchange rate. Apart from this difference, the same model is used, and the same (constant) values are given to the exogenous variables of the model.

We observe several features of the dynamics of the exchange rate move-ments. First, these movements show a complex pattern with many 'rallies' of the exchange rate in one or the other direction. Second, the movements of the exchange rate are unrelated to movements of the underlying fundamental vari-ables, since these are kept constant all the time. It looks as if exchange rate move-ments have a life of their own. This feature comes from the speculative dynamics in which sometimes speculation uses forward-looking rules, and at other times backward-looking rules. Third, the sensitivity to initial conditions shows in the difference of the time pattern of the exchange rate in the two figures. We observe that small differences in initial conditions can generate very different timing for the ups and downs of the exchange rate. Note, however, that these differences do not affect the qualitative nature of the exchange rate dynamics. (The latter shows up in the fact that the phase diagrams of the two time series in Figs 9.5 and 9.6 are identical (see Fig. 9.7).)

The preceding evidence suggests that a relatively simple 'non-linear' monetary model is capable of generating a complex dynamics of exchange rate movements in which the latter, as a rule, are disconnected from the movements of the fun-damental variables. This feature creates the impression that the exchange rate is continuously shocked by disturbances in the fundamental variables ('news'), although no shocks occur. This result is related to the fact that the model does not have a unique solution. Rather it produces a 'strange attractor', which defines the space within which the exchange rate moves in an erratic way.

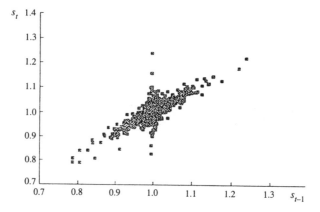

FIG. **9.7.** Phase diagram of the model in the $S_t - S_{t-1}$ space
Source: P. De Grauwe, *et al.* (1993), 136

In reality, 'news' of course does occur. It is, therefore, interesting to analyse the workings of the model when shocks in the fundamental variables (for example, money stock) occur. There is another reason why 'news' matters. As will be made clear in the next section, the movements in the fundamental variables affect the strange attractor, and therefore the long-run movements of the exchange rate.

Box 9.2. Some notions of chaos theory

The theory of chaotic behaviour has become quite popular in recent years. It has been applied in many scientific fields including economics. The basic idea is very simple. The implementation is much more difficult. The idea is as follows. Relatively simple non-linear models are capable of producing extremely complex behaviour of the endogenous variables of the model. Let us take an example, the so-called logistic model. This model has its origin in the biological sciences and describes the growth dynamics of a population:

$$x_t = b\, x_{t-1}(1 - x_{t-1}) \tag{9.9}$$

where x_t is a normalized population that takes values between 0 and 1.
   We can also rewrite this equation as follows

$$x_t = b\, x_{t-1} - b(x_{t-1})^2. \tag{9.10}$$

   We observe that population in period t is driven by two terms, a linear term and a non-linear one. The linear one expresses the fact that a high population in the previous period leads to a high population today (for the simple reason that there will be many births today). The second non-linear term expresses the phenomenon that a high population in the previous period will deplete natural resources thereby leading to starvation and thus less population today.
   A steady state solution is found by setting $x_t = x_{t-1}$ and solving

$$x^* = b\, x^* (1 - x^*). \tag{9.11}$$

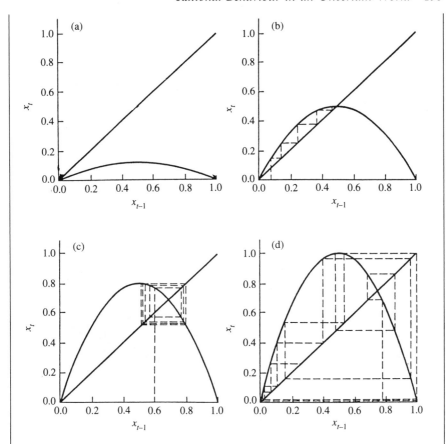

FIG. 9.8. Chaos and the logistic model

This yields two solutions, the trivial one $x^* = 0$, and $x^* = 1 - 1/b$.

The dynamics of this model can be very complex. In order to analyse these dynamics we use the phase diagram of the model, which is constructed as follows. We set out x_t on the vertical axis, and x_{t-1} on the horizontal axis. The non-linear relationship is the graphical representation of logistic equation (9.9). The equilibrium is obtained when $x^* = x_t = x_{t-1}$. This is obtained at the inter-section of the non-linear relationship and the 45 degree line.

We show the solution and the dynamics of the model for different values of b (see Fig. 9.8a–d). For $0 < b < 1$ the mapping will always converge to $x^* = 0$ (see Fig. 9.8a). For $1 < b < 3$ the mapping yields a steady state solution $x^* = 1 - 1/b$ (see Fig. 9.8b for the example $b = 2$). Note that in this case only the solution $x^* = 1 - 1/b$ is stable; the solution $x^* = 0$ is unstable.

The dynamics of the model gets more complicated when $3 < b < 4$. Two cases arise. When $3 < b < 3.45$ we obtain a limit cycle solution (in our case a two-cycle). This means that the solution for x will oscillate between two values x_1^* and x_2^*. What has happened here is that the second solution of the mapping has

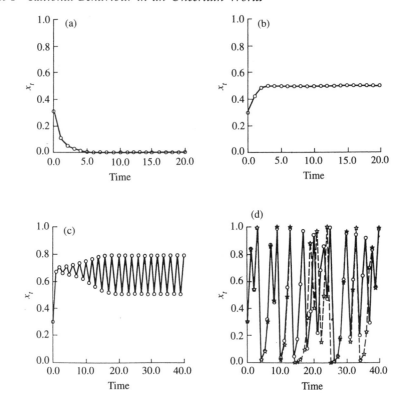

FIG. **9.9.** The logistic model in the time domain

become unstable as soon as b exceeds 3. Such a change in the stability behaviour of the solution is called a *bifurcation*. For larger values of b the two-cycle becomes unstable and one observes the development of a four-cycle, eight-cycle, sixteen-cycle, and so on. It has been shown by Feigenbaum that this cascade of bifurcations stops when b reaches the value of 3.570. For $b > 3.570$ the dynamics becomes even more complex. We enter the chaotic region (see Fig. 9.8d).

In Fig. 9.9a–d we show the dynamics of x_t in the time domain corresponding to the different values of b used in Fig. 9.8a–d. We observe that in Fig. 9.9d ($b > 3.57$) the behaviour of x_t becomes very complex and that it has the appearance of being unpredictable, despite the fact that the underlying model is deterministic. In Fig. 9.9d we also show the effect of a small change in the initial conditions on the time path of x_t. We observe that after a short period the new time series of x_t tends to diverge from the initial one.

From the example of the logistic model some aspects of chaotic behaviour can be distilled.

- In the chaotic regime seemingly random, or highly irregular, signals are produced from a completely deterministic process.
- In a chaotic regime there is *sensitivity to initial conditions*. This means that small initial disturbances can completely change the time path of x_t. Sen-

sitivity to initial conditions does not mean that we cannot predict the outcome of a chaotic system. It means that we can predict the results for a relatively short period only. It should be stressed that the sensitivity to initial conditions does not affect the overall dynamic behaviour of the system (represented by the phase space).

- The chaotic regime is associated with the existence of a strange attractor, i.e. the phase space shows a figure or distribution of points that is characterized by a fractal or non-integer dimension.[7]

The chaotic exchange rate model developed in this chapter has the same qualitative structure as the logistic model discussed here. The logistic model is driven by a positive feedback rule (the positive linear term in equation (9.10)) and a negative feedback rule (the negative quadratic term in equation (9.10)). The first one is a source of instability (explosive behaviour), the second one tends to bring the population variable back to the equilibrium value. This combination of positive and negative feedback is at the root of chaotic behaviour. In our exchange rate model we have a similar structure. The chartist behaviour is like a positive feedback rule which is a source of instability. The fundamentalist behaviour works like a negative feedback rule and is a source of stability in the model as it tends to drive the exchange rate back to its equilibrium value. The interaction of chartist and fundamentalist behaviour then produces the chaotic dynamics.

5. Chaos and news

In this and the following paragraphs we analyse the behaviour of the model when stochastic shocks occur in one of the exogenous variables. We will limit ourselves to an analysis of 'news' in the domestic money stock. Most of the results discussed in this section carry through when disturbances occur in other exogenous variables.

We assume that the stochastic process driving the domestic money stock is a random walk, and we feed this random walk into the model. As an example, we present the simulated exchange rate and the domestic money stock in the time domain in Fig. 9.10.

As can be seen, over a time horizon of 1,000 periods, the correlation between the exchange rate and the domestic money stock (the fundamental) is quite close. A simple regression analysis confirms this (see Table 9.2). From this table we also find the theoretically expected value of the parameter of the money stock. This is equal to 1, as the theory predicts, i.e. a 1 per cent increase in the money stock leads to a depreciation of the currency by 1 per cent. (Note that in all these simulations the foreign money stock is kept unchanged.)

Suppose now that a researcher who wants to know the underlying structural relationship between the money stock and the exchange rate, has at his disposal a much shorter sample period, say fifty periods. He then uses regression analysis to detect this relationship. How well will he do?

---

[7] There are other properties of chaotic systems that are discussed in De Grauwe, *et al.* (1993).

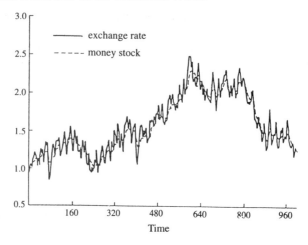

FIG. 9.10. Exchange rate and domestic money stock
Source: P. De Grauwe, *et al.* (1993), 157

TABLE 9.2. *Regression of the exchange rate on the domestic money stock (1,000 observations)*

Constant	Money stock	rho	R^2	DW
0.02	0.99	0.91	0.99	1.3
(0.5)	(32.8)	(70.3)		

TABLE 9.3. *Regression of the exchange rate on the money stock (50 observations)*

	Constant	Money stock	rho	R^2	DW
Sample period: 900–950					
	0.00	0.97	0.83	0.85	0.9
	(0.0)	(3.6)	(12.9)		
Sample period: 950–1000					
	0.46	0.65	0.90	0.9	1.4
	(1.4)	(2.7)	(12.6)		
Sample period: 1000–1050					
	–0.12	1.07	0.91	0.93	1.2
	(–0.4)	(5.0)	(15.2)		

In Table 9.3 we present the results of regressing the simulated exchange rate on the money stock using small sample periods of fifty periods. A first thing to observe is the substantial variability of the coefficient of the money stock for these different sample periods. This has to do with the fact that the chaotic model produces a lot of endogenous noise. This can also be seen from Fig. 9.11

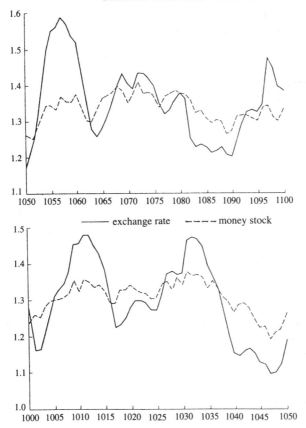

FIG. 9.11. Exchange rate and money stock
Source: P. De Grauwe, *et al.* (1993), 159

which shows the exchange rate and the money stock during these small sample periods. One observes that, although in the long run there is a relatively close fit between the exchange rate and the money stock, in the short run this relationship is weak. The variability of the exchange rate is much larger than that of the underlying money stock, and many of the cyclical movements of the exchange rate are not explained by the movements of the money stock.

Note that this feature has also been observed in empirical studies of the relation between money stock and the exchange rate. Over a sufficiently long period of time the correlation between exchange rate and money stocks (and for that matter price levels also) tends to be relatively strong. This strong link tends to disappear over shorter periods.

The next step in the analysis consisted of asking the question how well a forecaster would fare if he were to use the estimated equations of Table 9.3 to forecast the exchange rate out of sample. Does knowledge of the underlying stochastic process of the domestic money stock allow him to make good forecasts?

TABLE **9.4**. *RMSEs of forecasts with structural models and with random walk (in per cent)*

	Structural model	Random walk
Period 950–1000	7.9	4.2
Period 1000–1050	9.2	3.9
Period 1050–1100	11.6	4.4

(Note that this was also the question Meese and Rogoff asked in their celebrated empirical study of exchange rates.)

We analyse this question by comparing the 'out-of-sample' forecasts, using the regression models of Table 9.3, with a simple random walk forecast. The latter forecasts next period's exchange rate to be equal to the current exchange rate. The results are presented in Table 9.4, which shows the root mean squared errors (RMSE) of these forecasts. We observe that the RMSEs of the simple random walk forecasts are much smaller than the forecasts based on the regression models. It should also be noted that the latter assume that the forecaster knows the value of future exogenous variables exactly. Thus, even if the forecasters know the future value of the money stock, the use of a structural model leads to inferior forecasts compared to the random walk model which does not use that information. Note that we obtain this result despite the fact that there is no exogenous noise in the model. The forecaster uses the correct future values of the domestic money stock. And yet this knowledge does not help him to predict how the exchange rate will move.

Our results have the following interpretation. The complex dynamics of the chaotic model has the effect of obscuring the transmission of the exogenous money shocks to the exchange rate. It is as if the chaotic model works as a scrambling device which erases the short-term influences of money shocks. (This feature is related to the sensitivity to initial conditions.) At the same time, however, the monetary disturbance shifts the position of the strange attractor, so that permanent monetary shocks will affect the level of the exchange rate *on average*. Thus, 'in the long run' (i.e. if we have enough observations to eliminate the endogenous noise created by the speculative dynamics) permanent shocks in the money stock affect the exchange rate.

This difficulty in the use of structural models to explain and to predict exchange rates has been widely observed in reality.[8] Our model gives an explanation for this result. This explanation is not based on the possibility that the researcher uses the wrong structural model. In our analysis the regressions were based on the correct monetary model. Nor is the explanation to be found in exogenous noise. In our experiments the forecaster uses the correct values of all exogenous variables, and yet this does not help him to predict the short-term effects of these exogenous shocks. The factor that obscures the relationship

---

[8] See Meese and Rogoff (1983).

between the money stock and the exchange rate is the speculative dynamics which introduces a complex (chaotic) behaviour of the exchange rate.

These results obtained in our chaotic model also help to explain why we were unable to find a strong and stable relationship between such exogenous variables as fiscal and monetary policies and the exchange rate. The speculative dynamics based on near-rational behaviour interferes with the normal transmission channel from these exogenous variables to the exchange rate.

The results of our chaotic model have another important implication. One of the features of the model is the sensitivity to initial conditions. This means that very small changes in the initial conditions can completely change the future time path of the exchange rate. We illustrated this feature in Figs 9.5 and 9.6. The same sensitivity to initial conditions also implies that a very small error made in the estimation of the underlying model will completely change the path of estimated exchange rates, much in the same way as a small change in the initial conditions does. This feature has profound informational consequences. It implies that the slightest error made in estimating the underlying model of the exchange rate will make that model useless for forecasting purposes. Put differently, we would need an almost infinite precision in estimating the underlying model to make the whole exercise useful.

This casts doubt on the use of the rational expectations assumption if the world is chaotic. This assumption requires agents to estimate the underlying model and to use that information to predict the future. However, the slightest error in this estimation exercise will make the exercise useless for predictive purposes. We have come full circle. We started out with the idea that speculators do not trust economic models to estimate the equilibrium exchange rate most of the time. They therefore use simple decision rules to make their forecasts. This assumption then leads to chaotic dynamics in the foreign exchange market which in turn validates the initial assumption, i.e. it makes it impossible for speculators to make useful inferences about the underlying economic model.

The view of the exchange market defended here also goes against a more sophisticated version of the rational expectations assumption. This version allows agents to learn from past forecasting performances and to update the information about the underlying model in a gradual way, so that they increasingly obtain better information about the underlying structure. The chaotic model presented here makes this 'Bayesian learning' model quite futile. The degree of precision needed to make this learning useful is so high that one would need infinite time to have some success.

We conclude this section by noting that simple models that incorporate the idea that expectations are near-rational are capable of mimicking some important features of the real life behaviour of the exchange rates. One is that exchange rates regularly, but inexplicably, seem to wander off from their fundamental value; second, that knowledge of the underlying fundamental variables often does not help us to predict movements of the exchange rates, on the contrary. All this, of course, does not yet prove that the model presented here is a correct

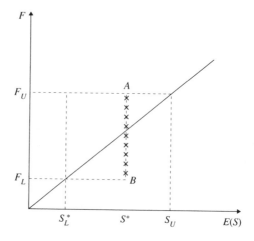

Fig. 9.12. Risk premiums and near-rationality

view of the world. It does suggest that it may be a useful way to understand what is going on.

6. Risk premiums and near-rational behaviour

In the previous section we presented a model based on the assumption of near-rational behaviour and argued that this model is capable of reproducing some important features of the movements of exchange rates. The theory of near-rationality also has important implications for the behaviour of risk premiums in the foreign exchange market.[9]

We can show these implications graphically as follows. In Fig. 9.12 we represent the observed forward rate on the vertical axis. The rationally expected future exchange rate is represented on the horizontal axis. (This is the exchange rate that agents have estimated using all available information, including the underlying model.) We also show the band of agnosticism $S_L S_U$ on the same horizontal axis. This means that as long as the observed forward rate remains within the bounds set by this band, speculators do not find it worthwhile to change their estimate of the true equilibrium exchange rate S^*. We show the disturbances in the forward rate with crosses on the vertical line segment AB. These disturbances do not lead to a re-evaluation of the estimated equilibrium rate S^*.

The existence of a band of agnosticism implies that as long as we remain within the band of agnosticism the movements in the forward rate and the rationally expected exchange rate are uncorrelated. Thus, when shocks occur in the equilibrium exchange rate (because of changes in the underlying fundamental variables) this will leave the forward rate unaffected. Similarly, shocks in

[9] For a similar analysis see Bryant (1995).

the forward rate occur without being accompanied by changes in the rationally expected exchange rate. This has the following implications for the risk premium. It will be remembered that the risk premium is defined as the difference between the forward rate and the rationally expected exchange rate, i.e.

$$\pi_t = f_t - E_t(s_{t+1}) \tag{9.12}$$

where π_t is the risk premium, f_t is the log of the forward rate and s_{t+1} is the log of the spot rate.

We can now immediately derive two propositions. First, when shocks occur in $E_t(s_{t+1})$ (and assuming they remain within the agnostic band), the risk premium will move in the opposite direction. Thus, the econometrician who duly estimates $E_t(s_{t+1})$ and π_t will note that the two variables are inversely correlated. As will be remembered this is also what we found in the previous chapter where we surveyed empirical studies of the risk premium. Almost all econometric studies have found that the risk premium and the rationally expected exchange rate are inversely correlated.

Second, within the band of agnosticism the variance of the risk premium will be larger than the variance of the rationally expected exchange rate. This can be seen by writing out the variance of the risk premium from (9.12):

$$\text{var}(\pi_t) = \text{var}(f_t) + \text{var}(E_t(s_{t+1})) - 2 \, \text{cov}(f_t, E_t(s_{t+1})) \tag{9.13}$$

As argued earlier the covariance between the forward rate and the rationally expected exchange rate is zero in the agnostic band. Therefore we must have

$$\text{var}(\pi_t) \geq \text{var}(E_t(s_{t+1})).$$

Again this has been confirmed by numerous studies of the behaviour of the risk premium (see appendix to Chapter 7). Up to now no satisfactory explanation has been given for these two features of the behaviour of risk premiums. Our theory allows us to understand these phenomena. It also makes clear that the risk premiums as measured by the econometrician have relatively little to do with true risk premiums. To see this, suppose a shock occurs in the rationally expected exchange rate. If this shock remains within the agnostic band, the speculator will not notice this and will not react to it. Later on the econometrician observes this shock. Since the forward rate does not change, the econometrician decides that the risk premium has changed (in the opposite direction). It is clear, however, that for the speculator nothing has changed and the true risk premium is unaffected. The econometrician has measured something that has nothing to do with true risk premiums (which are affected by fundamental variables such as the government budget, current accounts, etc.).

7. Exchange rates and 'fads'

The uncertainty about the relevant model to be used is great when the exchange rate is within the band of 'agnosticism'. This uncertainty makes it possible for many competing 'exotic' theories and fads to become important. When economic agents are uncertain about the fundamental variables which affect the exchange rate, they will more easily give weight to variables which economists would call irrelevant. In a sense, the band of agnosticism is also a breeding ground for fads which, in the absence of credible alternatives, are elevated to important theories.

These exotic theories become important to the extent that a sufficient number of individuals believe in their truth. Since the 'serious' theories are untested, and lack credibility, the likelihood that exotic theories are taken seriously increases. When agents act on their beliefs in a particular theory, this will be reflected in the exchange rate.

A good example of the importance of these fads is provided by the exchange rate story of the 1980s. During the first half of the 1980s exotic theories about supply side wonders were 'in vogue'. The US was seen as a dynamic and flexible economy, able to generate millions of additional jobs each year. The strong dollar inevitably reflected this dynamism of the US supply side. In Europe, however, there was labour market rigidity and 'Eurosclerosis'. This could only produce weak currencies.

After 1985, these explanations disappeared. Although the US continued to create millions of additional jobs, and labour market rigidity in Europe prevented unemployment from declining, the dollar became a weak currency. New fads emerged. Now the US economy was seen as weak and uncompetitive. Theories about the short-sightedness and insular attitudes of American management were resurrected. According to the new fad, this lack of competitiveness of the US economy inevitably produced a weak dollar. Conversely theories of Eurosclerosis were forgotten.

These theories certainly influenced the exchange rates. Although most economists would declare some of the variables, e.g. labour market flexibility, as irrelevant for explaining exchange rates, they became important because economic agents took the theories seriously. In addition, there was an element of self-fulfilling prophesy in these theories. During the early 1980s the prevailing theory of a strong America and a weak Europe led to a strong dollar. The strong dollar was then used by the proponents of this theory as evidence that America was strong and Europe weak. Exactly the opposite happened after 1985.

8. Conclusion

The theories of exchange rate determination which were developed during the 1970s were based on the idea that exchange rates are determined by the forward-looking behaviour of agents who forecast the implications of current and expected future events. This has led to models in which exchange rates react quickly to new information, and in which overshooting is a common feature. In previous chapters we argued that these models are unable to explain either the long swings in the exchange rates or the systematic bias in the forward exchange rate as a predictor of the future.

In this chapter we proposed an alternative way of modelling exchange rates. Instead of stressing forward-looking behaviour, we emphasized that in an uncertain environment, economic agents may prefer to use backward-looking rules (past and present movements of the exchange rates) for most of the time. We argued that such behaviour can be derived from the assumption of near-rationality. We also found that applying this idea in a simple model of the exchange rate is capable of reproducing some important features of the behaviour of exchange rates.

An important implication of the theory proposed in this chapter is that the movements of the exchange rates are largely disconnected from the underlying fundamental variables that drive the exchange rate in the long run (e.g. money stocks, inflation, etc.). As a result, it becomes nearly impossible to predict how particular disturbances in 'fundamental' variables affect the exchange rates. We should reduce our ambitions in this field. Movements of real exchange rates are, within certain bounds, unexplainable. All we can hope to do is to analyse the nature of the variability, without necessarily being able to explain why a particular movement (for example the appreciation of the dollar from 1982 to 1985) occurred.

In a sense the problem we face with predicting the behaviour of exchange rates is not unlike the problem in physics of predicting the behaviour of sub-atomic particles. It is impossible to predict the behaviour of individual particles. All we can do is to make probabilistic statements about this behaviour. The same can be said about the behaviour of individual exchange rates. There is an element of indeterminacy in their behaviour. In addition, and contrary to physics, where we can multiply the number of observations, in economics the number of observations is limited. As a result, even probabilistic statements are very difficult to arrive at.

APPENDIX. A SIMPLE CHAOTIC MODEL OF THE EXCHANGE RATE

In this appendix we describe the model used for the simulations discussed in the main text. For more detail, see De Grauwe, *et al.* (1993).

2.1. The money market equilibrium condition

Equilibrium in the money market is achieved when the demand for money is equal to the supply. We specify the demand for money in the traditional way, i.e.

$$M_{dt} = (Y_t a.) P_t (1 + r_t)^{-c} \qquad (A1)$$

where P_t is the domestic price level in period t, r_t is the domestic interest rate, Y_t is the (exogenous) level of domestic output. Note that if we take logarithms of this function we obtain the usual linear specification of the money demand function.

The process determining the supply of money, M_{st}, crucially depends on the policy regime. A policy of strict money supply targeting most often leads to large short-term volatility of the interest rate, so that most central banks in the world apply some interest rate smoothing procedure in the short run. We therefore assume that the authorities use some interest rate smoothing rule.

Equilibrium in the money market now implies:

$$M_{st} = M_{dt}. \qquad (A2)$$

2.2. The open interest parity condition

Assuming that the domestic financial markets are completely open to the rest of the world, the open interest parity condition can be used.

$$E_t(S_{t+1}) / S_t = (1 + r_t) / (1 + r_{ft}) \qquad (A3)$$

where S_t is the exchange rate in period t (the price of the foreign currency in units of the domestic currency), $E_t(S_{t+1})$ is the forecast made in period t of the exchange rate in period $t + 1$, and r_{ft} is the foreign interest rate.

2.3. Goods market equilibrium

Goods market equilibrium is characterized as follows. In the long run, purchasing power parity (PPP) is assumed to hold, i.e.:

$$S_t^* = P_t^* / P_{ft}^* \qquad (A4)$$

where S_t^* is the equilibrium (PPP) exchange rate, P_{ft} the foreign, and P_t the domestic price level in period t.

In the short run, however, one can have deviations from PPP. The short-term price dynamics is assumed to be determined as follows:

$$P_t / P_{t-1} = (S_t / S_t^*)^\lambda \qquad (A5)$$

where $k > 0$.

That is, when the exchange rate exceeds its PPP value, P_t, the domestic price level increases. Put differently, when the domestic currency is undervalued this leads to excess demand in the goods market tending to increase the price level. The opposite occurs when the exchange rate is below its PPP value (an overvalued domestic currency).

Note that we assume full employment so that adjustment towards equilibrium is realized through price changes. The parameter λ measures the speed of adjustment in the goods market. In general the size of this parameter depends on the choice of the units of time. If the unit of time in the model is, say, a week, then λ will be low compared to a model where the unit of time is a month or a quarter.

One can easily solve this structural model as follows. P_t from equation (A5) can be substituted into the money demand equation (A1). Together with the money market equilibrium condition, this yields an expression determining the domestic interest rate. The latter is then substituted into the open interest parity condition (A3). This yields the following expression for the exchange rate:

$$S_t = (Z_t^y.) \, E_t(S_{t+1})^f \qquad (A6)$$

where $Z_t = (M_{st} . Y_t^{-a}) \, P_{t-1}^{-x} \; (x = 1 / (1 + \lambda))$, and
$\quad f = 1 / (1 + \lambda / ((1 + \lambda)c))$.
$\quad y = (1 / c)f$.

2.4. Expectations formation

We use the equation incorporating chartist and fundamentalist behaviour as in (9.6) in the main text, which we rewrite here in multiplicative form.

$$\frac{E_t(S_{t+1})}{S_t} = \left[\left(\frac{S_t}{S_{t-1}} \right)^{c_1} \left(\frac{S_{t-1}}{S_{t-2}} \right)^{c_2} \cdots \right]^{m_t} \left[\left(\frac{S^*}{S_t} \right)^\lambda \right]^{1-m_t}. \qquad (A7)$$

For the chartist behaviour we assume a moving average of past exchange rate changes of three periods. The fundamental exchange rate S^* is obtained by solving equation (A6) forward, given the current and the future values of the exogenous variables. For the sake of simplicity, we set all these exogenous variables equal to one. This implies that the equilibrium exchange rate is equal to one. Note that PPP holds in equilibrium. We also set the speed of adjustment to the fundamental rate equal to the speed of adjustment in the goods market (λ).

We now turn to the analysis of how the weight m_t is determined. The near-rationality assumption implies that when the exchange rate is in the neighbourhood of the equilibrium rate, chartist behaviour dominates. As we depart more and more from the equilibrium rate fundamentalist analysis becomes more attractive. We approximate this behaviour by specifying a weighting function as follows:

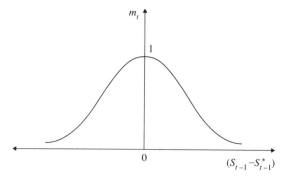

FIG. A9.1. The weighting function of chartists

$$m_t = 1 / (1 + b(S_{t-1} - S_{t-1}^*)^2) \tag{A8}$$

where m_t is the weight given to the chartists, and $b > 0$.

Graphically we can represent this specification as shown in Fig. A9.1. From Fig. A9.1 it can be seen that when the market exchange rate is equal to the fundamental rate the weight given to the chartist behaviour attains its maximum value of one. When the market rate deviates from the fundamental rate the weight given to the chartist behaviour tends to decline. For very large deviations it tends towards zero. Market expectations will then be dominated by the fundamentalist behaviour.

Note that the parameter b determines the speed with which the weight of the chartist behaviour declines. With a high value of b the curve in Fig. A9.1 becomes steeper. This means that the estimates of the true equilibrium rate made by speculators are very precise. As a result, relatively small deviations of the market rate from the true equilibrium rate lead to a strongly increasing influence by fundamentalist behaviour in the market. The opposite is true when b is low. In that case there is a lot of uncertainty in the market concerning the true equilibrium rate (the range of agnosticism is large).

We can now solve the model consisting of equations (A6) to (A8). This yields the following expression for the exchange rate:

$$S_t = Zy_t^{f_1 m_t + f_2(1 - m_t)} [S_{t-1} S_{t-2}^{f_3 m_t} S_{t-3}^{f_4 m_t}] \tag{A9}$$

with $y = (1 / c)q$
$q = 1 / (1 + \lambda / (1 + \lambda)c)$
$Z_t = m_{St} y_t^{-a} P_{t-1}^{-x}$
$x = 1 / (1 + \lambda)$.

This is the equation used in the simulations discussed in this chapter. Given the complexity of this dynamic equation numerical values are given to the coefficients of the model. These are described in De Grauwe, *et al.* (1993).

10

GOVERNMENTS AND THE EXCHANGE RATE MARKETS

1. Introduction

Although the exchange rate system which originated in the early 1970s is commonly called the flexible exchange rate system, this does not mean that monetary authorities have remained on the sidelines. In fact, monetary authorities have intervened heavily in the foreign exchange market, buying and selling foreign exchange in order to influence the movement of the exchange rates.[1] Paradoxically, the available evidence indicates that the amount of intervention during the flexible exchange rate regime has on average been larger than during the period of the Bretton Woods system. This is shown in Fig. 10.1 which presents the yearly changes of the foreign exchange reserves of the major industrialized countries.[2] We have deflated these changes by an average price index of the industrialized countries, so that we obtain yearly changes in 1960 prices. It can be seen that during the 1960s these yearly changes in the foreign exchange reserves were relatively small. The period 1971–3, which can be considered as a transition period from the fixed to the flexible exchange rate regime, was particularly turbulent. From 1973 on we observe yearly changes that are substantially higher than during the 1960s. Table 10.1 summarizes these results. It shows that the size of yearly interventions in the foreign exchange markets during the period of flexible exchange rates (1973–94) were more than twice the size of such interventions during the fixed exchange rate period (1960–70). This rather paradoxical situation leads to several questions which will be analysed in this chapter. First, there is the question whether, and under what conditions, official intervention in the foreign exchange market is effective in altering the path of the exchange rate compared to the path it would have taken under complete freedom. Second, what are the implications of the large-scale interventions

[1] Why they did this is outside the scope of the present chapter. It will be analysed in the next chapter when we take up some issues concerning the welfare implications of exchange rate variability.
[2] It is well known that the official statistics are unreliable. Quite often they tend to underestimate the true amount of intervention. This is the case in countries such as France, for example, where state companies have sometimes been urged by the authorities to borrow foreign exchange and to sell the proceeds in the foreign exchange market.

TABLE 10.1. *Mean absolute yearly change of foreign exchange reserves of industrialized countries*

	Billion SDRs, prices of 1960
1960–70	1.9
1971–2	13.0
1973–94	4.4

Source: IMF, *International Financial Statistics*

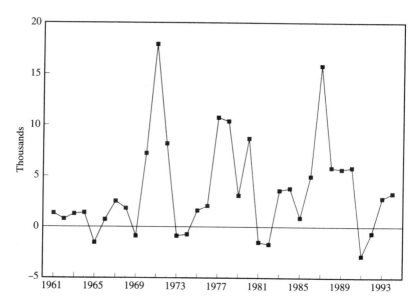

FIG. 10.1. Change in foreign exchange reserves of industrialized countries in billion SDRs (at 1960 prices)

Source: IMF, *International Financial Statistics*

observed during the floating exchange rate regime for monetary and financial relations between countries?

2. How effective are official interventions in the foreign exchange market? The theory

This important question has been analysed in great detail.[3] It has become customary to distinguish between two types of foreign exchange market intervention, i.e. sterilized and non-sterilized interventions.

[3] For an early survey of the literature see Crockett and Goldstein (1987) and the so-called *Jurgenson Report* (1983). A more recent survey of the issues is contained in Frankel and Rose (1994). See also Dominguez and Frankel (1993).

With non-sterilized intervention, the monetary authorities buy and sell foreign exchange in such a way that the domestic money stock is affected. Let us use an example to clarify how this works. Suppose the Japanese monetary authorities buy dollars in the foreign exchange market in order to stem a downward slide of the dollar against the yen. This purchase of dollars necessarily implies that yen are being sold, and that if nothing else happens the money stock in Japan increases. The reverse happens if the Bank of Japan sells dollars in the foreign exchange market.

Sterilized intervention implies that the central bank will offset these monetary effects of foreign exchange market interventions. Thus, in our example of the Bank of Japan buying dollars, the Japanese monetary authorities will take steps to avoid the Japanese money stock increasing. This can be done, for example, by open market operations, whereby the Bank of Japan sells government securities in exchange for cash.[4]

The implications of these two types of foreign exchange market intervention are quite different. In the case of non-sterilized intervention, the monetary authorities allow the automatic adjustment mechanism which we have discussed in the chapters on the fixed exchange rate system to work. In a sense, the 'rules of the game' are allowed to do their work. Let us take the example of the Bank of Japan again. When it buys dollars to stem its downward slide, and when it allows the money stock in Japan to increase, this will tend to reduce the interest rate in Japan. As a result, holdings of Japanese assets will be less attractive compared to dollar assets (*ceteris paribus*). This in turn will tend to increase the demand for dollars, and will help to stem the downward slide of the dollar. In addition, the expansionary monetary policies stimulate output and increase inflationary pressures. This should lead to an increase in imports, and therefore, to an increase in the demand for dollars.

It is this feature of non-sterilized intervention, which has led economists to conclude that this type of official intervention in the foreign exchange market is effective in influencing the exchange rate.

Things are quite different with sterilized intervention. The absence of a monetary effect of this kind of intervention considerably reduces its effectiveness. There is also now a consensus that in a world of large capital mobility, sterilized intervention has almost no effect on the exchange rate.[5] The reason is not difficult to understand. When, in our example, the Bank of Japan buys dollars using non-sterilized intervention, nothing is changed in the Japanese money market. In particular, Japanese interest rates do not change. Since in our example, the dollar is weak, presumably because economic agents find dollar

---

[4] Other techniques are possible. In some countries the central bank may increase reserve requirements. As a result, the excess reserves the banking system are accumulating, because of the foreign exchange market operation of the central bank, are prevented from having an expansionary effect on the money stock.

[5] See the *Jurgenson Report* (1983) again. See also Hans Genberg (1981), and Henderson (1984). In the latter papers it is also stressed that when assets are imperfect substitutes, sterilized intervention can have an effect on the exchange rate. The reason is that the change in the relative supplies of domestic and foreign assets changes their relative prices. This effect, however, is small and of little operational importance. A survey of recent experience by Obstfeld (1990) confirms this.

holdings relatively unattractive, the interventions of the Bank of Japan do nothing to change the relative attractiveness of dollar assets. As a result, investors are unlikely to change their bearish view about the dollar.

There is one channel through which sterilized intervention can have an effect on the exchange rate, however. This happens when the intervention acts as a signal that the authorities aim to change future economic policies (e.g. restrictive monetary policies). Thus, these intervention policies can be effective to the extent that agents believe that they will lead to future changes in fundamentals. This effect has been measured by Dominguez (1990, 1992), Lewis (1990, 1993), and Dominguez and Frankel (1993). See also the survey by Edison (1993). The impression today is that, although these signalling effects do occur, they are relatively rare.

3. Official interventions and commitments

In the Introduction, it was stressed that official interventions in the foreign exchange market have been sizeable during the floating exchange rate period. Have these interventions been effective in practice? From the theory, which we discussed in the previous section, it appears that the answer depends on whether this intervention was of the sterilized or non-sterilized type. Or, if of the former type, whether it generated expectations of future changes in monetary policies.

There is now considerable evidence indicating that the monetary authorities have often tried to use sterilized interventions, but that they have been only partly successful in doing so, so that quite often the foreign exchange market interventions did spill over into the money markets. Thus, it may appear that foreign exchange market interventions could have been effective in reducing the volatility of the exchange rates. Before we jump to this conclusion, however, let us first look at the empirical evidence.

The evidence that foreign exchange market interventions could not be fully sterilized by the monetary authorities can be obtained in an indirect way. Figs 10.2 and 10.3 show the movements of the money base in Germany and in Japan, and compare these with the movements of the DM/dollar and the yen/dollar rates, respectively. In the German case one observes a clear negative correlation between the movements of the dollar rate and of the German money base. This is especially evident during the 1970s up to the mid-1980s. Since the mid-1980s there is less evidence of such a negative correlation. The interpretation of this phenomenon (which has been analysed and documented in great detail by McKinnon (1982, 1984)) is the following. When the dollar was declining in value during the 1970s, the monetary authorities in Europe and Japan were intervening in order to slow down the dollar's depreciation. These interventions led to an increase in the money base in these countries. The opposite happened during the first half of the 1980s when the dollar was appreciating.

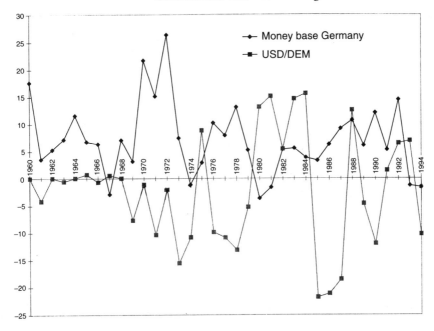

Fɪɢ. 10.2. Base money and dollar/DM rate (change in per cent per year)

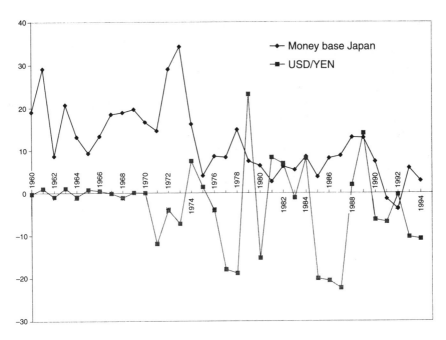

Fɪɢ. 10.3. Base money and dollar/yen rate (change in per cent per year)

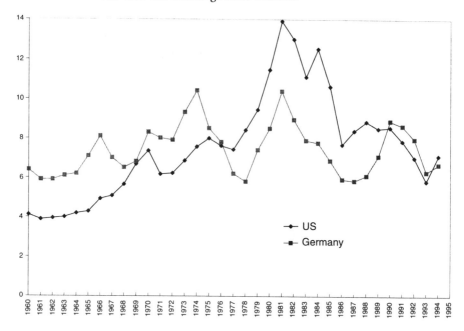

Fig. 10.4. Government bond yield, the US and Germany (in per cent per year)

As mentioned earlier this phenomenon is most pronounced in the case of Germany.[6] During 1970–3 and 1977–9 the dollar was declining rapidly against the mark. As a result, these were also periods of rapid monetary expansion in Germany. During the early 1980s, the opposite occurred. The dollar was appreciating and the rate of monetary expansion in Germany dropped significantly. Although less pronounced, we find a similar tendency in the case of Japan. As mentioned earlier these phenomena have been less pronounced since the mid-1980s suggesting that the Geman and Japanese monetary authorities have either intervened less or have been more successful in sterilizing these interventions.

One important effect of the previous phenomenon is that the movements of interest rates have been correlated across the major industrialized countries. We illustrate this in Figs 10.4 and 10.5, where we show government bond yields in the US, Germany, and Japan. Two facts stand out. First, the US has experienced a trend-like increase in the long-term government bond yield from 1960 to 1980. This phenomenon is not observed in Germany and Japan. Second, and more relevant for our analysis, the yearly movements of the German interest rate tended to coincide with those observed in the US. This is also the case with Japan, but to a lesser degree.

[6] In fact it is also true for most European countries. See Obstfeld (1983), and Herring and Marston (1977) on German intervention policies.

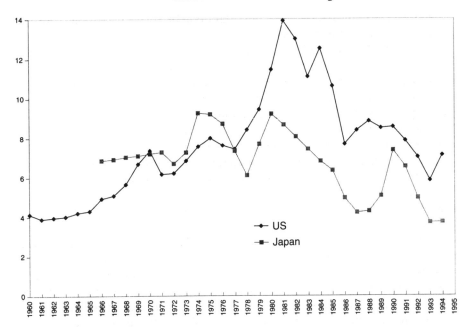

Fɪɢ. 10.5. Government bond yield, the US and Japan (in per cent per year)

Third, there does not seem to be much difference in the co-movements of the interest rates between the fixed and the flexible exchange rate periods. In the Japanese case, there seems to have been even less co-movement during the fixed exchange rate period than during the period of floating.[7]

From the preceding empirical observations one can conclude the following. The authorities of major countries (Japan, Germany) have often intervened heavily in the foreign exchange market. Although they may have tried to avoid these interventions affecting their domestic money markets, quite often they have not been successful in doing so. As a result, and quite paradoxically so, it can be said that during the period of floating exchange rates, the monetary authorities of these countries have been following the 'rules of the game', i.e. expanding the money stock when there was excess demand for their own currency (excess supply of dollars), and contracting it when there was excess supply of the domestic currency (excess demand for dollars). Such a policy reaction should have helped to stabilize the dollar exchange rate.

And yet one has a definite impression that even this type of intervention in the foreign exchange market was powerless in significantly stabilizing the long swings in the exchange rates. This impression is corroborated by several studies

[7] For a more formal test of the degree of covariation of interest rates, and other macroeconomic variables, see e.g. Swoboda (1983) and De Grauwe and Fratianni (1985). It appears from these studies that the movement from fixed to flexible exchange rates did not reduce the degree of interdependence between countries.

which have been made, the most important one being the Jurgenson report to which we made allusion earlier.[8]

Why has it been difficult for monetary authorities to have an effective influence on the large and protracted movements of the exchange rates, despite the fact that these interventions were quite often accompanied by the correct (i.e. stabilizing) monetary policies? In other words why did non-sterilized intervention work poorly to stabilize the exchange rate?

The answer has to do with a lack of commitment on the part of the monetary authorities to particular target exchange rates. Put differently, it appears from the available evidence that non-sterilized interventions in the foreign exchange market are insufficient to affect the exchange rates in a significant way. In order for these intervention policies to be effective they must be accompanied by clear commitments to a particular exchange rate (or range of exchange rates).

Why are commitments so important for stabilizing the exchange rates? Using the framework of the model of 'near-rationality' developed in the previous chapter, one can answer this question as follows. When, because of extreme uncertainty, fundamentals are given a low weight in predicting the future exchange rate, policies which change these fundamentals have little effect. Agents are unable to evaluate the importance of these policies for the exchange rate. The latter will continue to be driven by backward-looking rules and by occasional fads. This, as we have seen, leads to persistent movements away from the equilibrium exchange rates as predicted by economic models. This drift in the exchange rates cannot easily be stopped by the monetary authorities, even if they follow policies altering some important fundamentals.

Only by a commitment to a particular exchange rate can this mechanism of drifting exchange rates be broken. Commitments (if credible) work as anchors to fix expectations about the future exchange rate. Without such an anchor, the uncertainty faced by economic agents in predicting the future exchange rates becomes so high that these agents will revert to backward-looking rules in predicting the future. If the commitment succeeds in being credible, economic agents have no longer any reason to use backward-looking rules in predicting the future. The authorities' commitment anchors their expectations. As a result, the 'aimless drift' of the real exchange rates which has been so typical of the movements of the major currencies since the early 1970s will disappear.

The theory of near-rational behaviour also suggests that the traditional distinction between sterilized and non-sterilized intervention may only have limited practical importance. As will be remembered, the traditional theory tells us that sterilized intervention does not work whereas non-sterilized intervention does. The theory of near-rational behaviour tells us that this distinction between sterilized and non-sterilized intervention may not matter much. The

---

[8] See also Feldstein (1986a) and Takatoshi Ito (1986). Both these authors conclude that the Plaza Agreement of Sept. 1985 to pursue a policy of co-ordinated intervention among the G-5 countries had only a minimal impact in the exchange markets. In fact the decline of the dollar started in Feb. 1985, eight months before the agreement.

reason is that when agents are agnostic about the true underlying model and the fundamental variables that drive the exchange rate, interventions that change the fundamental variables may be no more effective than interventions that do not change the fundamental variables. In this near-rational expectations view interventions will only work if they are accompanied by commitments to keep the exchange rates close to some target.[9]

The importance of commitments is made clear by analysing the exchange rate policies of a number of European countries since the late 1970s. We first concentrate on two countries, Austria and Switzerland, which have used implicit exchange rate commitments. We then turn our attention to the European Monetary System (EMS) which has used explicit commitments to guide its exchange rate policies.

4. Austria and Switzerland: cases of implicit commitments

Austria and Switzerland are two countries which have followed policies based on pegging their exchange rates to the DM. This policy used an implicit commitment, in the sense that it was well understood in the market that the authorities were committed to a particular range of the exchange rate with the DM. Whereas Austria has used such a policy since the start of floating exchange rates, Switzerland has only recently (since the early 1980s) embarked on such an exchange rate policy. In contrast to the EMS countries, however, there was no explicit international agreement.

We first look at the Austrian case. In Fig. 10.6 the yearly movements of the DM/schilling exchange rate are shown, and are compared with the movements of the DM/dollar rate. The contrast between the stability of the DM/schilling exchange rate and the DM/dollar rate is remarkable.

The Swiss case is more subtle. During most of the 1970s, the Swiss Central Bank either let the Swiss franc float freely, or followed an independent float. Since the early 1980s, however, the exchange rate policies of the Swiss authorities have been geared towards following the movements of the DM. In Fig. 10.7 the movements of the DM/SF rate are presented together with those of the DM/dollar rate. One observes that during the 1970s the volatility of the Swiss franc against the mark was of the same order of magnitude as the volatility of the DM/dollar rate. Since 1982, however, a substantial reduction in the variability of the DM/SF rate has occurred. This happened at a time of increased volatility of the DM/dollar exchange rate.

---

[9] Using a chaotic model of the foreign exchange market such as the one discussed in Ch. 9, De Grauwe and Van Santen (1991) show that these two types of interventions (sterilized and non-sterilized) have approximately the same effects on the exchange rate.

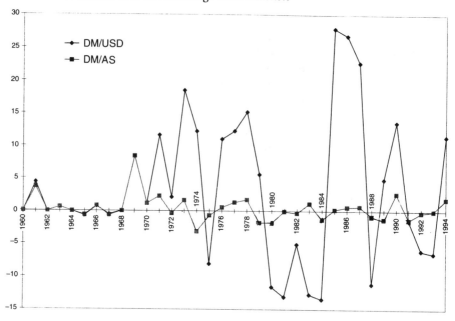

FIG. 10.6. DM/A. schilling exchange rate (yearly change in per cent)

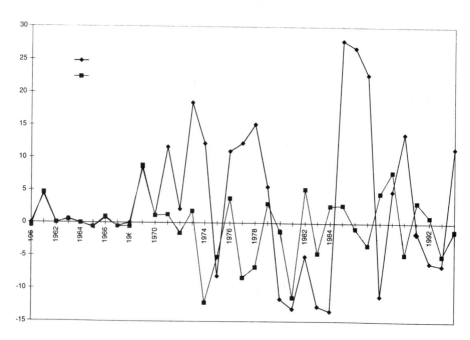

FIG. 10.7. DM/SF exchange rate (yearly change in per cent)

5. The European monetary system and the role of exchange rate commitments

The European Monetary System provides an interesting case-study about the role of commitments in stabilizing exchange rates and also about the limitations of these commitments. As was shown in Chapters 2 and 3 the EMS started out as a system of relatively flexible commitments. After 1987 it evolved into a truly fixed exchange rate regime. We argued in Chapter 3 that the rigidity into which the EMS evolved was the root cause of its undoing.

Let us therefore concentrate on the first and flexible period of the EMS to see what we can learn from the nature of these relatively flexible commitments. The main ingredients of this flexible commitment were the following. First, the early EMS was based on a commitment to maintain fixed margins of fluctuations for the intra-EMS exchange rates. These margins were 2.25 per cent above and below the official parities.[10] Second, this commitment was not a rigid one. It was understood that 'realignments' could and would be made if the need arose. Third, an implicit commitment evolved in that these realignments would be small, and typically not much larger than the total width of the intervention margins (4.5 per cent).

How effective was this exchange rate arrangement in stabilizing the exchange rates of the currencies of the EMS countries?

There is now enough empirical evidence to conclude that this early EMS was relatively successful in limiting the movements of its exchange rates.[11] In particular it avoided the large swings in the real exchange rates which have been so typical of the movements of the dollar versus the major currencies. We illustrate the difference between the movements of the exchange rates inside and outside the EMS in Table 10.2. The columns labelled 'Intra-EMS' measure the variability of the exchange rate of each currency against the other EMS currencies. The columns called 'Extra-EMS' measure the variability of the exchange rates of each currency against a group of industrialized countries outside the EMS. It can clearly be seen that during this flexible EMS period real exchange rate movements within the EMS were substantially smaller than the exchange rate movements of EMS currencies against the major currencies outside the EMS.

One of the interesting features about exchange rate policies based on a clearly perceived commitment by the central bank, is that the countries using these policies have had to intervene relatively little in the exchange markets, and yet their exchange rates have exhibited a relative stability during the times these policies have been in effect. This is illustrated for the EMS countries in Table 10.3. We can conclude from this table that the foreign exchange market interventions by EMS countries to maintain their intra-EMS exchange rates within the margins have been significantly smaller than the interventions these countries

---

[10] Italy had a special regime. The margins for the lira were 6 per cent above and below the official parity. When Spain, Portugal, and the UK joined they also used the 6 per cent margin.

[11] For empirical evidence, see e.g. Ungerer, *et al.* (1986).

TABLE **10.2.** *Standard deviation of the quarterly changes of the real effective exchange rates (per cent).*

	Intra-EMS		Extra-EMS	
	1973–8	1979–86	1973–8	1979–86
Belgium	1.3	1.3	2.9	3.1
Netherlands	1.7	1.2	3.0	3.5
Denmark	1.6	1.3	2.3	2.6
Germany	2.2	1.2	3.1	2.7
France	2.4	2.0	2.6	3.0
Italy	3.5	1.5	2.6	2.6

Note: The Extra-EMS countries consist of Austria, Canada, Japan, Norway, Sweden, Switzerland, US, and UK

Source: IMF, *International Financial Statistics*

TABLE **10.3.** *Foreign exchange market interventions by EMS countries* (in billion dollars)

	In dollar market	Intra-EMS
1979	23.6	7.9
1980	27.5	8.4
1981	42.6	19.5
1982	39.3	12.9
1983	32.5	26.4
1984	23.2	15.6
1985*	12.8	7.1

* First half of year

Source: Based on Stefano Micossi, 'The Intervention and Financing of the EMS and their Role for the ECU', *Banca Nazionale del Lavoro Quarterly Review*, Dec. 1985

have conducted in the dollar exchange market. This did not prevent the dollar from fluctuating much more against the EMS currencies than the EMS currencies among each other.

The contrast between the effectiveness of exchange rate policies based on implicit or explicit commitments and policies without commitments is spectacular. The former have been quite effective in stabilizing exchange rates. Compared to this standard, the effectiveness of the latter policies is very small indeed. This is the case, despite the fact that (as was noted earlier) the exchange rate policies of the major countries appear to have been accompanied by the right kind of stabilizing monetary policies (non-sterilized intervention).

The history of the EMS is also interesting in that it shows us that commitments that are too rigid will lack credibility and will cease to work. After 1987 the EMS evolved into a truly fixed exchange rate system. We have argued in

Chapter 3 that these rigid commitments undermined the credibility of the system and led to its collapse. Thus, the history of the EMS shows us that some forms of flexible commitments can indeed stabilize exchange rates. Too much ambition in commitments, however, can easily lead to disaster.

6. Speculators against central banks

The size of financial capital available for speculative purposes is staggering. The BIS has estimated that in 1994 the *daily* transactions in the foreign exchange markets amounted to 880 billion dollars, which is almost twice the stock of international reserves owned by all central banks together. This has led to the view that central banks are helpless when speculators decide to attack a currency. When a battle erupts between central banks and speculators, the former always lose because they are hopelessly outgunned by the speculators.

Is this popular view the correct one? The answer is no.

First, the estimates of the size of the foreign exchange transactions by the BIS vastly overestimates the *net* purchases and sales in the foreign exchange markets. Most of the transactions in the foreign exchange markets these days are made for hedging purposes, and do not add a net (up- or downward) pressure in the foreign exchange market. An example makes this clear. Suppose a speculator decides to buy dollars forward because he thinks the dollar will appreciate in the future. He must find a counterpart willing to take a reverse position (sell forward). The speculator typically will go to his bank and obtain forward dollars from the bank. The latter, however, does not want to keep an open position in dollars and will therefore immediately buy dollars spot. This spot operation in turn leaves someone else with an open position. This position will be closed by a reverse operation in the forward market. This will go on until someone is found in the market willing to take the reverse position of the speculator who started this chain of transactions. In the end, the size of the transactions in the foreign exchange market will be a multiple of the initial speculative purchase. It is only the latter that puts pressure on the exchange rate. All the intermediary transactions do not affect the exchange rate because they exactly offset each other.

Another example illustrates the same point. Suppose a multinational company wants to invest in a new plant in Germany and decides to finance this investment by raising the necessary capital in Germany. In order to do so it borrows, say, 10 million DM. The foreign exchange market will not be affected. This multinational company can however raise the capital in a different way, i.e. by a swap transaction involving dollars. This consists in borrowing dollars, selling the dollars spot in exchange for DM, and buying back dollars forward. If interest parity holds, the borrowing cost of the multinational company will be exactly the same as in the case of DM borrowing. In addition, this swap operation does not lead to a net capital movement, and therefore does not add pressure in the foreign exchange market. The BIS study, however, measures the increase in foreign exchange transactions, and gives the impression that the size of the movements of capital has increased. In this example, no such movement has occurred however.

All this confirms that the figures produced by the BIS vastly overestimate the importance of net capital movements in the world. While the BIS overestimates capital mobility, it is still true that this has become large. The next question then is whether, after correction for this overestimation, it is true that speculators always 'outgun' the central banks when they decide attack a currency? The answer is no. To see this, it is important to realize that when speculators attack a currency there are always two currencies involved, and therefore two central banks. When in 1993 speculators attacked the FF, they sold FF and bought DM. Thus, both the Banque de France and the Bundesbank were involved. We can now come to the following proposition: if the two central banks are willing to co-operate, then they can always 'outgun' the speculators. Let us return to the example of a speculative attack on the FF. The Banque de France will have to sell DM to the speculators. If the Bundesbank is willing to co-operate with the Banque de France, it can provide the DM in unlimited amounts because it manufactures DM. There is in principle no limit to the amount of DM the Bundesbank can create to counter a speculative attack. Thus, one can say that when central banks are willing to co-operate they can always beat the speculators.

The problem quite often is that they do not want to co-operate. In the case of the attack on the FF in 1993, the Bundesbank decided that the unlimited support it was giving to the Banque de France was interfering with its money supply target. As a result, it stopped sending marks to the Banque de France. At that moment, the Banque de France became a helpless victim of the speculators. Thus, if speculators often win the battle against the central banks, this is not due to the fact that they have more weapons (capital) than the central banks. They do not. The reason is that the central banks often do not want to use their superior weaponry. When speculators 'smell' this, their attacks will become more intense, and they will win. Ultimately, the problem is always the same: central bankers tend to lose against the speculators because their full commitment to the fixity of the exchange rate is in doubt.

7. Conclusion: lessons for exchange rate stabilization

Two schools of thought have emerged during the 1970s and the 1980s about the question of how exchange rates can be stabilized.[12] According to one school, the way to stabilize exchange rates and to avoid the wide swings in real exchange rates, consists in stabilizing economic policies. On this view, the misalignments of exchange rates are mainly the result of misaligned economic policies. Therefore,

---

[12] There is of course, a school of thought which disputes the need for exchange rate stabilization. We shall come back to the normative issue of how much flexibility is optimal. Here we discuss a positive issue: if the objective is to stabilize the exchange rate, how can one best achieve this objective.

the major countries have to co-ordinate their policies better if they want to avoid situations of extreme misalignments of exchange rates.

The need for the authorities to use exchange rate commitments in such a programme of exchange rate stabilization is denied. It is sufficient for the authorities to follow stable and predictable policies for stable exchange rates to follow. It is probably fair to say that this view now constitutes the majority view among academic economists.[13] It was also adopted during the 1970s by major international institutions, such as the IMF.

A second school of thought emphasizes the need to introduce exchange rate commitments as an essential ingredient of any policy aimed at the stabilization of exchange rates.[14] Although stable and predictable policies are necessary in any programme of exchange rates stabilization, they are insufficient to achieve this objective.

The first school bases its policy recommendation on forward-looking models where economic agents base their forecast of the future exchange rate on a knowledge of the fundamentals which drive the exchange markets. The task of the policy-makers is to stabilize the fundamentals, so that expectations become less volatile. In a stable policy environment, exchange rates will stop exhibiting large swings.

In this and the previous chapters we have argued that the floating exchange rate regime has led to a situation where a great deal of uncertainty exists about how fundamentals affect the exchange rate. As a result, economic agents tend to give a low weight to fundamentals in forecasting the future. This leads to situations where exchange rates tend to drift away from the fundamentals for prolonged periods of time.

The evidence concerning the effectiveness of foreign exchange market interventions, which we have discussed in this chapter, suggests that the relevance of fundamentals in exchange rate forecasting can only be restored if the authorities provide an anchor for exchange rate expectations by committing themselves to a particular range of exchange rates. This emphasis on commitments does not mean, however, that policy co-ordination should be de-emphasized. On the contrary, policy co-ordination is needed mainly to give credibility to the commitments. Without such credibility, any commitment will be defeated in the market-place.

A comparison of the early-EMS with the post-EMS regimes also revealed that some flexible commitments are quite capable of stabilizing exchange rates. The challenge is to find the right degree of commitment that is not so rigid that it leads to speculative attacks, nor so flexible that it is little different from a flexible exchange rate regime.

---

[13] A recent example is the CEPR report of 1995 which argues that if European countries outside the EMS were to follow inflation targeting policies this would stabilize the exchange rates in Europe. See Dewatripont, *et al.* (1995).

[14] Proponents of this view are John Williamson and Ronald McKinnon. See Williamson (1983) and McKinnon (1984). Both authors, however, differ in their view as to how exchange rate commitments should be implemented.

11

CONDITIONS FOR INTERNATIONAL MONETARY REFORM

1. Introduction

In the previous chapter we argued that a programme aimed at stabilizing the exchange rates must include some degree of commitment by the authorities to a range (or a rate of change) of exchange rates. In this chapter we first discuss what the minimal conditions are for such stabilization programmes to be successful. We then discuss some of the proposals that have been made to stabilize the exchange rate and analyse the question whether such proposals are likely to come about.

2. Exchange rate commitments and the $(n-1)$ problem

Every exchange rate commitment (even if it is a relatively flexible one) faces the liquidity problem ($(n-1)$ problem) that we discussed in Chapter 3. This means that some form of joint decision-making process about the nature of the monetary policies for the system as a whole becomes necessary.

The Bretton Woods System and the European Monetary System 'solved' this problem in an asymmetric way: one country took over responsibility for setting the monetary policy for the system as a whole. We argued that such an arrangement among sovereign nations does not withstand the passage of time. Sooner or later conflicts arise between the centre and the periphery leading to speculative crises and a collapse of the arrangement. A return to such an asymmetric arrangement at the international level seems out of the question. It would require a willingness on the part of the partners to accept a dominating position by one country in setting monetary policies. Presumably, this would have to be the US. It is doubtful that, at this moment, countries like Germany and Japan would be willing to submit their monetary policies to US dominance, even if this were to take a softer form than during the Bretton Woods period.

Another institutional arrangement which can be used to solve the (n − 1) problem is based on co-operation between the countries taking up an exchange rate commitment. The requirement that the authorities jointly determine the money stocks is the Achilles heel of the co-operative model. It appears to be extremely difficult for countries to arrive at such a solution. It is not that countries cannot occasionally come to an agreement. In fact, there are many cases of such agreements. An example is the agreement between the US, Germany, and Japan in 1986 to jointly reduce interest rates: the so-called Louvre Accord. Another famous effort at co-ordinating policies was the agreement between the US and Germany in 1977 whereby the latter agreed to play the role of locomotive for the world economy and to stimulate domestic demand. The problem is to achieve a stable and lasting co-operative solution to monetary policy-making.

Why is it difficult to achieve co-operative solutions which will stick? Modern game theory allows us to give some insights into the problem. Almost all co-operative agreements suffer from the 'free riding' problem. This means that once an agreement is reached between different partners, there are usually incentives for one or more of them to cheat, and to do something other than what was agreed upon. These incentives arise because, by cheating, the partners concerned expect to be better off. The condition for this expectation to be realized is that the other partners do not retaliate by reneging on the agreement.

The problem is the same as with price cartels. Firms or countries (for example, OPEC) come to an agreement to fix prices. When they go home, some of the firms (countries) realize that they can increase their profits even more by giving price discounts, thereby extending their market share. This profit calculation will be correct if the other partners in the agreement do not retaliate by lowering their prices.

It follows that the strength of a co-operative agreement depends on how well the actions of the partners can be monitored, and how quickly retaliation can be expected. If monitoring is easy, and if quick retaliatory action can be expected, co-operative agreements have a chance of lasting a long time. If these conditions are not met, co-operative agreements will break down easily.

There are good reasons to believe that these conditions are not met in international economic policy-making. First, the monitoring of policy actions is not always easy. The reason is that quite often the variables which are used as indicators of monetary (or for that matter fiscal) policies do not unambiguously reflect the true nature of policy actions. This problem was very acute in the US during the first half of the 1980s, when because of financial innovations, a traditional indicator of monetary policy, M1, lost much of its information content concerning the Fed's policy actions. Something similar happened in the UK during 1979–82, when different indicators of monetary policies (M1, M2, M3) moved in opposite directions. This confounded the UK policy-makers themselves who targeted M3, which was increasing very fast. As a result, considerable monetary deflation was applied. Later it became clear that M3 was overestimating the true amount of liquidity creation and was therefore the wrong variable to target. It also follows that the Bank of England probably applied more monetary restraint than it really wanted.[1] This historical episode illustrates a very general problem, which is that even experts can be wrong in judging the true nature of economic policies. In such an environment the monitoring of co-operative agreements is made difficult.

The second condition for successful co-operative efforts, i.e. a swift retaliatory action, is also unlikely to be fulfilled in the economic policy field. Policy decisions in modern democracies are usually the outcome of an elaborate and slow decision-making process. This has to do with the fact that in each country there are different and opposing interest groups. As a result, many decisions are the result of a painfully slow compromise between conflicting interests. This makes it very difficult for policy-makers to change their policy stance quickly when their partners in the agreement change theirs.[2]

The slowness of the decision-making process leads to another problem with international co-operative agreements. Quite often exogenous disturbances require a change in policies. Since most co-operative efforts take much time to be decided upon, they usually lack the flexibility to respond quickly to these shocks. A dramatic example of this problem is provided by the 'Locomotive' experiment of the late 1970s. As mentioned earlier, Germany agreed to stimulate its economy and started implementing this policy in 1978. A few months later the second oil shock broke out, requiring a completely different policy. The major countries were unable at that time to come up with a co-operative effort to deal with this new problem. As a result, the German action came at the wrong time, and influenced the German authorities in their refusal during the 1980s to participate in new co-operative efforts.

These problems with international co-operation in economic policy-making are well known. They therefore lead to a self-defeating mechanism. As it is known that co-operation between policy-makers does not easily stick, economic agents attach a low credibility to commitments by national governments to co-operate in setting their monetary policies. They will in fact expect that these joint efforts will quickly break down. This expectation in turn speeds up the breakdown of the co-operative agreement. One can conclude that credible international monetary policies between the major industrialized countries aimed at deciding on the level of the world money stock in a co-operative way are very unlikely to come about very soon.

This is a rather pessimistic conclusion. One may ask the question whether less ambitious agreements do not have a better chance of achieving credibility. Some of the looser arrangements which have been proposed are analysed in the following sections.

---

[1] See Patrick Minford and Kent Matthews (1987).

[2] See Putman and Henning (1986) for an historical account of the domestic politicking which led to the Locomotive agreement between the US and Germany in 1977.

3. The target zone proposal

The best-known formula has been proposed by John Williamson (1983 and 1985). The central idea is that the authorities would announce a 'target zone', within which the exchange rate would fluctuate freely. The target zone would be obtained from a calculation of an equilibrium exchange rate, which in turn would be determined by fundamental variables (such as inflation rates and the balance of payments). This zone could be up to 20 per cent wide.

The idea of target zones is in essence the same as in the EMS. The major difference between the Williamson proposal and the EMS is that in the former the authorities do not commit themselves to defend the target zone. Thus, if the exchange rate is driven outside the zone, 'the authorities are unhappy to see the rate move, despite not being prepared to pre-commit themselves to prevent such movements' (Williamson (1985), p. 64). The authorities are, however, prepared to use their monetary policies in order to discourage the exchange rate from diverging too much from the zone.

In addition, and again in contrast to the EMS arrangement, the target zone would be a 'crawling one', i.e. it would move up or down depending on the movement of the 'fundamental equilibrium exchange rate' (FEER). The latter depends on fundamental variables such as inflation rates, and disequilibria in the balance of payments. In Box 11.1 we go a little deeper into the question of how this FEER is computed.

Box 11.1. The determination of the fundamental equilibrium exchange rate (FEER)

The Williamson proposal requires the determination of the FEER. The latter generally changes over time so that the target zone will have to move accordingly. How can one estimate this FEER?

In order to answer this question it is useful to look at the theory underlying the FEER. The easiest way to do this is to use the Swan diagram which we introduced in Chapter 4. It is shown here in Fig. 11.1.

As we have seen in Chapter 4, the upward-sloping line represents external equilibrium, and the downward-sloping line internal equilibrium. The intersection of these two lines allows us to find the real exchange rate which is consistent with both internal and external equilibrium. In Fig. 11.1 this is R_1. This is also the FEER. It can therefore be interpreted as follows. It is the value of the real exchange rate that makes sure that not only the current account is in equilibrium (external equilibrium), but also that the domestic economy is in equilibrium. Two points should be made here: one relates to the external equilibrium, the other to the internal equilibrium. In Williamson's proposal the concept of equilibrium in the current account is enlarged to mean a sustainable current account position. This means that a country can have a current account deficit today if the future debt repayment flows which result from having a current account deficit are sustainable. Second, domestic equilibrium implies that demand and supply of domestic goods occurs at a non-accelerating rate of inflation.

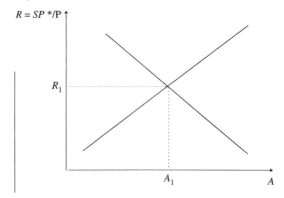

Fig. 11.1. The fundamental equilibrium exchange rate in the Swan diagram

The theory underlying the estimation of the FEER is relatively simple. The actual measurement, however, is much less so.[3] Many practical problems arise when one wants to implement this theory. For example, it is not easy to determine what the sustainable level of the current account deficit is. The determination of this level requires an extrapolation of the future debt repayment flows. It also requires an answer to the question whether these flows are sustainable. This question is difficult because it necessitates estimating the future growth of GDP and of domestic spending.

As a result of these difficulties, great uncertainty exists about the precise value of the FEER. This creates difficulties in the practical implementation of the Williamson proposal. As the value of the FEER is only known with a large margin of error, discussion and controversies about this FEER are likely to occur. This will reduce the credibility of the target zone proposal.

4. A minimal reform

Although the target zone proposal is relatively flexible, putting a minimum of constraints on domestic policies, it has some drawbacks.[4] A first one is the need to compute equilibrium exchange rates. As stressed in Box 11.1, it is very difficult to achieve a consensus on what these equilibrium exchange rates are.[5] If

[3] For more detail about the practical problems in estimating the FEER see Williamson (1994).
[4] For some criticism see Genberg (1984), Marston (1987*b*), and Frenkel and Goldstein (1986). See also Corden (1994).
[5] In a recent publication edited by Williamson (1994) it appeared that experts could not agree on the method to be used for determining the fundamental equilibrium exchange rate, let alone on a numerical value.
See Bayoumi, *et al.* (1994) and Stein (1994). Another example of the divergence of opinion is provided by the estimates made in 1986 concerning the equilibrium dollar/yen rate. The estimates varied between 100 and 200 yen to the dollar (see Loopesko and Johnson (1987)).

officials of the major countries have to agree periodically on what these equilibrium rates must be, one can expect constant bickering and 'political' determination of the equilibrium rates.

A second criticism of the Williamson proposal is that there is not sufficient commitment where commitment matters. That is, there is no rule that governs how large the exchange rate adjustments in the future will be.[6] We have argued earlier that the source of the success of the early EMS resided in an implicit commitment to limit the realignments to (approximately) the size of the intervention margin. Such a commitment is of crucial importance to anchor economic agents' expectations about the future. It also helps economic agents to focus their expectations on the fundamentals, instead of on past movements of the exchange rates (technical analysis).

Taking this criticism of the target zone proposal into account, a revised reform proposal could then consist of the following two rules.

(1) Each central bank declares an official exchange rate and a band of free fluctuation. In the spirit of Williamson's proposal this could be fixed at 10 per cent above and below the parity rate. Central banks commit themselves to defend these parities. This commitment, however, is not absolute. When the need arises the parities may be adjusted.

(2) Each central bank commits itself to limit these adjustments in the parities to a maximum of say 10 per cent per year. In contrast to the first commitment, this is absolute.

It will be noted that this proposal is very loose. Its looseness has the great advantage that no explicit agreements on the conduct of monetary policies in the system will be necessary. The size of the intervention band is so large that it can accommodate relatively large differences in monetary policies on the part of the participants. As a result, such an arrangement can achieve credibility, the *conditio sine qua non* for its success.

In such an exchange rate arrangement, the periodic computation of an equilibrium exchange rate is also unnecessary (except at the start of the arrangement). The market participants take over this task. And the role of the monetary authorities is to provide the necessary anchor. This anchor then is a commitment that the currencies will not be devalued or revalued during a given period of time by more than a certain percentage (10 per cent). It is this feature on which no compromise is possible which will be able to stabilize expectations.

In such a world, economic agents will regularly re-evaluate the question whether the existing parities correspond to their fundamental values. If they do not believe this to be the case, the speculative pressure becomes a sign for the monetary authorities to change the parities. The limited size of the adjustments, however, makes the occurrence of unusual speculative profits impossible. This is so because adjustments in the parities must remain smaller than the size of

---

[6] In a recent addendum to his original proposal Williamson has added such a rule (see Williamson and Henning (1994)).

the band of free fluctuation. As a result, after a realignment, the exchange rate does not make a jump.

5. The McKinnon proposal for international monetary reform

In a number of influential articles Ronald McKinnon of Stanford University has proposed a drastic reform of the international monetary system. It consists of a co-operative agreement between the US, Germany, and Japan aimed at stabilizing the respective exchange rates. In addition, the n − 1 problem of such a fixed exchange rate arrangement is solved by these three countries jointly targeting a price index of tradable goods. This would allow the world price level to be 'anchored'.

The McKinnon proposal is nothing but a fixed exchange rate commitment, and a very tight one. One is entitled to remain sceptical about the feasibility of such international co-operative efforts. Since the McKinnon rule is a fixed exchange rate arrangement, it too will suffer from the credibility problems we identified in the chapter on fixed exchange rate arrangements.

6. Controls on capital mobility

The liberalization of capital movements which was set in motion during the 1980s has increased the amount of funds available for speculative purposes and has also enlarged the policy options of the authorities (see Chapter 8). All this has led to a strong perception that the world-wide integration of capital markets has increased the fragility of the international monetary system, and that it has led to greater variability of the exchange rates. As a result, it has again become popular to propose the reintroduction of capital controls. The best known proposal was formulated by Tobin (1978), and has reappeared in different forms (see Eichengreen and Wyplosz (1994)). The proposal made by Tobin consists in imposing a 1 per cent tax on all foreign exchange transactions, in order 'to put sand in the wheels of international finance'. How can a 1 per cent tax halt speculative movements? The answer given by Tobin is that a 1 per cent tax on very short-term capital movements (say one week) reduces the rate of return on these short-term investments substantially. It barely affects the rate of return on long-term investments in foreign assets. As a result, this 'Tobin tax' will discourage short-term capital movements while leaving long-term movements relatively unaffected. And this is precisely the objective of the proposal. Long-term capital movements are generally guided by differences in long-term profitability of investments in different countries. These movements generally increase

TABLE **11.1.** *Measures of exchange rate variability*

	Standard deviation of monthly changes			Mean average monthly changes		
	DM/$	Yen/$	Sterling/$	DM/$	Yen/$	Sterling/$
1970s	3.5	3.2	2.8	2.5	2.0	2.1
1980s	3.6	3.5	3.6	2.9	2.8	2.8
1990s	3.3	2.9	3.5	2.4	2.3	2.5

Note: The 1970s span the period 1973–9 of floating exchange rates
Source: IMF, *International Financial Statistics*

world welfare. Short-term capital movements on the other hand are not related to differentials in long-term rates of return but are motivated by ephemeral and often self-fulfilling speculative gains. These will be discouraged by the Tobin tax.

Eichengreen and Wyplosz (1994) have formulated a similar proposal. However, instead of imposing a tax on foreign exchange transactions, they propose to impose a requirement for banks to deposit the counterpart of their net foreign exchange exposure in an interest-free account at the central bank. It should also be noted that the proposal made by Eichengreen and Wyplosz was formulated in the context for the workings of the EMS. In their view the major reason for the collapse of the EMS was the abolition of capital controls in the early 1990s (see Chapter 5 for a discussion of this view). Their proposal, therefore, aims at making the EMS less fragile.

What are we to think about these proposals to reintroduce capital controls in the international monetary system? Several problems arise with these proposals. The first has to do with the question of whether the liberalization of capital movements has increased the variability of exchange rates, and concomitantly whether a reintroduction of capital controls will reduce exchange rate variability. The second question deals with the practicability of reintroducing capital controls.

6.1. Capital controls and exchange rate variability

The proposals to reintroduce capital controls are predicated on the view that the liberalization of capital movements, that became a reality in many countries during the 1980s and 1990s, has increased the degree of volatility of exchange rates. Is there any evidence for this?

In Table 11.1 we show some measures of exchange rate variability during these decades.[7] We compare these measures with those observed in the 1970s. We find that there is practically no difference in the degree of variability of exchange rates during the 1970s, 1980s, and 1990s. In fact we find a slight decline

[7] Ideally one should use measures of conditional variability. Note, however, that the standard deviation of monthly changes can be interpreted as the variability of the exchange rate conditional on the exchange rate being a random walk.

of the degree of exchange rate variability during the 1990s compared to the 1980s. This is surprising since the degree of capital market integration has probably increased in the 1990s compared to the 1980s. Thus, it is safe to conclude that the greater degree of capital mobility does not seem to have led to greater exchange rate variability.

This finding tends to undermine the basic rationale for a reintroduction of capital controls, which is predicated on the presumption that the liberalization of capital movements has led to greater turbulence in foreign exchange markets. There does not seem to be evidence to substantiate this.[8]

6.2. Practical problems of a reintroduction of capital controls

The practical problems of a reintroduction of capital controls are formidable.[9] Take the Tobin tax for example which would tax all transactions passing through the foreign exchange markets (presumably both spot and forward markets). It is clear, however, that the increasing sophistication of the financial markets now allows speculators to bypass the foreign exchange market and yet to take a speculative position. An example will clarify this. A speculator who expects the dollar to decline can sell dollars spot (or forward). In that case he will pay the Tobin tax. He can, however, also make a swap transaction exchanging, say, the future interest revenue on a dollar security for future interest returns on a DM security. When he does this, he will not pay the Tobin tax.

Another way to speculate is to change the timing of the payments for imports and exports. For example, speeding up the payment of imports and delaying the repatriation of export receipts when one expects the foreign currency to increase in price, has the same effect in the foreign exchange market as an outright purchase of foreign currency. And yet such a reshuffling of the payment periods will not be taxed.

Another important practical problem of the Tobin tax has to do with the fact that in order to impose such a tax, a world-wide agreement is necessary involving all countries. This will be very difficult to achieve because there will always be free-riding countries who will find it attractive not to participate in the agreement so as to attract a disproportionate amount of financial transactions to their country. In other words, there will be many Luxembourgs and Switzerlands that will decide not to play the game of the Tobin tax.

For all these reasons it is highly unlikely that such a proposal will ever be put into practice. Not only is it not obvious that the Tobin tax (or other capital control measures) will reduce the degree of exchange rate variability, the practical problems of implementing such a proposal in a world of increasing financial sophistication are overwhelming.

---

[8] For a survey of the empirical evidence, see IMF (1995*b*).
[9] For a recent analysis see Charles Goodhart (1995) and Frenkel (1996).

7. Conclusion

In order for exchange rate commitments to work, rules must be established for setting the system-wide money stocks (and interest rates). If the asymmetric model which was typical of the Bretton Woods system and of the EMS, cannot be used between the major industrialized countries, explicit co-operation must be used to solve this (n – 1) problem. We have argued in this chapter that stable co-operative agreements are unlikely to come about. As a result, credible exchange rate commitments between the major industrialized countries are equally unlikely to be realized in the near future.

All this leads to a rather pessimistic view about the possibilities for reform of the international monetary system. Major changes are not to be expected soon, and we are likely to have to live with high variability of the exchange rates of the major currencies for some time. But what is wrong with the present system that so many people want to reform it? This is the question we deal with in the next chapter.

12

COSTS OF EXCHANGE RATE VARIABILITY

1. Introduction

In the previous chapter we concluded that it is very unlikely that credible exchange rate agreements between the major industrialized countries will come about soon. Should we worry about this? Is there really a need for such stabilization schemes? In discussions on international monetary reform, this question has loomed large. Whereas during the 1960s a consensus existed that there was not enough exchange rate flexibility, the large swings in real exchange rates experienced since the early 1970s have created a new consensus that the degree of exchange rate flexibility may now be excessive. In this chapter we evaluate the arguments of those who claim that exchange rates have become excessively variable and of those who see nothing special to worry about.

2. Two schools of thought

As was mentioned in Chapter 10 there are basically two schools of thought about the causes of the high variability of exchange rates. According to the 'fundamentalist' view exchange rate variability reflects variability in economic fundamentals. This view is also consistent with the rational expectations, perfect foresight model. In this model, exogenous disturbances lead economic agents to calculate the effects of these shocks on the exchange rate. This process will often require overshooting of the exchange rate. As a result, in this model disturbances in fundamentals have amplified effects on the exchange rate. In general, however, the ensuing exchange rate variability will reflect variability of the underlying fundamentals.

According to the second school of thought, exchange rate movements often do not reflect movements of fundamentals. There are many versions of this school. The most popular one is to say that economic agents are irrational and do not attach importance to fundamentals. Another version is the speculative bubble theory which was discussed in Chapter 7. A third version has been presented in this book. Its main feature is that economic agents are extremely uncertain about the underlying economic model driving the exchange rate. As a result, most often they do not find it worthwhile to use 'fundamental information'. They will use simple rules (like the past patterns of exchange rate movements) to forecast exchange rates. In such a 'near-rational' world exchange rate movements most often do not reflect movements in the fundamentals.

It is clear that these two schools of thought have drastically different implications, not only for the question of how exchange rates can be stabilized (as we discussed in Chapter 10), but also for the question of the welfare effects of these exchange rate movements.

3. The welfare effects of exchange rate variability: the 'fundamentalist' model

The basic insight provided by the fundamentalist model can be formulated as follows. Exchange rate variability reflects the variability of the exogenous variables in the system (for example, the variability of monetary and fiscal policies, oil price shocks, etc.).[1] As a result, attempts at stabilizing the exchange rate while nothing is done to reduce the variability of these 'fundamentals' will generally not improve economic welfare. Trying to fix the exchange rate may sometimes increase welfare. However, it may also lead to the opposite result.

The first formalization of this basic insight can be found in an important article by William Poole written in 1970. Although William Poole did not ask the question whether it is good to fix exchange rates, he analysed a related question, i.e. whether fixing the interest rate or fixing the money stock (and thereby allowing the interest rate to float freely) is the optimal policy rule.

Since that article was published, many refinements have been added. The basic insight of the original Poole article, however, remains valid. Let us, therefore, analyse in greater detail what he had in mind. We shall, first, discuss the logic of the argument within the framework of Poole's original objective of determining whether fixing the interest rate is optimal in a world of many stochastic disturbances in the exogenous variables. We shall then apply the same logic to the question of whether fixing the exchange rate is optimal.

Let us assume, as Poole did, that the authorities have as their objective the stabilization of output. In other words, they want to follow a policy rule which minimizes fluctuations in output. What, then, is the optimal rule? Fixing the interest rate, or allowing it to float freely while fixing the money stock? The

---

[1] In Ch. 7 we referred to econometric studies that give very little empirical foundation for this view. For example, the recent study by Flood and Rose (1994*a*) shows that the variability of the fundamentals has on average *not* been higher in flexible exchange rate systems than in fixed exchange rate regimes.

answer given by Poole is that it depends on the nature of the shock which hits the economy.

Let us take two examples of disturbances to illustrate what Poole had in mind. Take first an expansion of aggregate demand due to a boom in the business cycle. (In the framework of the *IS–LM* analysis this is a rightward shift in the *IS* curve.) If the monetary authorities fix the interest rate, they will be forced to increase the money stock. This is so because the increase in real income increases the demand for money and exerts upward pressure on the interest rate. In order to keep the interest rate constant, the authorities will have to increase the money stock. This policy, however, will tend to fuel the boom conditions and to exacerbate the business cycle.

An alternative approach for the authorities is to fix the money stock and to allow the interest rate to 'float freely'. In this case this will be a better policy than fixing the interest rate. Why? When aggregate demand increases, a free-floating interest rate policy will make it possible for the interest rate to increase. This increase then tends to dampen the business cycle. Thus, it can be concluded more generally that when the shock originates in the goods market it is better to allow free floating of the interest rate (fixing the money stock) than fixing the interest rate, if the objective is to stabilize output. Fixing the interest rate will lead to more variability in output than a policy which allows the interest rate to move freely. Put differently, more stability in the interest rate is obtained at the cost of more variability in output.

Things are quite different if the shock originates in the financial markets. Suppose that the velocity of money declines (the demand for money increases). If the authorities fix the money stock the interest rate will increase. This will then feed back into the goods market, and lead to a decline in aggregate demand. The result may be a recession. If, on the other hand, the authorities fix the interest rate, they will have to increase the money stock. This is now the best possible response. Since economic agents wish to hold more money, the authorities supply more. The interest rate remains constant, and there are no effects in the goods market. Thus, the effects of a purely financial disturbance are contained in the financial markets. This was not the case when the authorities followed a flexible interest rate policy.

We can now come to a more fundamental insight. Since the economy is hit by financial *and* real shocks most of the time, the optimal response will almost never be one of fixing the interest rate rigidly, or of letting it be determined completely freely. A mixed policy will usually be optimal. In the context of our discussion, we can say that attempts at fixing the interest rate will usually lead to more volatility in some other variable, *in casu* the output level.

The previous analysis can almost literally be used to study the optimality of fixing or 'flexing' the exchange rate. All we have to do is to translate interest rate into exchange rate. The conclusions are the same: if a shock occurs in the goods markets it will generally be better to allow the exchange rate to adjust than to fix it. Thus, if there is an expansion of aggregate demand, fixing the money stock leads to both a higher domestic interest rate and to an appreciation

of the currency. This appreciation will dampen the effects of the c
on the output level. On the other hand, fixing the exchange rate
interest rate will increase the impact of the boost to aggregate dei
it forces the authorities to increase the money stock. More genera
are demand disturbances, fixing the exchange rate will lead to n
in output.

The opposite occurs when the shock is financial in nature. For example, if
there is an increase in the demand for money (a reduction of velocity), the
higher interest rate also leads to an appreciation of the domestic currency.
Allowing the exchange rate to float will then transmit the financial shock to the
goods market through the appreciation of the currency. The same is true when
the demand for money declines. Letting the currency depreciate allows a pure
financial shock to lead to inflationary pressures in the goods market.

These propositions can be shown more formally using a simple *IS–LM* framework. This is done in Box 12.1.

Box 12.1. The optimal exchange rate flexibility in the *IS–LM* model

The model used here is the same as the one which was used in Chapter 6. It
is, of course, very simple, and more sophisticated models have been developed.[2]
The essence of the conclusions of the simple model, however, carries over to
the more complicated world.

We use the same version of the *IS–LM* model which was used in Chapter 6.
On the vertical axis we have the exchange rate, on the horizontal axis the output level. It will be remembered that when we analyse the *IS–LM* model in the
exchange rate–output space, the *IS* curve is a positively sloped line, because a
depreciation of the currency (an increase in *S*) increases aggregate demand and
therefore requires an increase in output to equilibrate the goods market. The *LM*
curve is a negatively sloped line for the following reason. A depreciation of the
currency increases the domestic price level. This reduces the supply of real cash
balances. As a result, the level of real income must decline in order to reduce
the (transactions) demand for money.

We can now analyse the effects of shocks under the two exchange rate regimes.
Suppose, first, we have shocks in the *IS* curve (these are shocks in the goods market). We represent these by movements of the *IS* curve within the band IS_L–IS_U.
Fixing the exchange rate then implies that the output level fluctuates between the
limits given by Y_L and Y_U. To make this result clear, consider the leftward movement of the *IS* curve to IS_L. In order for the exchange rate to remain fixed, the
authorities have to reduce the money stock, so that the *LM* curve intersects the
IS_L curve at *A*. As a result, the new equilibrium is located at *A*. When the *IS* curve
shifts to IS_U, the new equilibrium point becomes *B*.

If, however, the authorities fix the money stock, and therefore allow the
exchange rate to fluctuate freely, the fluctuations of the output level will be
reduced to the band between Y_L' and Y_U'. Thus, a policy of free exchange rate
movements reduces the variability of output when the disturbances originate in

---

[2] See Frenkel and Aizenman (1982), Fischer (1977), Henderson (1982), Turnovsky (1982).

Costs of Exchange Rate Variability

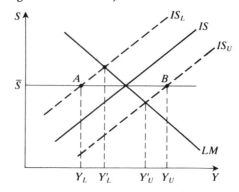

Fɪɢ. 12.1. *IS–LM* model: stochastic disturbances in goods market

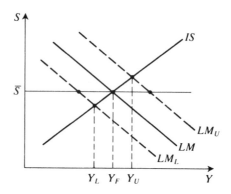

Fɪɢ. 12.2. *IS–LM* model: stochastic disturbances in money market

the goods market. The reason is that when aggregate demand increases/declines the currency appreciates/depreciates, thereby reducing/increasing aggregate demand.

When the shocks occur in the *LM* curve we obtain the opposite results. We represent this in Fig. 12.2. The *LM* curve now fluctuates between the limits LM_L and LM_U. If the authorities let the exchange rate float, the result will be that the output level fluctuates between the limits Y_L and Y_U. If the exchange rate is fixed, however, the output level will not be affected at all. It is fixed at Y_F. This is due to the fact that when the *LM* curve shifts to the right (for example because of a reduction in the demand for money), a fixed exchange rate system leads to an outflow of international reserves. This reduces the supply of money, and shifts the *LM* curve back to the left, leaving the output market unaffected. This contrasts with the floating exchange rate regime, where the same reduction in the demand for money leads to a depreciation of the currency, which in turn stimulates aggregate demand.

In general, the economy is hit by disturbances in both the goods market and the money market. As a result, the optimal policy will usually not be a complete fixity nor a complete flexibility of the exchange rate. A managed floating (limited flexibility) will be optimal.

The previous model is certainly extremely simplified. As mentioned earlier, however, more complex models which allow for rational expectations, and for objective functions which include other variables than output, lead to the same result, i.e. that limited flexibility will generally be better than either fixed or completely flexible exchange rates.[3] As mentioned in the previous chapter, these models generally imply that in order to reduce the variability of the exchange rate, it is necessary and sufficient to reduce the variability of the fundamental variables (the shifts in the *IS* and *LM* curves).

The previous discussion allows us to conclude that exchange rate agreements which are too rigid, and which do not allow for adjustments in the exchange rates when certain disturbances occur, will not be optimal. At the same time, we learn from this literature on the optimal degree of exchange rate flexibility that complete flexibility will not be optimal either, because it will frequently amplify the effects of financial disturbances in the goods markets.

Although this literature provides important insights, it can also be said that it gives few, if any, practical guidelines for the authorities in their conduct of exchange rate policies. The main reason is that the authorities generally do not know the source of the disturbance when they observe a movement in the exchange rate. Since the theory tells them that knowledge of the source of the shock is crucial in devising an optimal exchange rate policy, it will be very difficult to implement such optimal policy responses. In a sense it can be said that this theory has little practical relevance because it requires the authorities to process more information than is possible.

4. An alternative view

The second school of thought leads to quite a different analysis. Let us start from the theory which we have developed in Chapter 9. On this view, economic agents are unable to detect how the exchange rate is influenced by fundamentals, as long as the exchange rate does not deviate too much from its fundamental value. Within this band of 'agnosticism' the exchange rate will be driven mainly by backward-looking rules. This will produce drift in the exchange rate which will show no clear tendency to return to its equilibrium value. It follows from this theory that exchange rate volatility is quite often not the result of exogenous disturbances in fundamentals.

In this view of the world there are costs to exchange rate variability which are not the price we pay for having less variability in other variables. Thus, whereas

---

[3] See Frenkel and Aizenman (1982) for an illustration.

in the 'fundamentalists'' view of the world attempts at reducing exchange rate variability will usually lead to more variability of other economic variables (e.g. output or prices), this is not the case when exchange rate variability is disconnected from the variability of the underlying fundamentals. In the latter case, one can reduce the variability of the exchange rates without increasing variability somewhere else in the system.

If we accept this second school of thought we have to conclude that exchange rate variability has been costly for the world economy. What is the nature of these costs? How important have these costs been empirically? These are the two questions which are analysed in the remainder of this chapter.

5. Costs of exchange rate variability

Many problems of the world economy have been blamed on the volatility of exchange rates.[4] Some should be taken seriously. Others have very little to do with the existence of flexible exchange rates. Let us analyse some of these problems.

5.1. Floating exchange rates and world inflation

During the first decade after the switch to floating exchange rates in 1973, the rate of inflation in the industrialized countries increased significantly. Whereas during 1960–73 the yearly inflation rate in the industrialized world was on average 3.7 per cent, it increased to 7.9 per cent during 1973–86. This increase in inflation led to many different theories showing that the flexibility of the exchange rates by itself was a source of world-wide inflation.[5] Since the middle of the 1980s, however, industrialized countries have on average been quite successful in reducing their yearly inflation to the level observed during the Bretton Woods system (see Fig. 12.3). As a result, most of these theories have been shelved since then. It can be interesting, however, to discuss some of the theories that were taken seriously in the past.

Two mechanisms in the flexible exchange rate system which could, in principle, have stimulated inflation, have been stressed. One is a ratchet effect. The other is a discipline effect.

The *ratchet effect* works as follows. A depreciation of one currency always means that some other currencies must be appreciating. The country of the depreciating currency should experience an acceleration of its inflation, while the countries of the appreciating currencies should experience a decline in their inflation rates. As a result, exchange rate fluctuations should have a neutral effect on the average inflation rate in the world. However, if there are asymmetries in wage and price flexibility, i.e. if prices and wages are less flexible downwards than upwards, the decline in the rate of inflation of the appreciating country may

---

[4] For an excellent overview of some of the issues see IMF (1984), and Goldstein (1980).

[5] A well-known proponent of this view was Triffin. See Triffin (1983). For a criticism, see Goldstein (1980).

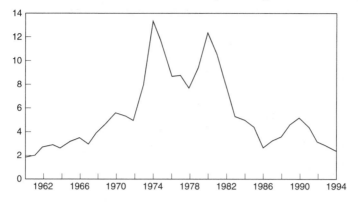

FIG. **12.3.** Inflation: industrial countries (early growth CPI)
Source: IMF, International Financial Statistics

not match the increase in the depreciating country. This asymmetry then leads to a net increase in average inflation when exchange rates become more variable.

A second source of inflation in the flexible exchange rate system comes from the fact that in such a system, countries do not face a foreign exchange constraint. There is, therefore, a loosening of the *discipline* exerted on the conduct of monetary policies. This may then give an incentive to the authorities to follow more inflationary monetary policies.[6] This discipline effect has been stressed very much in the context of the EMS. We discussed this in Chapter 4 where we studied the cases of countries like Italy and Spain which tried to reduce their inflation rates by pegging their currencies to the DM.

Although it cannot be denied that the ratchet and discipline effects may have played a role, the evidence now indicates that these effects have been weak in practice. This is especially true of the discipline effect. (In Chapter 4 we discussed some theoretical reasons why this discipline effect has not worked well.) Some evidence is obtained by comparing the experience of EMS countries with the industrialized countries outside the EMS. The former pegged their bilateral exchange rates, the latter did not have such explicit exchange rate arrangements. In Fig. 12.4, we show the average inflation rates in both groups of countries during 1973–92. It can clearly be seen that despite the fact that the EMS countries had tied their currencies to each other since 1979, their inflation rates did not decline faster than outside the EMS. Thus, the existence of (quasi) fixed exchange rates among a relatively large group of countries in Europe did not seem to facilitate the dis-inflationary process, compared to the experience of a group of countries which maintained a regime of flexible exchange rates.[7]

---

[6] In a well-known paper Rogoff (1985) has argued the opposite. Using a theoretical model he found that countries with a fixed exchange rate can in fact have stronger incentives to produce inflation than countries with a flexible exchange rate.

[7] It should be noted that some countries in the non-EMS group pegged their exchange rates informally to the EMS. This is the case for Austria and Switzerland.

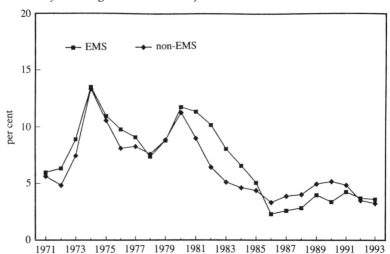

FIG. 12.4. Average yearly inflation in the EMS and in non-EMS industrial countries

Note: The EMS and non-EMS inflation rates are weighted averages of national inflation rates using GDP as weights

Source: OECD, 'Economic Outlook'

The main argument against the view that floating exchange rates lead to a reduction in monetary discipline is that the overshooting of the exchange rate is itself a source of discipline exerted by the financial markets.[8] Thus, if the domestic authorities engage in a policy of monetary expansion, the currency will depreciate and overshoot its long-run value. This overshooting of the currency is the financial markets' method of disciplining the monetary authorities. As a result, it is very difficult to conclude that fixed exchange rate systems provide more monetary discipline than floating exchange rate regimes.

5.2. Floating exchange rates and the slowdown of economic growth

Since the inception of floating exchange rates in 1973, the industrialized world has experienced a significant decline in the growth rate of output. Whereas during the period 1960–73 the GNP of the industrial countries grew at an average yearly rate of 4.4 per cent, this growth rate dropped to 1.7 per cent during 1973–90.

It is tempting to find a causality between the variability of exchange rates and the slow-down of economic growth. In order to see whether such a causal link exists, it is necessary to investigate first what the transmission mechanism

---

[8] We have argued in Chapter 8 that the flexible exchange rate regime (together with free capital mobility) may have reduced budgetary discipline.

is from exchange rate variability to economic growth. Can one find theoretical arguments to predict that exchange rate variability leads to a slow-down in economic growth?

Exchange rate variability can influence economic growth via its effect on international trade. Here also one observes that since the start of the floating exchange rate regime, the growth of international trade among industrialized countries has slowed down significantly. Whereas during the 1960s trade flows were growing on average by more than 10 per cent annually in the industrialized world, this growth rate has dropped to less than 5 per cent since 1973. Can the increased variability of exchange rates be held responsible for this phenomenon? Two potential channels through which this may have occurred have been stressed in the literature.

Uncertainty and International Trade   A first effect of exchange rate variability is to increase uncertainty in international trade. Uncertainty leads risk-averse individuals to reduce their effort in these more risky activities and to retrench into domestic (less risky) activities. As a result, the uncertainty created by more variable exchange rates has a negative effect on international trade. It also follows that one of the engines of post-war growth in the industrialized countries is slowed down.

One may object to this view that financial markets allow traders to hedge against the increased exchange risk. Traders can buy futures and options contracts. In addition, these contracts have become more and more sophisticated. Although it cannot be denied that financial markets provide these insurance services, it is also true that these services are not costless. Traders who want to hedge have to pay a price. Therefore, the increased risk in international trade can also be considered to have the same effect as an increase in tariffs, i.e. it will slow down international trade.

Despite its obvious plausibility, it has been surprisingly difficult to find empirical confirmation of this theory. Numerous empirical studies have been undertaken to test it. A survey by the IMF (1984) concludes that the majority of existing econometric studies have been unable to detect such a negative influence of exchange rate uncertainty on trade. Only a relatively small number of econometric studies have been able to uncover such negative effects of exchange rate variability on trade.[9] It is unclear, however, whether in these studies it is the uncertainty effect which produces these results, or whether other mechanisms are at work (see next section).

Although the theory about the negative effects of uncertainty on trade sounds extremely plausible, it must be stressed that the modern theory of production and consumption under risk does not allow one to derive clear-cut conclusions about the effect of increased risk on the volume of trade.[10] One reason is the following. When the price (exchange rate) increases unexpectedly, the firm

---

[9] See De Grauwe (1988), De Grauwe and de Bellefroid (1987), and Kenen and Rodrik (1986).

[10] This has been stressed by De Grauwe (1988) and Gros (1987). See also Newbery and Stiglitz (1981).

increases its output to profit from the higher price. Thus, its profits increase because average revenue increases, and because the firm increases output. When the price declines, however, the firm cuts back its output. Thus, profits decline because the average revenue declines. The firm however limits this loss by reducing quantities. One can say that with a higher price risk, profits will on average be higher.[11] As a result, risk-neutral individuals will be attracted by these higher profit opportunities.

This positive effect of risk must now be contrasted with the negative effect of risk aversion which has been stressed by the traditional theory. Risk-averse individuals give a lower utility value to profits that are uncertain than to less risky profits. One can conclude that increased uncertainty leads to a fundamentally ambiguous effect on trade: greater profit opportunities attract individuals; the greater risk of these profits inhibits risk-averse individuals. It should therefore not be surprising that empirical studies have been unable to find significant negative effects of the increased exchange rate risk on international trade.

The Political Economy of Exchange Rate Variability   There is a second channel of transmission from exchange rate variability to trade which appears to be more promising in explaining the slow-down of international trade. This second channel can be explained as follows.

Exchange rate changes that wander away from purchasing power parities for long periods of time lead to 'real' effects in the economy. These 'misalignments' lead to a boom in the traded-goods sectors of countries whose currencies have become undervalued. In the countries whose currencies have become overvalued as a result of the swing in the real exchange rate, the traded goods sectors are squeezed, leading to a loss of output and employment that is not easily absorbed in the short run by the other sectors of the economy.[12]

The political economy part of this story is set in motion when, as a result of output and employment losses, individuals hurt by these developments organize to pass projectionist legislation. As a result, markets become more protected, so that international trade is negatively affected.[13]

This hypothesis only makes sense if there is some asymmetry in the protectionist tendencies—for example, when protectionist legislation passed when the currency tended to be overvalued is kept in place when the currency is in the undervaluation part of the cycle. If such asymmetries are present, then swings in real exchange rates will lead to a trend-like increase in protectionism and will negatively affect international trade. Thus, in general, this theory predicts that volatility of real exchange rates over periods exceeding a few months or quarters is likely to lead to a reduction in the growth of international trade.

---

[11] Technically this effect follows from the convexity of the profit function in the output price. Thus, when the price increases, profits increase by more than they decline when the price drops.

[12] For a thorough analysis of the costs of these misalignmnents see Williamson (1983). See also Bergsten and Williamson (1983).

[13] Empirical evidence on the determinants of protectionist pressure is provided by Cline (1984) and Clifton (1985).

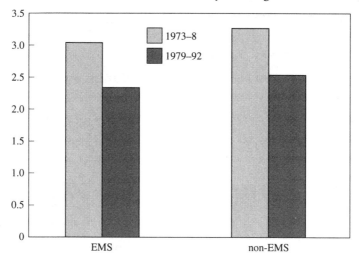

Fɪɢ. **12.5.** Real growth GNP in EMS and non-EMS

Although the evidence is still skimpy, there has been an increasing number of empirical studies documenting that the long swings in real exchange rates may have affected international trade negatively.[14] There is now a growing realization that if the floating exchange rate system has led to negative effects on trade, it is through this political economy effect of exchange rates that tend to be misaligned for long periods of time.

There are still a number of puzzles, however. First, although significant, the effect of the long-run variability of real exchange rates on international trade appears to be relatively limited and is able to explain only a small part of the total decline in the growth rate of trade.[15] Second, the experience of the EMS countries leads to puzzling questions concerning the effects of exchange rate variability.

The EMS and international trade As mentioned in the previous chapter, the EMS countries have been relatively successful in avoiding the large misalignments of their currencies against each other. Has this success enabled these countries to avoid the deceleration in the growth rate of their trade and of their GNP?

Some evidence is provided in Figs 12.5 and 12.6. In Fig. 12.5 the average yearly growth rate of GNP of the EMS countries is compared with the growth rate in the non-EMS industrialized countries, before and after 1979. In both groups of countries one observes a deceleration of economic growth since 1979.

Fig. 12.6 presents evidence on the growth of trade within the EMS. It shows the average yearly growth of intra-EMS trade before and after 1979. At the same time the growth of trade of the EMS countries with the non-EMS industrial countries is presented. The most striking feature of these growth rates is the

---

[14] See the above-mentioned studies by De Grauwe (1988), De Grauwe and de Bellefroid (1987), and Kenen and Rodrik (1986).　　　　[15] See De Grauwe (1988) on this.

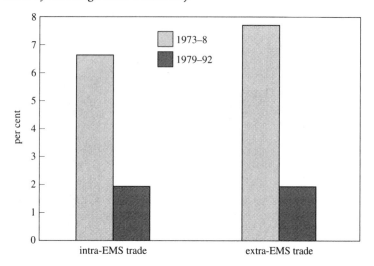

FIG. 12.6. Average yearly growth of trade

Notes: Extra-EMS trade: trade (exports + imports) of EMS countries with non-EMS industrial countries
Extra-EMS (ex. US): same as previous except that trade with US is excluded
Source: IMF, *Direction of Trade*

deceleration of the intra-EMS trade since 1979 which has been stronger than that observed in the case of the extra-EMS trade. This has happened despite the fact that the EMS countries experienced more exchange rate stability.

The previous evidence suggests that if more stable exchange rates within the EMS had a positive influence on the growth rates of output and trade, these positive effects have been more than compensated by negative forces, which have been strong enough to swamp the beneficial effects of exchange rate stability. These negative forces have been widely studied. They are, first, the restrictive fiscal policies pursued by the major EMS countries and, second, the supply side problems of many European countries.[16]

One can learn an important lesson from the experience of the EMS. This is that stable exchange rates are not sufficient to obtain better growth prospects. The latter seem to be relatively independent of the exchange rate regime. Put differently, growth in output and in trade is influenced by a host of factors, the stability of exchange rates being a relatively unimportant one.

5.3. Floating exchange rates and the adjustment problem

The Achilles' heel of the Bretton Woods system was its lack of flexibility. The fixity of the exchange rates made it difficult for countries to correct external

[16] For an analysis of demand and supply side problems in Europe, see e.g. Blanchard, *et al.* (1985), Modigliani, *et al.* (1986).

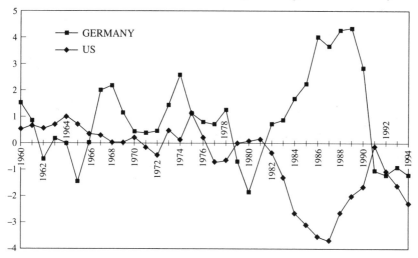

FIG. **12.7.** Current account balance, the US and Germany (per cent of GDP)

disequilibria without coming into conflict with domestic policy objectives. The move to flexible exchange rates carried with it the hope that these external disequilibria could more easily be dealt with. For, in such a system, depreciations and appreciations of the currency would not be prevented, and would help to eliminate current account deficits and surpluses in a smoother way than was possible in the Bretton Woods system.

Has this hope been realized? In Figs 12.7 and 12.8 we present the current accounts of the US, Germany, and Japan (as a percentage of their GNP). It is immediately clear that there has been no tendency for current account surpluses and deficits to become smaller after 1973. On the contrary, since the early 1980s the deficits and surpluses of the three major industrialized countries have increazed in size.

This is a rather surprising situation. If anything, the strength of the flexible exchange rate system was seen initially as consisting in an ability to correct current account disequilibria. What are the reasons for this surprising failure of the flexible exchange rate system to solve the 'adjustment' problem which haunted the fixed exchange rate regime?

First of all it should be stressed that part of the problem may reside in the fact that the oil shocks of the 1970s coincided with the existence of exchange rate flexibility. These oil shocks by themselves produced large current account imbalances. This was especially clear in the case of Germany during 1979–80 (see Fig. 12.7). Nevertheless, the largest current account disequilibria emerged during the 1980s when most of the current account effects of the oil shocks had dissipated.

Second, since the 1970s budget deficits have tended to increase substantially in many countries. In addition, as was illustrated in Chapter 8, fiscal policies have

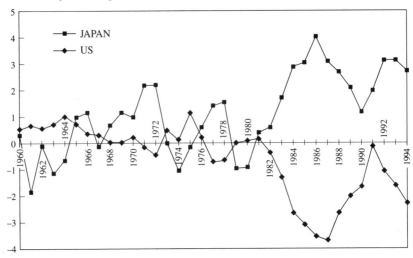

FIG. 12.8. Current account balance, the US and Japan (per cent of GDP)

had a tendency to be less co-ordinated among major industrialized countries during the floating exchange rate period than during the fixed exchange rate period. This lack of co-ordination of fiscal policies has been most pronounced during the 1980s when the US followed an expansionary fiscal policy, whereas many of the other industrial countries engaged in fiscal contraction. These large and unco-ordinated fiscal policies are a major reason why current account balances have been so difficult to achieve since the world moved to flexible exchange rates.

This explanation leads to new questions, however. First, there is the question whether the existence of floating exchange rates may have given incentives to countries to 'go their own way' in the fiscal policy field. If this is the case (and in Chapter 8 we argued that it is), the greater variability and lack of co-ordination of fiscal policies is not exogenous, but is itself the result of the existence of more exchange rate flexibility. Thus, it can be argued that the flexibility of exchange rates may have contributed to larger current account imbalances through the incentives it gave to fiscal policy authorities to follow more independent policies.

A second question arises from the fact that even if the new nature of fiscal policies may have contributed to larger current account imbalances, one could still have expected that the flexibility of the exchange rates would have corrected the current account consequences of these fiscal policies. As argued earlier, this was the general expectation of economists during the Bretton Woods system. It was then widely expected that the flexible exchange rate regime would allow for more national independence in the economic policy area, and that the current account consequences would easily be dealt with by variations in the exchange rates. The model which we used in Chapter 4 (the Swan diagram) synthesized this view.

It has, therefore, come as a surprise to many economists that the current accounts have shown such a small and slow response to real exchange rate movements during the flexible exchange rate period.

Many econometric studies have been undertaken to measure the response of trade flows to exchange rate changes. For surveys see Leamer and Stern (1970), and Kenen (1975) on the earlier literature. During the 1950s economists generally believed that the price elasticities in international trade were low. During the 1960s, this 'elasticity pessimism' gave way to a greater optimism about the ability of exchange rate changes to significantly affect exports and imports. This change in attitude was to a certain extent due to the successes of the devaluations in the UK (1967) and in France (1969) in correcting current account deficits.[17]

Experience since the early 1970s appears to have triggered a new 'elasticity pessimism'. Many of the more recent econometric studies of the effects of exchange rate changes on trade flows give some basis for this renewed pessimism. In general one finds that the large depreciations and appreciations of the dollar, the yen, and other major currencies have had effects on trade flows which appeared with a considerable lag only.[18] These studies have also uncovered the existence of so-called J curves. The latter describe the dynamics of the current account after a devaluation of the currency. When exports and imports are slow to react to the devaluation the initial effect of the latter may be to deteriorate the current account before an improvement sets in. There is now substantial evidence that these J curves are important.

Is there any reason to believe that the price sensitivity of international trade may have been affected by the exchange rate regime? In other words, is it conceivable that the move to more variable exchange rates may have reduced the price sensitivity of exports and imports, thereby reducing the ability of real exchange rate changes to correct current account imbalances?

In order to analyse this question a very simple model of an exporter in imperfectly competitive markets is presented in the next section. The model will allow us to show that when exchange rates become more variable, and when the exchange rate variations are perceived to be transitory, the sensitivity of trade flows with respect to exchange rate movements has a tendency to decline.

6. The exporter in an uncertain environment

Consider a firm selling a product in two markets, one domestic and the other foreign. The product is produced in the domestic country. Let us assume that the firm operates in imperfectly competitive markets. This means that it is selling a differentiated product, and that it faces a downward-sloping demand curve for its product in both the domestic and the foreign markets.

---

[17] This change in attitude was also the result of econometric studies indicating that the previously estimated price elasticities were biased downwards. See Leamer and Stern (1970).

[18] See e.g. Wilson and Takacs (1980), Japan, Economic Planning Agency (1979), Hooper and Mann (1987).

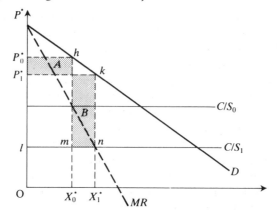

Fig. **12.9.** Effect of currency depreciation in imperfectly competitive market

We know from the microeconomic theory of the firm that the optimal pricing in the two markets will be given by the following rules:[19]

$$P = C\frac{\varepsilon}{\varepsilon - 1} \tag{12.1}$$

$$P^* = \frac{C}{S}\frac{\varepsilon^*}{\varepsilon^* - 1} \tag{12.2}$$

where P is the domestic currency price of the output sold in the home country; C is the marginal cost in domestic currency; ε is the price elasticity of demand in the domestic market; P^* is the foreign currency price of the output sold in the foreign market; C/S is the marginal cost translated into foreign currency terms; ε^* is the price elasticity of demand in the foreign market.

From equation (12.1) it is clear that the price in the domestic market (expressed in domestic currency) is not affected by exchange rate changes.[20] The foreign price, however, will be affected, because the marginal cost (in foreign currency) of selling the product in the foreign market is influenced by exchange rate changes.

The model of the foreign market is presented in Fig. 12.9. The foreign demand curve is represented by the line D, and the marginal revenue curve by MR. The marginal cost curve is assumed to be horizontal. When the exchange rate increases (i.e. the domestic currency devalues), the marginal cost in the foreign currency declines (C/S declines). This then leads to a downward shift of the marginal cost curve.

[19] Note that different prices in the two markets are only possible if there are impediments to trade, making it difficult to arbitrage between the two markets.

[20] We disregard the possibility that the change in the exchange rate changes the price elasticity in the domestic market. In addition, the effect of the exchange rate change on the marginal cost, c, when the firm imports foreign inputs is disregarded.

Let us assume an initial exchange rate S_0. The optimal combination of price and output in the foreign market is then given by P_0^* and X_0^*. Suppose now that the domestic currency depreciates unexpectedly. The exchange rate increases to S_1. The new optimal mix of price and output becomes P_1^* and X_1^*.

The question we now want to analyse is whether the firm will change its price if there are some 'menu' costs in doing so. Keeping the price unchanged after the unexpected increase in the exchange rate results in the profit represented by the area $P_0^* hml$. Changing the price to the new optimal value yields a profit given by the area $P_1^* knl$. Thus the gain in profit from changing the price is equal to $B - A$ (which must be positive since P_1^* is the profit maximizing price). It is clear, however, that this gain is of a 'second order' of magnitude. This has to do with the fact that the gain in revenue resulting from the increase in output (the shaded area B) is partly compensated by the revenue loss resulting from the price decline (the shaded area A).[21]

We can now come to the following rule. If the gain in profit is smaller than the menu cost, the firm will not adjust its price following the unexpected increase in the exchange rate, i.e. if

$$B - A < z$$

where z is the menu cost.

The gain in profit $B - A$ is really a one period gain. In reality the firm will compare the present value of the gains in all future periods from changing the price today with the (once and for all) cost of changing the price. It is then crucial to specify whether the unexpected increase in the exchange rate is perceived to be permanent or transitory. Let us take two extreme examples. First, we assume that the increase observed today is expected to last indefinitely. The firm will then decide to keep the price unchanged if

$$\sum_{i=0}^{n} \frac{B - A}{(1 + r)^i} < z \tag{12.3}$$

i.e. if the present value of the current and future gains from changing today's price is smaller than the menu cost z.

In the second assumption of a purely transitory shock, the firm expects the increase in the exchange rate to last only for one period. After that period, the exchange rate is expected to return to its initial level, so that the optimal price becomes P_0^* again. The firm will then decide to keep today's price fixed if

$$(B - A) + \frac{A - B}{1 + r} < z + \frac{z}{1 + r}. \tag{12.4}$$

Comparing (12.3) with (12.4), it is obvious that the firm is more likely not to adjust its price if the exchange rate change is perceived to be temporary than

---

[21] Technically, we say that the profit function is convex in the price level. Around the equilibrium, changes in the price level have only second order effects on the level of profits. See Ackerlof and Yellen (1987), Mankiw (1985), and our discussion in Ch. 9.

if the firm believes the change to be permanent. More generally, if the temporary component of the change is perceived to be high, it is more likely that the firm will find it profitable not to adjust its price.

The previous theory allows us to list the factors which influence the sensitivity of trade flows to exchange rate changes. First, and foremost, the distinction between the temporary and the permanent nature of exchange rates matters. In an environment where exchange rates move up and down as they have since 1973, a relatively large component of any given exchange rate change will be perceived to be temporary. As a result, such movements in the exchange rates will lead to relatively small price changes, and will have a small effect on trade flows. When, however, the exchange rates change in an environment of exchange rate stability (e.g. the Bretton Woods regime, or the EMS), such changes are likely to be perceived as permanent and will lead to more pronounced price and quantity adjustments.

A second factor is the degree of competition. In markets of highly differentiated goods, price and quantity stickiness will be higher than in perfectly competitive markets. This can be seen from Fig. 12.8. The higher the degree of competition, the flatter the demand curve faced by the individual producer. The *B* area increases relative to the *A* area, increasing the gain from price changes.

There is a lot of empirical evidence to substantiate this theoretical prediction. Krugman (1987) found that the large appreciation of the dollar during the period 1980–5 had a very small influence on the US prices of German export goods of the differentiated type (machinery, cars). In other words, the German exporters of these differentiated products were 'pricing them to the market' in which they were sold. Thus the price of the same German car sold in the US and in Germany was relatively sticky, and changed little with the movements of the dollar/DM. In a perfectly competitive market, the US price would have had to decline and/or the German price would have had to increase following the appreciation of the dollar relative to the German mark. This failed to occur in differentiated goods markets.[22]

The same Krugman study also reveals that this phenomenon of price stickiness ('pricing to market') was not observed in the homogeneous goods sectors (chemicals, textiles). Similar evidence was found by Isard (1977), and by Richardson (1978).

A third factor influencing price stickiness in international trade is the level of the interest rate. As can be seen from equation (12.3), the expected gain from price adjustments declines when the interest rate increases. Thus, during periods of high interest rates (for example, the 1980s) price stickiness in international trade will be more pronounced than during periods of low interest rates. This may help to explain why trade flows appear to have been particularly unresponsive to exchange rate movements during the 1980s. More empirical evidence needs to be produced, however, before we can trust this result.

[22] For more empirical evidence see Hooper and Mann (1987) and Feenstra (1987). The latter author finds that price stickiness has increased during the 1980s, when the exchange rate variability increased relative to the 1970s. See also the recent study of Engel and Rogers (1996).

7. The law of one price

The 'law of one price' says that the price of the same product in two markets will be the same when expressed in a common currency. Thus, the same Mercedes or BMW should have the same price tag in New York or in Hamburg when translated in a common currency. An important implication of the theory developed in the previous sections (and its empirical confirmations), is that deviations from the 'law of one price' become more important when exchange rates become more variable, and when products are more differentiated.

It has always been known that impediments to trade (transport costs, tariffs) introduce price differentials, and therefore, deviations from the 'law of one price'. Up to recently, however, it was not widely known that these price differentials change when the exchange rates change, and that this phenomenon is important for the differentiated goods sectors. Thus, the price differential between a Mercedes sold in New York and in Hamburg varies with movements in the dollar/DM exchange rate (see Engel and Rogers (1996)).

8. Lessons to be learned

From the evidence of the 1970s, the 1980s, and the 1990s, it appears that floating exchange rates have not been instruments facilitating external adjustment. We identified two main reasons. One is that the flexibility of the exchange rates may have given incentives to the authorities to follow more independent fiscal policies, thereby exacerbating current account imbalances. It was generally believed that the latter 'would be taken care of' by depreciations and appreciations of the currency. This, however, did not happen easily. Thus, we identified a second major reason why exchange rate movements did not produce the expected current account adjustments. In an environment of high exchange rate variability, the sensitivity of trade flows to given movements of the exchange rate declines, because of the uncertainty whether these exchange rate movements will last.

All this leads to the following paradox. During the fixed exchange rate regime, countries found themselves lacking an instrument, the exchange rate, to equilibrate the current account. As a result, they were forced to rely on fiscal (and monetary) policies to correct an external disequilibrium when the latter had become too large to be sustainable. In a flexible exchange rate environment, the exchange rate loses its cutting edge as an instrument to equilibrate the current account. This leads to the paradoxical situation that countries may be forced to rely on domestic fiscal policies to correct disequilibria in the current account, despite the fact that the exchange rate is left free to perform this duty.

The most dramatic example of this paradox is the experience of the US since 1985. In the middle of the 1980s the US found itself confronted with large current account deficits which were built up during the early 1980s. The extremely large depreciations of the dollar which occurred after 1985 failed to change the current account outlook. The unsustainability of these external deficits has therefore put pressure on the US authorities to use the fiscal policy instrument in order to return to current account balance. This is certainly an irony of history. As pointed out earlier, such situations where countries would be pressured to use domestic fiscal policies for purposes of external balance, were thought to be restricted to fixed exchange rate regimes. Surprisingly, this also occurs in countries where the exchange rate is flexible.

9. Conclusion

From the discussion of this chapter it appears that the variability of the exchange rates, and especially the large misalignments that have occurred since the early 1970s have been costly for the world economy. Sizeable adjustments between traded and non-traded goods sectors have been forced on many countries when the currencies moved through cycles of overvaluation and undervaluation. Although hard evidence is difficult to gather, there is a presumption that these cycles may have stimulated protectionist pressures thereby harming international trade. Ultimately, this may have contributed to the major slow-down of economic growth observed in the industrialized world since 1973. More empirical evidence will have to be collected, however, to find out how important this effect has been.

At the start of the floating exchange rate period, it was generally expected that the flexibility of exchange rates would eliminate the balance of payments adjustment problem which had undermined the Bretton Woods system. It must now be admitted that the predictions of most economists were wrong. The adjustment problem has not abated. If anything, current account disequilibria have vastly increased in size.

In this and in the previous chapter it was argued that there are two reasons for this failure of the floating exchange rate system to correct external imbalances. One is that the flexibility of exchange rates has given incentives to governments to 'go their own way' in the budgetary field, without much consideration for the current account implications. Second, the high variability of the exchange rates has reduced the effectiveness of the latter in changing prices and quantities in international trade.

Thus, there are many reasons to argue for a return to more fixity in exchange rates of the major currencies. Unfortunately, it must immediately be added that although desirable, exchange rate stabilization is unlikely to happen soon. The historical analysis of this book tells us why. Sustainable exchange rate stabilization requires credible commitments, i.e. a commitment that even if the fixity of exchange rates hurts, the authorities will stick to it. The Bretton Woods system and the EMS foundered on the lack of credibility of the fixed exchange rate arrangement. This lack of credibility of fixed exchange rate commitment will continue to exist as long as independent nations pursue domestic objectives that can come into conflict with the exchange rate target.

In addition, fixed exchange rate arrangements require rules governing the system-wide monetary policy. This necessitates either a formidable amount of co-ordination of policies, or a very asymmetric relation between partners. These conditions do not seem to be satisfied today. Even the looser 'fixed' exchange rate systems proposed by Williamson and by McKinnon face this problem of how the major countries will be able to agree on the conduct of system-wide monetary policy. In an environment where the monetary authorities of the major countries maintain their full independence there will always be doubts about the robustness of an agreement once it is achieved.

History teaches us that there are no examples of lasting monetary co-operation between nations without some form of political and institutional integration. Agreements between independent national institutions to fix exchange rates or to conduct jointly a monetary policy suffer from an inevitable lack of credibility. There will always come a moment when the exchange rate commitment is perceived to go counter to some national interest. The incentive for the national authorities to override a prior commitment will then be overwhelming, and will lead to a speculative crisis.

There are two ways out of this dilemma. The first is that countries who aim at stabilizing their exchange rates take steps towards political and institutional integration. This is the strategy favoured by the proponents of monetary integration in Europe.[23] It is, however, too far-fetched as a strategy for the major industrial countries (US, Germany, Japan).

The second strategy is less ambitious. It recognizes that only loose commitments among independent nations can have credibility. This then suggests that agreements to limit the size of exchange rate changes, without eliminating them, might have a chance of success. Such a scheme was proposed in the previous chapter. Even if such agreements can be worked out, however, exchange rate changes will remain sizeable. Private and official agents will, therefore, have to learn to live with considerable exchange rate variability in the future.

---

[23] For an analysis of issues relating to monetary union see De Grauwe (1994), Gros and Thygesen (1992), Fratianni and von Hagen (1992).

REFERENCES

Akerlof, George, and Yellen, Janet, 'Rational Models of Irrational Behaviour', *American Economic Review*, May 1987.

Allen, P. R., and Taylor, M., 'Charts, Noise and Fundamentals: A Study of the London Foreign Exchange Market', *CEPR Discussion Paper*, 341, 1989.

Axelrod, Robert, *The Evolution of Cooperation*, Basic Books, 1984.

Bagehot, Walter, *Lombard Street*, London, John Murray, 1917 (New Edition).

Baillie, R. T., and McMahon, P., 'The Foreign Exchange Market: Theory and Econometric Evidence', Cambridge, Cambridge University Press, 1989.

Balassa, Bela, 'The Purchasing Power Parity Doctrine: A Reappraisal', *Journal of Political Economy*, 1964.

Balbach, Anatol, 'The Mechanics of Intervention in Exchange Markets', Federal Reserve Bank of St Louis, *Review*, Feb. 1978.

Barro, Robert, 'Are Government Bonds Net Wealth?' *Journal of Political Economy*, Nov./Dec. 1974.

—— and Gordon, David, 'Rules, Discretion and Reputation in a Model of Monetary Policy', *Journal of Monetary Economics*, 12, 1983.

Baye, M., De Grauwe, P., and de Vries, C., 'An Oligopoly Model of Free Banking: Theory and Tests', *De Economist*, 141, 4, 1993.

Bayoumi, T., Clark, P., Symansky, S. M., and Taylor, M., 'The Robustness of Equilibrium Exchange Rate Calculations to Alternative Assumptions and Methodologies', in John Williamson (ed.), *Estimating Equilibrium Exchange Rates*, Institute for International Economics, Washington, 1994.

Bergsten, Fred, and Williamson, John, 'Exchange Rates and Trade Policy', in William Cline (ed.), *Trade Policy in the 1980s*, Washington, Institute for International Economics, 1983.

Bertola, G., and Svensson, L., 'Stochastic Devaluation Risk and the Empirical Fit of Target-Zone Models', *Review of Economic Studies*, 60, 689–712, 1993.

Bilson, J., 'The Monetary Approach to the Exchange Rate: Some Empirical Evidence', *IMF Staff Papers*, 25, 48–75, Mar. 1978.

Blanchard, Olivier, 'Speculative Bubbles, Crashes and Rational Expectations', *Economic Letters*, 1979.

—— Dornbusch, Rudiger, Drèze, Jacques, Giersch, Herbert, Layard, Richard, and Monti, Mario, 'Employment and Growth in Europe: A Two-Handed Approach', *CEPS Papers*, 21, Brussels, 1985.

Bloomfield, Arthur, *Monetary Policy under the International Gold Standard: 1880–1914*, Federal Reserve Bank of New York, 1959.

Bomhoff, Eduard, 'The Dollar–Yen Exchange Rate', *Monetary and Economic Studies*, Bank of Japan, Dec. 1987.

Borensztein, Eduardo, 'Alternative Hypotheses about Excess Return on Dollar Assets', *IMF Staff Papers*, Mar. 1987.

Branson, William, 'Asset Markets and Relative Prices in Exchange Rate Determination', *Sozialwissenschaftliche Annalen*, 1977.

Brock, W. A., Dechert, W. D., and Scheinkman, J. A., 'A Test for Independence Based on the Correlation Dimension', SSRJ Working Paper, 8762, Department of Economics, University of Wisconsin-Madison, 1987.

Bruno, Michael, 'The Two-Sector Open Economy and the Real Exchange Rate', *American Economic Review*, 1976.

Bryant, R., 'The Exchange Risk Premium, Uncovered Interest Parity and the Treatment of Exchange Rates in Multicountry Econometric Models', mimeo, The Brookings Institution, 1995.

Bui, Nhuong, and Pippinger, John, 'Excessive Exchange Rate Volatility', Paper presented at the Meetings of the European Economic Association, Copenhagen, Aug. 1987.

Buiter, Willem, 'A Guide to Public Sector Debt and Deficits', *Economic Policy*, Nov. 1985.

Cassel, Gustave, *Money and Foreign Exchange after 1914*, London, Constable, 1922.

Caves, Richard, and Jones, Ronald, *World Trade and Payments*, New York, Little, Brown, 1985.

Clarke, Stephen V., 'The Reconstruction of the International Monetary System: The Attempts of 1922 and 1933', *Princeton Studies in International Finance*, 33, 1973.

Clifton, Eric, 'Real Exchange Rates, Import Penetration, and Protectionism in Industrial Countries', *IMF Staff Papers*, Sept. 1985.

Cline, William, *Exports of Manufactures from Developing Countries*, Washington, The Brookings Institution, 1984.

Collins, Susan, 'The Expected Timing of Devaluation: A Model of Realignment in the European Monetary System', mimeo, Harvard University, 1986.

Cooper, Richard, 'The Gold Standard: Historical Facts and Future', *Brookings Papers on Economic Activity*, 1, Washington, The Brookings Institution, 1982.

Corden, Max, *Economic Policy, Exchange Rates and the International System*, Oxford, Oxford University Press, 1994.

—— and Neary, Peter, 'Booming Sector and De-industrialization in a Small Open Economy', *Economic Journal*, 1982.

Crockett, Andrew, and Goldstein, Morris, 'Strengthening the International Monetary System', *IMF Occasional Paper*, 50, 1987.

Cutler, Poterba, and Summers, J., 'Speculative Dynamics: The Role of Feedback Traders', *NBER Working Paper*, 2442, 1989.

De Grauwe, Paul, 'Exchange Rate Oscillations and Catastrophe Theory', in Emile Claassen and Pascal Salin (eds.), *Recent Issues in the Theory of Flexible Exchange Rates*, Amsterdam, North-Holland, 1983.

—— 'Exchange Rate Variability and the Slowdown in Growth of International Trade', *IMF Staff Papers*, Mar. 1988.

—— 'On the Nature of Risk in the Foreign Exchange Markets', CEPR Discussion Paper, London, 1989.

—— 'The Cost of Disinflation and the European Monetary System', *Open Economies Review*, 1, 147–73, 1990.

—— *The Economics of Monetary Integration*, 2nd edn., Oxford, Oxford University Press, 1994.

—— and de Bellefroid, B., 'Long Run Exchange Rate Variability and International Trade', in Sven Arndt and David Richardson (eds.), *Real Financial Linkages among Open Economies*, Cambridge, Mass., MIT University Press, 1987.

—— De Wachter, H., and Embrechts, M., *Exchange Rate Theory: Chaotic Models of the Foreign Exchange Markets*, London, Basil Blackwell, 1993.

—— and Fratianni, Michele, 'Interdependence, Macro-economic Policies and All That', *The World Economy*, Mar. 1985.

—— Janssens, Marc, and Leliaert, Hilde, 'Real Exchange Rate Variability from 1920 to 1926 and 1973 to 1982', in *Princeton Studies in International Finance*, 56, 1985.

—— and Peeters, Theo, *Exchange Rates in Multi-Country Econometric Models*, London, Macmillan, 1984.

—— and Verfaille, Guy, 'Exchange Rate Variability, Misalignment and the European Monetary System', in Richard Marston (ed.), *Misalignment of Exchange Rates*, Chicago, Chicago University Press, 1988.

—— and Van Santen, Kris, 'Speculative Dynamics and Chaos in the Foreign Exchange Markets', in R. O'Brien and S. Hewin (eds.), *Finance and the International Economy: 4*, Oxford, Oxford University Press, 79–103, 1991.

De Long, J., Bradford, B., Schleiffer, A., Summers, L., and Waldman, R., 'Noise Trader Risk in Financial Markets', *Journal of Political Economy*, 1990.

Dellas, Harris, and Stockman, Alan, 'Self-fulfilling Expectation, Speculative Attack and Capital Controls', *Journal of Money, Credit and Banking*, 25, 721–30, 1993.

Despres, Emile, Kindleberger, Charles, and Salant, Walter, 'The Dollar and World Liquidity: A Minority View', *The Economist*, Feb. 1966.

Devenow, A., and Welch, I., 'Rational Hedging in Financial Economics', *European Economic Review*, forthcoming, 1996.

Dewatripont, M., Giavazzi, F., von Hagen, J., Harden, I., Persson, T., Roland, G., Rosenthal, H., Sapir, A., and Tabellini, G., 'Flexible Integration: Towards a More Effective and Democratic Europe', *Monitoring European Integration*, 6, CEPR, London, 1995.

Dixit, A., and Norman, V., 'Theory of International Trade: A Dual General Equilibrium Approach', Welwyn, James Nesbit, 1980.

Dominguez, K., 'The Informational Role of Foreign Exchange Intervention Operations: The Signalling Hypothesis', in *Exchange Rate Efficiency and the Behavior of International Asset Markets*, New York, Garland Publishing Company, 1992.

—— 'Market Responses to Coordinated Central Bank Intervention', *Carnegie Rochester Series on Public Policy*, vol. 32, 1990.

—— and Frankel, J., *Does Foreign Exchange Intervention Work?* Institute for International Economics, Washington, DC, 1993.

Dornbusch, Rudiger, 'Expectations and Exchange Rate Dynamics', *Journal of Political Economy*, 1976.

—— 'Exchange Rate Economics: Where do we Stand?' *Brookings Papers on Economic Activity*, 1980.

—— 'Equilibrium and Disequilibrium Exchange Rates', *Zeitschrift für Wirtschaft- und Sozialwissenschaften*, 1982.

—— and Fisher, Stanley, 'Exchange Rates and the Current Account', *American Economic Review*, 1980.

Drazen, Allan, and Masson, Paul, 'Credibility of Policies versus Credibility of Policymakers', *Quarterly Journal of Economics*, 109, 735–54, 1994.

Edison, Hali, 'The Effectiveness of Central Bank Intervention: A Survey of the Post-1982 Literature', *Essays in International Finance*, Princeton, NJ, 1993.

Eichengreen, B., *A History of the International Monetary System*, Leuven, Leuven University Press, 1995.

—— Tobin, J., and Wyplosz, C., 'Two Cases for Sand in the Wheels of International Finance', *Economic Journal*, Jan. 1995.

—— and Wyplosz, C., 'The Unstable EMS', *CEPR Discussion Paper*, 817, 1993.

——, —— 'How to Save the EMS', in C. Johnson and S. Collignon (eds.), *The Monetary Economics of Europe*, 166–83, London, Pinter, 1994.

Engel, Charles, 'The Forward Discount Anomaly and the Risk Premium: A Survey of Recent Evidence', *NBER Working Paper*, 5312, 1995.

—— and Hamilton, D., 'Long Swings in the Dollar', *American Economic Review*, 80, 689–713, 1990.

—— and Rogers, John, 'Regional Patterns in the Law of One Price: The Roles of Geography vs. Currencies', *International Finance Discussion Papers*, 533, Board of Governors of the Federal Reserve System, Jan. 1996.

European Commission, 'Annual Economic Report for 1995', *European Economy*, 59, Brussels, 1995.

Fama, Eugene, 'Inflation, Output and Money', *Journal of Business*, Apr. 1982.

—— 'Forward and Spot Exchange Rates', *Journal of Monetary Economics*, Nov. 1984.

—— and Gibbons, Michael, 'Inflation, Real Returns and Capital Investments', *Journal of Monetary Economics*, May 1982.

Feenstra, Robert, 'Symmetric Pass-through of Tariffs and Exchange Rates under Imperfect Competition: An Empirical Test', *NBER Working Paper*, 2453, Dec. 1987.

Feldstein, Martin, 'New Evidence on the Effects of Exchange Rate Intervention', *NBER Working Paper*, 2052, Oct. 1986*a*.

—— 'The Budget Deficit and the Dollar', *NBER Macroeconomic Annual*, 1986*b*.

—— 'Tax Policy and International Capital Flows', *NBER Working Paper*, 4851, Sept. 1994.

—— and Horioka, Charles, 'Domestic Savings and International Capital Flows', *Economic Journal*, 90, 314–29, June 1980.

Fischer, Stanley, 'Stability and Exchange Rate Systems in a Monetarist Model of the Balance of Payments', in Robert Aliber (ed.), *The Political Economy of Monetary Reform*, London, Macmillan, 1977.

Flood, Robert, and Garber, Peter, 'Collapsing Exchange Rate Regimes: Some Linear Examples', *Journal of International Economics*, 17, 1–14, 1984.

—— and Rose, K., 'Fixing Exchange Rates', *NBER Working Paper*, 4503, 1993.

——, —— 'Fixes: Of the Forward Discount Puzzle', *NBER Working Paper*, 4928, 1994.

Frankel, Jeffrey, 'On the Mark: A Theory of Floating Exchange Rates based on Real Interest Differentials', *American Economic Review*, 69, 610–22, 1979.

—— 'In Search of Exchange Risk Premium: A Six Currency Test Assuming Mean-Variance Optimization', *Journal of International Money and Finance*, Dec. 1982.

—— 'Tests of Monetary and Portfolio Balance Models of Exchange Rate Determination', in J. Bilson and R. Marston (eds.), *Exchange Rate Theory and Practice*, Chicago, Chicago University Press, 1984.

—— 'Six Possible Meanings of "Overvaluation": The 1981–85 Dollar', *Princeton Essays in International Finance*, 159, Dec. 1985.

—— 'The Sources of Disagreement among the International Macro Models and Implications for Policy Co-ordination', *NBER Working Paper*, 1925, May 1986.

—— 'Measuring International Capital Mobility: A Review', *American Economic Review*, May 1992.

—— 'How Well do Foreign Exchange Markets Function: Might a Tobin Tax Help?' *NBER Working Paper*, 5422, 1996.

—— and Andrew, Rose, 'A Survey of Empirical Research on Nominal Exchange Rates', *NBER Working Paper*, 4865, 1994.

—— and Froot, Kenneth, 'The Dollar as a Speculative Bubble: A Tale of Fundamentalists and Chartists', *NBER Working Paper*, 1854, May 1986a.

——, —— 'Interpreting Tests of Forward Discount Bias Using Survey Data on Exchange Rate Expectations', *NBER Working Paper*, no. 1963, 1986b.

——, —— 'Short-Term and Long-Term Expectations of the Yen/Dollar Exchange Rate: Evidence from Survey Data', *NBER Working Paper*, 2216, Apr. 1987.

——, —— 'Chartists, Fundamentalists and the Demand for Dollars', *Greek Economic Review*, 10, 49–102, 1988.

—— and Meese, Richard, 'Are Exchange Rates Excessively Variable?' *NBER Working Paper*, 2249, Apr. 1987.

Fratianni, Michele, Hur, Hyung-Doh, and Kang, Heejong, 'Random Walk and Monetary Causality in Five Exchange Markets', *Journal of International Money and Finance*, 6, 1987.

—— and von Hagen, J., *The European Monetary System and European Monetary Union*, Boulder, Colo., Westview Press, 1992.

Frenkel, Jacob, 'A Monetary Approach to the Exchange Rate: Doctrinal Aspects and Empirical Evidence', *Scandinavian Journal of Economics*, 78, 200–24, 1976.

—— 'The Collapse of PPP during the Seventies', *European Economic Review*, 1981.

—— and Aizenman, Joshua, 'Aspects of the Optimal Management of Exchange Rates', *Journal of International Economics*, Nov. 1982.

—— and Goldstein, Morris, 'A Guide to Target Zones', *IMF Staff Papers*, 1986.

—— and Mussa, Michael, 'Asset Markets, Exchange Rates and the Balance of Payments', in R. Jones and P. Kenen (eds.), *Handbook of International Economics*, vol. 2, ch. 14, Amsterdam, North-Holland, 1985.

—— and Razin, A., 'Budget Deficits and Rates of Interest in the World Economy', *American Economic Review*, May 1986a.

——, —— 'The International Transmission and Effects of Fiscal Policies', *American Economic Review*, May 1986b.

Friedman, Milton, 'The Role of Monetary Policy', *American Economic Review*, May 1968.

Fukao, Mitsuhiro, 'The Theory of Exchange Rate Determination in a Multi-Currency World', *Monetary and Economic Studies*, Bank of Japan, Oct. 1983.

—— 'A Risk Premium Model of the Yen-Dollar and DM-Dollar Exchange Rates', *OECD Economic Studies*, 9, Autumn 1987.

Genberg, Hans, 'Effects of Central Bank Intervention in the Foreign Exchange Market', *IMF Staff Papers*, 1981.

—— 'On Choosing the Right Rules for Exchange Rate Management', *The World Economy*, Dec. 1984.

Giavazzi, F., and Giovannini, A., 'Models of the EMS: Is Europe a Greater Deutsche-Mark Area?' unpublished, Jan. 1987.

——, —— *Limiting Exchange Rate Flexibility: The European Monetary System*, Cambridge, Mass.: MIT Press, 1989.

—— and Pagano, M., 'The Advantage of Tying One's Hands: EMS Discipline and Central Bank Credibility', *European Economic Review*, 32, 1055–82, 1988.

Goldstein, Morris, 'Have Flexible Exchange Rates Handicapped Macroeconomic Policy?' *Special Papers in International Economics*, Princeton University, 1980.

—— 'The Exchange Rate System and The IMF: A Modest Agenda', *Policy Analyses in International Economics*, 39, Washington, Institute for International Economics, 1995.

Goodhart, C., 'News and the Foreign Exchange Market', *LSE Financial Markets Group Discussion Paper*, 71, 1989.

—— 'Financial Globalization, Volatility and the Challenge for the Policies of the Central Banks', Financial Markets Group, London School of Economics, 1995.

—— and Figliuoli, L., 'Every Minute Counts in the Foreign Exchange Markets', *Journal of International Money and Finance*, 10, 23–52, 1991.

Gros, Daniel, 'The Effectiveness of Capital Controls: Implications for Monetary Autonomy in the Presence of Incomplete Market Separation', *IMF Staff Papers*, 35, 3, Sept. 1987a.

—— 'Exchange Rate Variability and Foreign Trade in the Presence of Adjustment Costs', Brussels, CEPS, 1987b.

—— 'A Note on the Effectiveness of Capital Controls', Brussels, CEPS, 1987c.

—— and Thygesen, Niels, *European Monetary Integration: From the European Monetary System towards Monetary Union*, London, Longman, 1992.

Guillaume, D., 'A Low Dimensional Fractal Attractor in the Foreign Exchange Market?' *International Discussion Papers*, 99, Leuven, Catholic University of Leuven, 1993.

Haberler, Gottfried, and Willett, Thomas, 'US Balance of Payments Policies and International Monetary Reform: A Critical Analysis', Washington, DC, American Enterprise Institute, 1968.

Hakkio, Craig, 'Does the Exchange Rate Follow a Random Walk?' *Journal of International Economics*, June 1986.

Hayek, F. von, *Denationalizing Money: The Argument Refined*, London, The Institute of Economic Affairs, 1978.

Heller, Peter, Haas, Richard, and Monsur, Ahsan, 'A Review of the Fiscal Impulse Variable', *IMF Occasional Paper*, 44, 1986.

Henderson, Dale, 'The Role of Intervention Policy in Open Economy Financial Policy: A Macroeconomic Perspective', *International Finance Discussion Paper*, 202, Board of Governors of the Federal Reserve System, Feb. 1982.

—— 'Exchange Market Intervention Operations: Their Role in Financial Policy and their Effects', in John Bilson and Richard Marston (eds.), *Exchange Rate Theory and Practice*, NBER, Chicago University Press, 1984.

Herring, Richard, and Marston, Richard, *National Monetary Policies and International Financial Markets*, Amsterdam, North-Holland, 1977.

Hewson, John, and Sakakibara, Eisuke, 'The Impact of US Controls on Capital Outflows on the US Balance of Payments: An Exploratory Study', *IMF Staff Papers*, Mar. 1975.

Hirschleifer, D., and Welch, I., 'Institutional Memory, Inertia and Impulsiveness', *Working Paper*, University of California at Los Angeles, 1995.

Hooper, Peter, and Mann, Catherine, 'The US External Deficit: Its Causes and Persistence', *International Finance Discussion Paper*, 316, Board of Governors of the Federal Reserve System, Nov. 1987.

—— and Morton, John, 'Fluctuations in the Dollar: A Model of Nominal and Real Exchange Rate Determination', *Journal of International Money and Finance*, 1, 39–56, 1982.

IMF, 'The Exchange Rate System: Lessons from the Past and Options for the Future: A Study by the Research Department of the IMF', *Occasional Paper*, 30, 1984.

—— 'Issues in International Exchange and Payments Systems', *World Economic and Financial Surveys*, Washington, Apr. 1995a.

—— 'International Capital Markets, Developments, Prospects and Policy Issues', Washington, *Occasional Paper*, Aug. 1995b.

Isard, Peter, 'How Far can we Push the Law of One Price?' *American Economic Review*, 1977.

—— *Exchange Rate Economics*, Cambridge, Cambridge University Press, 1995.

Ito, Takatoshi, 'The Intra-Daily Exchange Rate Dynamics and Monetary Policies after the G5 Agreement', *NBER Working Paper*, 2048, Oct. 1986.

Japan, Economic Planning Agency, *Economic White Paper*, 1979.

Jurgenson Report, Working Group on Exchange Market Intervention, Report, Mar. 1983.

Kenen, Peter (ed.), *International Trade and Finance: Frontiers for Research*, Cambridge, Cambridge University Press, 1975.

—— 'Ways to Reform Exchange Rate Arrangements in Bretton Woods Commission', *Bretton Woods: Looking to the Future*, Conference Proceedings, Washington, 1995.

—— and Rodrik, Danny, 'Measuring and Analysing the Effects of Short-Term Volatility in Real Exchange Rates', *Review of Economics and Statistics*, May 1986.

Kindleberger, Charles, *The World in Depression, 1929–39*, University of California Press, 1973.

Klein, B., 'The Competitive Supply of Money', *Journal of Money, Credit and Banking*, 6, 423–53, Nov. 1974.

Kouri, Pennti, 'The Exchange Rate and the Balance of Payments in the Short Run and in the Long Run', *Scandinavian Journal of Economics*, 1976.

Krause, Lawrence, 'A Passive Balance of Payments Strategy for the US', *Brookings Papers on Economic Activity*, 3, 1970.

Kravis, Irving, and Lipsey, Robert, 'The Assessment of National Price Levels', in Sven Arndt and David Richardson (eds.), *Real Financial Linkages among Open Economies*, Cambridge, Mass., MIT Press, 1987.

Krugman, Paul, 'A Model of Balance of Payments Crises', *Journal of Money, Credit and Banking*, 11, Aug. 1979.

—— 'Pricing to Market When the Exchange Rate Changes', in Sven Arndt and David Richardson (eds.), *Real Financial Linkages among Open Economies*, Cambridge, Mass., MIT University Press, 1987.

—— 'Target Zones and Exchange Rate Dynamics', *Quarterly Journal of Economics*, 1991.

—— and Miller, Marcus (eds.), 'Exchange Rate Targets and Currency Bands', Centre for Economic Policy Research and Cambridge University Press, 1992.

Kydland, F., and Prescott, E. C., 'Rules rather than Discretion: The Inconsistency of Optimal Plans', *Journal of Political Economy*, June 1977.

Laidler, David, 'Free Banking: Theory', in P. Newman, M. Milgate, and J. Eatwell (eds.), *The New Palgrave Dictionary of Money and Finance*, 196–7, London, Macmillan, 1992.

Leamer, Edward, and Stern, Robert, *Quantitative International Economics*, Allyn and Bacon, 1970.

Levich, Richard, 'Overshooting in the Foreign Exchange Market', *Occasional Paper*, 5, New York, Group of Thirty, 1981.

—— 'Empirical Studies of Exchange Rates: Price Behavior, Rate Determination and Market Efficiency', in R. Jones and P. Kenen (eds.), *Handbook of International Economics*, vol. 2, ch. 19, Amsterdam, North-Holland, 1985.

Lewis, Karen, 'Occasional Intervention to Target Rates', *NBER Working Paper*, 3398, 1990.

—— 'Are Foreign Exchange Intervention and Monetary Policy Related and Does it Really Matter?' *NBER Working Paper*, June 1993.

Loopesko, Bonnie, and Johnson, Robert, 'Realignment of the Dollar/Yen Exchange Rate: Aspects of the Adjustment Problem in Japan', *International Finance Discussion Paper*, 311, Board of Governors of the Federal Reserve System, Aug. 1987.

Lucas, Robert, 'Interest Rates and Currency Prices in a Two-Country World', *Journal of Monetary Economics*, Nov. 1982.

McDougall, Sir Donald, *The World's Dollar Problem*, London, Macmillan, 1957.

McKinnon, Ronald, 'Currency Substitution and Instability in the World Dollar Market', *American Economic Review*, 3, 1982.

—— 'An International Standard for Monetary Stabilization', *Policy Analyses in International Economics*, 8, Washington, DC, Institute for International Economics, 1984.

Magee, Stephen, 'Currency Contracts, Pass-through and Devaluation', *Brookings Papers on Economic Activity*, 1, 1973.

Mankiw, Gregory, 'Small Menu Costs and Large Business Cycles: A Macroeconomic Model of Monopoly', *Quarterly Journal of Economics*, May 1985.

Marris, Stephen, *Deficits and the Dollar: The World Economy at Risk*, Institute for International Economics, Dec. 1985.

Marston, Richard, 'Real Exchange Rates and Productivity Growth in the US and Japan', in Sven Arndt and David Richardson (eds.), *Real Financial Linkages among Open Economies*, Cambridge, Mass., MIT Press, 1987*a*.

—— 'Exchange Rate Policy Reconsidered', *NBER Working Paper*, 2310, 1987*b*.

Meade, James, *Theory of International Economic Policy: The Balance of Payments*, Oxford, Oxford University Press, 1951.

Meese, Richard, and Rogoff, Kenneth, 'Empirical Exchange Rate Models of the Seventies: Do They Fit Out of Sample', *Journal of International Economics*, 1983.

Minford, Patrick, and Matthews, Kent, 'Mrs. Thatcher's Economic Policies 1979–87', *Economic Policy*, Oct. 1987.

Modigliani, Franco, Mon, Mario, Drèze, Jacques, Giersch, Herbert, and Layard, Richard, 'Reducing Unemployment in Europe: The Role of Capital Formation', *CEPS Papers*, 28, Brussels, 1986.

Mundell, Robert, 'A Theory of Optimal Currency Areas', *American Economic Review*, Sept. 1961.

—— 'Inflation and Real Interest Rate', *Journal of Political Economy*, June 1963.

Mussa, Michael, 'The Exchange Rate, the Balance of Payments and Monetary and Fiscal Policies under a Regime of Controlled Floating', *Scandinavian Journal of Economics*, 1976.

—— 'Empirical Regularities in the Behaviour of Exchange Rates and the Theories of the Foreign Exchange Market', in Carnegie-Rochester Conference Series on Public Policy, *Journal of Monetary Economics*, 1979.

Newbery, David, and Stiglitz, Joseph, *The Theory of Commodity Price Stabilization: A Study in the Economics of Risk*, Oxford, Clarendon Press, 1981.

Niehans, Jurg, *The Theory of Money*, Johns Hopkins University Press, 1978.

—— *International Monetary Economics*, Johns Hopkins University Press, 1985.

Nurske, Ragnar, *International Currency Experience: Lessons of the Interwar Period*, Princeton, NJ, League of Nations, 1944.

Obstfeld, Maurice, 'Exchange Rates, Inflation, and the Sterilization Problem: Germany 1975–81', *European Economic Review*, 1983.

—— 'Rational and Self-fulfilling Balance of Payments Crises', *American Economic Review*, 76, 72–81, 1986.

—— 'Peso Problems, Bubbles and Risk in the Empirical Assessment of Exchange Rate Behavior', *NBER Working Paper*, 2203, Apr. 1987.

—— 'The Effectiveness of Foreign Exchange Intervention: Recent Experience, 1985–88', in W. Branson, *et al.*, *International Policy Coordination and Exchange Rate Fluctuations*, Chicago, Chicago University Press, 197–237, 1990.

—— and Stockman, Alan, 'Exchange Rate Dynamics', in R. Jones and P. Kenen (eds.), *Handbook of International Economics*, vol. 2, ch. 18, Amsterdam, North-Holland, 1985.

OECD, 'Economic Outlook', *Occasional Studies*, Paris, June 1983.

—— 'Economic Outlook', Paris, Dec. 1994.

Okina, K., 'Empirical Tests of Bubbles in the Foreign Exchange Market', *Monetary and Economic Studies*, Bank of Japan, May 1985.

Padoa-Schioppa, Tommaso, 'Efficiency, Stability and Equity: A Strategy for the Evolution of the Economic System of the EC', Commission of the European Communities, Brussels, Apr. 1987.

Peters, E. E., 'Chaos and Order in the Capital Markets: A New View of Cycles, Prices, and Market Volatility', J. Wiley, 1991.

Portes, R., 'EMS and EMU after the Fall', *World Economy*, 16, 1–16, 1993.

Putman, Robert, and Henning, Randall, 'The Bonn Summit of 1978: How does International Economic Policy Coordination Actually Work?' *Brookings Discussion Paper*, 53, Oct. 1986.

Ricardo, David, 'Funding System', in P. Sraffa, *The Works and Correspondence of David Ricardo*, Cambridge, Cambridge University Press, 1951.

Richardson, J. D., 'Some Empirical Evidence on Commodity Arbitrage and the Law of One Price', *Journal of International Economics*, May 1978.

Rogoff, Kenneth, 'Can Exchange Rate Predictability be Achieved without Monetary Convergence? Evidence from the EMS', *European Economic Review*, 1985.

—— 'Can International Monetary Policy Cooperation be Counterproductive?' *Journal of International Economics*, 1985.

Rosenberg, Michael, *Currency Forecasting*, Chicago and London, Irwin, 1996.

Sachs, Jeffrey, and Wyplosz, Charles, 'The Economic Consequences of President Mitterand', in *Economic Policy*, Apr. 1986.

Shiller, Robert, 'Do Stock Prices Move too Much to be Justified by Subsequent Changes in Dividends?' *American Economic Review*, 71, 1981.

Solomon, Robert, *The International Monetary System, 1945–1976: An Insider's View*, Harper and Row, 1977.

Stein, J., 'The Natural Real Exchange Rate of the US Dollar and Determinants of Capital Flows', in John Williamson (ed.), *Estimating Equilibrium Exchange Rates*, Institute for International Economics, Washington, 1994.

Stockman, Alan, 'A Theory of Exchange Rate Determination', *Journal of Political Economy*, 1980.

—— 'The Equilibrium Approach to Exchange Rates', *Economic Review*, Federal Reserve Bank of Richmond, Mar./Apr. 1987.

Svensson, Lars, 'Currency Prices, Terms of Trade, and Interest Rates: A General Equilibrium Asset-Pricing, Cash in Advance Approach', *Journal of International Economics*, 1985.

—— 'Assessing Target Zone Credibility: Mean Reversion and Devaluation Expectations in the ERM, 1970–92', *European Economic Review*, 37, 763–802, 1993.

—— 'Why Exchange Rate Bands? Monetary Independence in Spite of Fixed Exchange Rates', *Journal of Monetary Economics*, 33, 157–99, 1994.

Swan, Trevor, 'Longer Run Problems of the Balance of Payments', in H. W. Arndt and Max Corden (eds.), *The Australian Economy: A Volume of Readings*, Melbourne, Cheshire, 1963.

Swoboda, Alexander, 'Exchange Rate Regimes and US–European Policy Interdependence', *IMF Staff Papers*, 30, 1, 1983.

Taylor, Mark, 'Exchange Rate Economics', *Journal of Economic Literature*, 1994.

—— and Allen, Helen, 'The Use of Technical Analysis in the Foreign Exchange Market', *Journal of International Money and Finance*, 11, 304–14, 1992.

Tinbergen, Jan, *On the Theory of Economic Policy*, Amsterdam, North-Holland, 1952.

Tobin, James, 'Money and Economic Growth', *Econometrica*, Oct. 1965.

Triffin, Robert, *Europe and the Money Muddle*, Yale University Press. 1957.

—— *Gold and the Dollar Crisis*, Yale University Press, 1960.

—— 'A Proposal for International Monetary Reform', Eastern Economic Journal, 4, 153–9, July–Oct. 1978.

—— 'How to End the World Infession: Palliatives of Fundamental Reforms', *CEPS Working Documents*, 1, Brussels, 1983.

Turnovsky, Stephen, 'Exchange Market Intervention in a Small Open Economy', in J. Bhandari and B. Putman (eds.), *The International Transmission of Economic Disturbances*, Cambridge, Mass., MIT University Press, 1982.

Ungerer, Horst, Evans, Owen, Mayer, Thomas, and Young, Philip, 'The European Monetary System: Recent Developments', *IMF Occasional Paper*, 48, 1986.

Van der Wee, Herman, *Prosperity and Upheaval: The World Economy during 1945–80*, Penguin, 1985.

Welch, I., 'Sequential Sales, Learning and Cascades', *Journal of Finance*, 47–2, 695–732, 1992.

Williamson, John, *The Open Economy and the World Economy*, Basic Books, 1983.

—— 'The Exchange Rate System', *Policy Analyses in International Economics*, 5, Washington, Institute for International Economics, 1983.

—— (ed.), *Estimating Equilibrium Exchange Rates*, Institute for International Economics, Washington, 1994.

—— and Henning, Randall, 'Managing the Monetary System', in Peter Kenen (ed.), *Managing the World Economy: Fifty Years after Bretton Woods*, Washington, 1994.

Wilson, Charles, 'The Impact of Anticipated Shocks in Professor Dornbusch's Model of "Expectations and Exchange Rate Dynamics"', *Journal of Political Economy*, June 1979.

Wilson, John, and Takacs, Wendy, 'Expectations and the Adjustment of Trade-Flows under Floating Exchange Rates: Leads and Lags, and the J-Curve', *International Finance Discussion Paper*, 160, Board of Governors of the Federal Reserve System, Apr. 1980.

INDEX